IBM USERS TAKE NOTE...

If you like *More Than 32 BASIC Programs for the IBM Personal Computer,* you will appreciate having the programs on a disk which is ready to run on your IBM Personal Computer. The software has a 'forever guarantee' (any problems, simply return the disk with $5 and we will send you a new one). Not only will it save you typing time, the disk will save you time fretting about errors that are so easy to make. Interested?

☐ You bet I'm interested! Please send the the disk, 32 BASIC Programs for the IBM Personal Computer.

☐ Please find my check in the amount of $19.95 and rush my disk to the address below.

☐ Charge my disk to my _____ VISA _____ M/C and send to the address below.

ACCT # _____ Exp. Date _____

Signature _____

Name _____

Address _____

City, State, Zip _____

(To expedite your order, phone 1-800-547-1842 and charge to your VISA or M/C)

☐ Please send me your catalog entitled Brain Food.

More than 32 BASIC Programs
for the IBM® Personal Computer

More than 32 BASIC Programs for the IBM® Personal Computer

Tom Rugg and Phil Feldman

dilithium Press
Beaverton, Oregon

10   9   8   7   6   5   4   3   2   1

Library of Congress Cataloging in Publication Data
Rugg, Tom.
   More than 32 BASIC programs for the IBM Personal Computer.

   Bibliography: p.
   1. IBM Personal Computer—Programming. 2. Basic (Computer program language) I. Feldman, Phil. II. Title. III. Title: More than thirty-two BASIC programs for the IBM personal computer. IV. Title: More than 32 B.A.S.I.C. programs for the IBM personal computer.
QA76.8.I2594R84 1983   001.64'2   83-7712
ISBN 0-88056-078-9
IBM is a registered trademark of the International Business Machines Corporation.
dilithium Press
8285 S.W. Nimbus
Suite 151
Beaverton, Oregon 97005

Acknowledgements

Our thanks to the following for their help and encouragement: Our families, Merl and Patti Miller, Asenatha McCauley, The Ranger, Jim Rugg (W6DVZ), Wes Steele, and especially QT and the Buug.

AN IMPORTANT NOTE

The publisher and authors have made every effort to assure that the computer programs are accurate and complete. However, this publication is prepared for general readership, and neither the publisher nor the authors have any knowledge about or ability to control any third party's use of the programs and programming information. There is no warranty or representation by either the publisher or the authors that the programs or programming information in this book will enable the reader or user to achieve any particular result.

Preface

You have just bought yourself an IBM Personal Computer (or maybe you just have access to one at school or work). You will soon find that the most frequent question you are asked goes something like this: "Oh, you got a computer, eh? Uh...what are you going to do with it?"

Your answer, of course, depends on your own particular situation. Maybe you got it for mathematical work, or for your business, or for home usage, or to enable you to learn more about computers. Maybe you got it for a teaching/learning tool or for playing games.

Even if you bought the computer specifically for only one of these reasons, you should not neglect the others. The computer is such a powerful tool that it can be used in many different ways. If it is not being used for its "intended" function right now, why not make use of it in some other way?

A personal computer is so small and portable that you can, say, take it home from work over the weekend and let the kids play educational games. They will have fun *and* learn a lot. After they go to bed, you can use it to help plan your personal finances. Or, you can let your guests at a party try to outsmart the computer (or each other) at some fascinating games. The possibilities are endless.

All these things can be done with your computer, but it cannot do any of them without the key ingredient—a computer program. People with little or no exposure to computers may be in for a surprise when they learn this. A computer without a program is like a car without a driver. It just sits there.

So you ask, "Where can I get some programs to do the things I want my computer to do?" Glad you asked. There are several alternatives.

1. Hire a computer programmer. If you have a big budget, this is the way to go. Good programmers are expensive and hard to find (and you will not know for sure if they're really good until after the job is finished). Writing a couple of programs that are moderately complex will probably cost you more than you paid for the computer itself.
2. Learn to program yourself. This is a nice alternative, but it takes time. There are lots of programming books available — some are good, some are not so good. You can take courses at local colleges. If you can afford the time and you have a fair amount of common sense and inner drive, this is a good solution.
3. Buy the programs you want. This is cheaper than hiring your own programmer because all the buyers share the cost of writing the programs. You still will not find it very cheap, especially if you want to accumulate several dozen programs. Each program might cost anywhere from a few dollars to several hundred dollars. The main problem is that you cannot be sure how good the programs are, and, since they are generalized for all possible buyers, you may not be able to easily modify them to do exactly what *you* want. Also, they have to be written in a computer language that *your* computer understands. Even if you find a program written in the BASIC language, you will soon learn that your computer's BASIC is not the same as other versions. Variations between versions of the same language typically result in the program not working.

This book gives you the chance to take the third alternative at the lowest possible cost. If you divide the cost of the book by the number of programs in it (use your computer if you like), you will find that the cost per program is amazingly low. Even if there are only a few programs in the book that will be useful to you, the cost is pretty hard to beat.

Just as important is the fact that these programs are written specifically for your IBM Personal Computer. If you type them in exactly as shown, they will work! No changes are needed. In addition, we show you exactly what to change in order to make some simple modifications that may suit your taste or needs. Plus, if you have learned a little about BASIC, you can go even further and follow the suggestions about more extensive changes that can be made. This approach was used to try to make every program useful to you, whether you are a total beginner or an old hand with computers.   .

But enough of the sales pitch. Our main point is that we feel a computer is an incredibly flexible machine, and it is a shame to put it to only one or two limited uses and let it sit idle the rest of the time. We are giving you a wide range of things to do with your computer, and yet we are really only scratching the surface.

So open your eyes and your mind! Play a mental game against the computer (WARI, JOT). Evaluate your next financial decision (LOAN, DECIDE). Expand your vocabulary or improve your reading speed (VOCAB, TACHIST). Solve mathematical equations (DIFFEQN, SIMEQN).

But please, don't leave your computer asleep in the corner too much. Give it some exercise.

How to Use This Book

Each chapter of this book presents a computer program that runs on a 64K (or more) IBM Personal Computer with one disk drive and the color/graphics display interface with an 80 column CRT monitor. However, most of the programs will also work with the monochrome display, or on a 16K cassette system. Refer to the Appendix for details.

Each chapter is made up of eight sections that serve the following functions:

1. **Purpose:** Explains what the program does and why you might want to use it.
2. **How To Use It:** Gives the details of what happens when you run the program. Explains your options and the meanings of any responses you might give. Provides details of any limitations of the program or errors that might occur.
3. **Sample Run:** Shows you what you will see on the screen when you run the program.
4. **Program Listing:** Provides a *listing* (or *print-out*) of the BASIC program. These are the instructions to the computer that you must provide so it will know what to do. You must type them in extremely carefully for correct results.
5. **Easy Changes:** Shows you some very simple changes you can make to the program to cause it to work differently, if you wish. You do not have to understand how to program to make these changes.
6. **Main Routines:** Explains the general logic of the program, in case you want to figure out how it works. Gives the BASIC line numbers and a brief explanation of what each major portion of the program accomplishes.

7. **Main Variables:** Explains what each of the key variables in the program is used for, in case you want to figure out how it works.
8. **Suggested Projects:** Provides a few ideas for major changes you might want to make to the program. To try any of these, you will need to understand BASIC and use the information provided in the previous two sections (Main Routines and Main Variables).

To use any of these programs on your computer, you need only use the first four sections. The last four sections are there to give you supplementary information if you want to tinker with the program.

RECOMMENDED PROCEDURE

Here is our recommendation of how to try any of the programs in this book:

1. Read through the documentation that came with the computer to learn the fundamentals of communication with it. This will teach you how to turn the computer on, enter a program, correct mistakes, run a program, etc. At a minimum, be sure you have read the first three sections of the *Guide to Operations* manual (especially "Using BASIC") and the first two chapters of the BASIC manual.
2. Pick a chapter and read Section 1 ("Purpose") to see if the program sounds interesting or useful to you. If not, move on to the next chapter until you find one that is. If you are a beginner you might want to try one of the short "Miscellaneous Programs" first.
3. Read Sections 2 and 3 of the chapter ("How To Use It" and "Sample Run") to learn the details of what the program does. Look at line 130 of the Program Listing (or the Appendix) to be sure you have the right computer configuration.
4. Get into the proper version of BASIC and enter the NEW command to eliminate any existing program that might already be in your computer's memory. Using Section 4 of the chapter ("Program Listing"), *carefully* enter the program into the computer. Be particularly careful to get all the punctuation characters right (e.g., commas, semicolons, colons, quotation marks, etc.). You may find it easiest to

use the **AUTO 100** command to have the computer enter the BASIC line numbers for you. Use **CTRL BREAK** to end **AUTO**.

5. After the entire program is entered into the computer's memory, use the LIST command to display what you have entered so you can double check for typographical errors, omitted lines, etc. Don't mistake a semicolon for a colon, or an alphabetic I or O for a numeric 1 or 0 (zero). *Take a minute to note the differences in these characters before you begin.* Using **CAPS LOCK** may help you avoid typing a lowercase l instead of the number 1.

6. Before trying to RUN the program, use the SAVE command to save the program temporarily on cassette or disk. This could prevent a lot of wasted effort in case something goes wrong (power failure, computer malfunction, etc.). If the computer "hangs up" when you enter RUN, you can simply reset it, reload the program from cassette or disk, and look for typing errors.

7. Now RUN the program. Is the same thing happening that is shown in the Sample Run? If so, accept our congratulations and go on to Step 9. If not, stay cool and go to Step 8.

8. If you got a SYNTAX ERROR in a line, LIST that line and look at it closely. Something is not right. Maybe you interchanged a colon and a semicolon. Maybe you typed a numeric 1 or 0 instead of an alphabetic I or O. Maybe you misspelled a word or omitted one. Keep looking until you find it, then correct the error and go back to Step 7.

   If you got some other kind of error message, consult the computer's documentation for an explanation (Appendix A in the BASIC manual). Keep in mind that the error might not be in the line that is pointed to by the error message. It is not unusual for the mistake to be in a line immediately preceding the error message line. Another possibility is that one or more lines were omitted entirely. In any event, fix the problem and go back to Step 7.

   If there are no error messages, but the program is not doing the same thing as the Sample Run, there are two possibilities. First, maybe the program isn't *supposed* to do exactly the same thing. Some of the programs are designed to do unpredictable things to avoid repetition (primarily the game programs and graphic displays). They should be doing the same *types* of things as the Sample Run, however.

The second possibility is that you made a typing error that did not cause an error message to be displayed, but simply changed the meaning of one or more lines in the program. This can be a little tricky to find, but you can usually narrow it down to the general area of the problem by noting the point at which the error takes place. Is the first thing displayed correct? If so, the error is probably after the PRINT statement that caused the first thing to be displayed. Look for the same types of things mentioned before. Make the corrections and go back to Step 7.

9. Continue running the program, trying to duplicate the Sample Run. If you find a variation that cannot be accounted for in the "How To Use It" section of the chapter, go to Step 8. Otherwise, if it seems to be running properly, SAVE the program on cassette or disk.

10. Read Section 5 of the chapter ("Easy Changes"). Try any of the changes that look interesting. If you think the changed version is better, SAVE it on cassette or disk, too. You will probably want to give it a slightly different name and title in the first REM statement to avoid future confusion.

Be careful not to confuse similar looking characters when typing the programs into your computer. This photo compares some of the most frequently confused characters, as they appear on a 40 characer graphics screen.

A NOTE ON THE PROGRAM LISTINGS

A line on the computer screen is either 40 or 80 characters long, depending on which type of CRT you have and whether you have used the WIDTH 40 or WIDTH 80 commands. If you use the WIDTH 40, lines from our Program Listings may take two lines on your screen. If a line is exactly 40 characters long, be sure to press the **ENTER** key after typing it even though the cursor has already jumped to the next line. The **ENTER** key must be used to end *every* line.

In order for the listings to fit properly in this book, lines that are over 50 characters long have been split into two lines. This is *only* for the purpose of fitting on the page. You should type a split line as though it is one long line.

Contents

Section 3 – GAME PROGRAMS
Match wits with the computer or a friend.

Section 4 – GRAPHICS DISPLAY PROGRAMS
Dazzling visual diversions.

Section 5 — MATHEMATICS PROGRAMS
For math, engineering, and statistical uses.

Section 6 — MISCELLANEOUS PROGRAMS
Short programs that do interesting things.

Appendix — Memory and Configuration Requirements

Bibliography

Errata Offer

Section 1

Applications Programs

Good practical applications are certainly a prime use of personal computers. There are a myriad of ways the computer can help us to do useful work. Here are eight programs for use around the home or business.

Financial considerations are always important. LOAN will calculate interest, payment schedules etc. for mortgages, car loans, or any such business loan. Do you ever have trouble balancing your checkbook(s)? CHECKBOOK will enable you to rectify your monthly statements and help you find the cause of any errors. With the many types of investments available today, there is often confusion about their true annual yields. ANNUAL will make sure you don't have this problem any more.

Perhaps you find yourself compiling various lists at home or work. These could be lists of names, words, phrases, etc. The chore of alphabetizing such a list is duck soup for SORTLIST.

Fuel usage is a constant concern for those of us who drive. MILEAGE will determine and keep track of a motor vehicle's general operating efficiency.

The tedium of analyzing questionnaires and examinations can be greatly relieved with the aid of your computer. In particular, teachers and market researchers should find QUEST/EXAM useful.

Often we are faced with difficult decisions. DECIDE transforms your computer into a trusty advisor. Help will be at hand for any decision involving the selection of one alternative from several choices.

Before anything else, you might want to consult BIO-RHYTHM each day. Some major airlines, and other industries, are placing credence on biorhythm theory. If you agree, or "just in case," simply turn on your computer and load this program.

ANNUAL

PURPOSE

Suppose you put $1000.00 into an investment that pays ten percent interest. How much interest will you earn by the end of one year?

Generally the answer is *not* simply $100.00 (the interest rate times the principal). The amount of interest earned per year depends on how often the interest is compounded (calculated) and paid. If it is done only once at the end of the year, you really do earn only ten percent. But if it is done more often (each month, for example) you earn more. This is because the interest after the first month begins earning interest too.

This program shows you the annual yield of any interest rate for various compounding techniques, assuming that the interest is added to the principal as it is calculated. Be aware that some savings institutions use different techniques for calculating annual yield. Their published figures may differ from the ones calculated here.

HOW TO USE IT

Simply enter the interest rate you want to evaluate. The program shows the annual yield for annual, semi-annual, quarterly, monthly, weekly, and daily compounding. Then it asks you for another interest rate to evaluate. If you have no more, enter zero or a negative number to end the program.

Due to the way numbers are represented inside the computer, you may occasionally notice the last significant digit or two to be inaccurate. Fortunately, there is seldom any need to know the annual yield beyond two or three decimal places, so this should be no problem. An Easy Change below shows how to increase the accuracy.

SAMPLE RUN

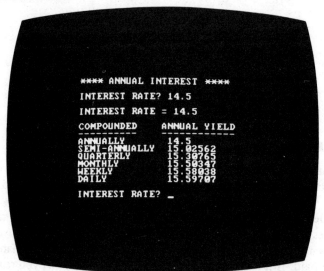

```
**** ANNUAL INTEREST ****
INTEREST RATE? 14.5
INTEREST RATE = 14.5

COMPOUNDED      ANNUAL YIELD
----------      ------------
ANNUALLY        14.5
SEMI-ANNUALLY   15.02562
QUARTERLY       15.30765
MONTHLY         15.50347
WEEKLY          15.58038
DAILY           15.59707

INTEREST RATE? _
```

The program asks what interest rate should be evaluated. The operator provides it, and the program shows the annual yield for six different compounding techniques.

PROGRAM LISTING

```
100 REM: ANNUAL
110 REM: Compute annual interest yields.
120 REM: COPYRIGHT 1982 Tom Rugg and Phil Feldman.
130 REM: Any BASIC, any CRT.
140 KEY OFF:SCREEN 0,0:WIDTH 40:COLOR 7,0:CLS
150 PRINT"**** ANNUAL INTEREST ****"
160 PRINT
170 INPUT"INTEREST RATE";R
180 PRINT:IF R<=0 THEN END
190 PRINT"INTEREST RATE =";R
200 PRINT
210 PRINT"COMPOUNDED";TAB(15);
220 PRINT"ANNUAL YIELD"
230 PRINT STRING$(10,45);TAB(15);STRING$(12,45)
240 RESTORE
250 READ N$,N
260 IF N$="END" OR N$="end" THEN 330
270 PRINT N$;TAB(15);
```

```
280 T=R/100:W=T/N:S=1
290 S=(1+W)^N
300 S=(S-1)*100
310 PRINT S
320 GOTO 250
330 PRINT
340 GOTO 170
350 DATA ANNUALLY,1
360 DATA SEMI-ANNUALLY,2
370 DATA QUARTERLY,4
380 DATA MONTHLY,12
390 DATA WEEKLY,52
400 DATA DAILY,365
410 DATA END,999
```

EASY CHANGES

1. If you have a printer, you can send the output to it very easily. Just change every **PRINT** in lines 190 through 330 to **LPRINT**.
2. Adding another compounding technique is done by inserting another DATA statement between lines 350 and 410. For example, bimonthly compounding would mean once every two months, or six times per year. To include it, add this statement:

   375 DATA BIMONTHLY,6

3. The program can be changed to make calculations for a whole series of interest rates without stopping. If you have a printer, you may want to create your own reference tables. To do so for, say, interest rates from 10 to 12 percent in increments of one-quarter percent, make these changes:

   170 FOR R = 10 TO 12 STEP .25
   340 NEXT

4. If you want more precise results, make these changes:

   145 DEFDBL R – W
   290 FOR J = 1 TO N
   295 S = S + S*W:NEXT

MAIN ROUTINES

140-160	Initializes screen and displays title.
170-180	Gets interest rate. Ends program if zero or negative.
190-230	Displays rate and column headings.

240-340	Makes calculation and displays result for each compounding technique.
350-410	DATA statements for each compounding technique.

MAIN VARIABLES

R	Interest rate supplied by operator (as percentage).
N$	Name of compounding technique.
N	Number of times per year to compound.
T	Interest rate (as decimal).
W	Interest rate per compounding period.
S	Sum of interest earned for the year.

SUGGESTED PROJECTS

1. Take inflation and taxes into account and show the "real" gain or loss of the investment. For example, a person in a 50 percent tax bracket during a year of nine percent inflation needs to make about an 18 percent annual yield just to break even at the end of the year.
2. Change the program to display (or print) a table of annual yields. Show a column for each compounding technique, and a row for each interest rate.

BIORHYTHM

PURPOSE

Did you ever have one of those days when nothing seemed to go right? All of us seem to have days when we are clumsy, feel depressed, or just cannot seem to force ourselves to concentrate as well as usual. Sometimes we know why this occurs. It may result from the onset of an illness or because of an argument with a relative. Sometimes, however, we find no such reason. Why can't we perform up to par on some of those days when nothing is known to be wrong?

Biorhythm theory says that all of us have cycles, beginning with the moment of birth, that influence our physical, emotional, and intellectual states. We will not go into a lot of detail about how biorhythm theory was developed (your local library probably has some books about this if you want to find out more), but we will summarize how it supposedly affects you.

The physical cycle is twenty-three days long. For the first 11½ days, you are in the positive half of the cycle. This means you should have a feeling of physical well being, strength, and endurance. During the second 11½ days, you are in the negative half of the cycle. This results in less endurance and a tendency toward a general feeling of fatigue.

The emotional cycle lasts for twenty-eight days. During the positive half (the first fourteen days), you should feel more cheerful, optimistic, and cooperative. During the negative half, you will tend to be more moody, pessimistic, and irritable.

The third cycle is the intellectual cycle, which lasts for thirty-three days. The first half is a period in which you should have greater success in learning new material and pursuing creative,

intellectual activities. During the second half, you are supposedly better off reviewing old material rather than attempting
to learn difficult new concepts.

The ups and downs of these cycles are relative to each individual. For example, if you are a very self-controlled, unemo-
tional person to begin with, your emotional highs and lows may
not be very noticeable. Similarly, your physical and intellectual
fluctuations depend upon your physical condition and intellectual capacity.

The day that any of these three cycles changes from the plus
side to the minus side (or vice versa) is called a "critical day."
Biorhythm theory says that you are more accident-prone on
critical days in your physical or emotional cycles. Critical days in
the intellectual cycle aren't considered as dangerous, but if they
coincide with a critical day in one of the other cycles, the poten-
tial problem can increase. As you might expect, a triple critical
day is one on which you are recommended to be especially
careful.

Please note that there is quite a bit of controversy about biorhythms. Most scientists feel that there is not nearly enough evi-
dence to conclude that biorhythms can tell you anything meaningful. Others believe that biorhythm cycles exist, but that they
are not as simple and inflexible as the 23, 28, and 33 day cycles
mentioned here.

Whether biorhythms are good, bad, true, false, or anything
else is not our concern here. We are just presenting the idea to
you as an interesting theory that you can investigate with the
help of your computer.

HOW TO USE IT

The program first asks for the birth date of the person whose
biorhythm cycles are to be charted. You provide the month and
day as you might expect. For the year, you only need to enter the
last two digits if it is between 1900 and 1999. Otherwise, enter all
four digits.

Next the program asks you for the start date for the biorhythm chart. Enter it in the same way. Of course, this date cannot be earlier than the birth date.

After a delay of about a second, the program clears the screen
and begins plotting the biorhythm chart, one day at a time. The

left side of the screen displays the date, while the right side displays the chart. The left half of the chart is the "down" (negative) side of each cycle. The right half is the "up" (positive) side. The center line shows the critical days when you are at a zero point (neither positive nor negative).

Each of the three curves is plotted with an identifying letter — P for physical, E for emotional, and I for intellectual. When the curves cross, an asterisk is displayed instead of either of the two (or three) letters.

Eighteen days of the chart are displayed on one screen, and then the program waits for you to press a key. If you press the E key, the current chart ends and the program starts over again. If you press the **ESCAPE** key, the program ends. If you press the **SPACE** key (or almost any other key), the program clears the screen and displays the next eighteen days of the chart.

The program will allow you to enter dates from the year 100 A.D. and on. We make no guarantees about any extreme future dates, however, such as entering a year greater than 3000. We sincerely hope that these limitations do not prove to be too confining for you.

SAMPLE RUN

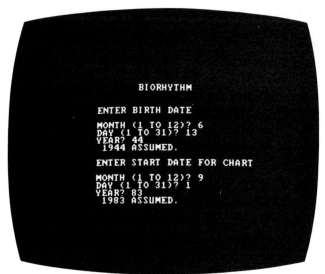

The operator enters his or her birth date and the date for the beginning of the chart.

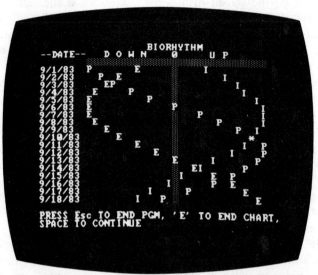

The program responds with the first 18 days of the operator's biorhythm chart, then waits for a key to be pressed.

PROGRAM LISTING

```
100 REM: BIORHYTHM
110 REM: Display biorhythm charts.
120 REM: COPYRIGHT 1982 Tom Rugg and Phil Feldman.
130 REM: Any BASIC, 80 column CRT.
140 DEFINT K,L:DEFDBL B,J,M-Z
150 L=0:Z=.99999:T=33:P=3.14159:I=1
160 KEY OFF:SCREEN 0,0:WIDTH 80:COLOR 7,0:CLS
170 PRINT TAB(8);"BIORHYTHM"
180 GOSUB 1000:PRINT:PRINT
190 PRINT"ENTER BIRTH DATE"
200 GOSUB 450
210 GOSUB 550
220 JB=JD
230 PRINT:PRINT"ENTER START DATE FOR CHART"
240 GOSUB 450
250 GOSUB 550
260 JC=JD
270 IF JC>=JB THEN 310
280 PRINT"CHART DATE CAN'T BE EARLIER"
290 PRINT"THAN BIRTH DATE.   TRY AGAIN."
300 GOTO 180
```

```
310 FOR K=1 TO 1000:NEXT
320 GOSUB 630
330 N=JC-JB
340 V=23:GOSUB 690
350 V=28:GOSUB 690
360 V=33:GOSUB 690
370 GOSUB 850
380 PRINT TAB(1);C$;TAB(9);L$
390 JC=JC+1:L=L+1:IF L<18 THEN 330
400 PRINT:PRINT"PRESS Esc TO END PGM, 'E' TO
    END CHART, SPACE TO CONTINUE";
410 R$=INKEY$:IF LEN(R$)=0 THEN 410
420 IF ASC(R$)=27 THEN END
430 IF R$="E" OR R$="e" THEN 150
440 L=0:GOTO 320
450 PRINT
460 INPUT "MONTH (1 TO 12)";M
470 M=INT(M):IF M<1 OR M>12 THEN BEEP:GOTO 460
480 INPUT "DAY (1 TO 31)";D
490 D=INT(D):IF D<1 OR D>31 THEN BEEP:GOTO 480
500 INPUT "YEAR";Y
510 Y=INT(Y):IF Y<0 THEN 500
520 IF Y>99 THEN 540
530 Y=Y+1900:PRINT Y;"ASSUMED."
540 RETURN
550 W=INT((M-14)/12+Z)
560 JD=INT(1461*(Y+4800+W)/4)
570 B=367*(M-2-W*12)/12
580 IF B<0 THEN B=B+Z
590 B=INT(B):JD=JD+B
600 B=INT(INT(3*(Y+4900+W)/100)/4)
610 JD=JD+D-32075-B
620 RETURN
630 CLS
640 PRINT TAB(T+5);"BIORHYTHM"
650 PRINT TAB(1);"--DATE--";TAB(5+INT(T/2));
660 PRINT
    "D O W N";TAB(9+T);"O";TAB(8+INT(1.5*T));"U P"
670 PRINT TAB(9);U$
680 RETURN
690 W=INT(N/V):R=N-W*V
700 IF V<>23 THEN 730
710 L$=STRING$(T,32)+CHR$(176)+STRING$(T,32)
720 IF V=23 THEN C$="P"
730 IF V=28 THEN C$="E"
740 IF V=33 THEN C$="I"
750 W=R/V:W=W*2*P
760 W=T*SIN(W):W=W+T+1.5
770 W=INT(W):A$=MID$(L$,W,1)
780 IF A$="P" OR A$="E" OR A$="*" THEN C$="*"
790 IF W=1 THEN 830
```

```
800  IF W=T+T+1 THEN 840
810  L$=LEFT$(L$,W-1)+C$+RIGHT$(L$,T+T+1-W)
820  RETURN
830  L$=C$+RIGHT$(L$,T+T):RETURN
840  L$=LEFT$(L$,T+T)+C$:RETURN
850  W=JC+68569!:R=INT(4*W/146097!)
860  W=W-INT((146097!*R+3)/4)
870  Y=INT(4000*(W+1)/1461001!)
880  W=W-INT(1461*Y/4)+31
890  M=INT(80*W/2447)
900  D=W-INT(2447*M/80)
910  W=INT(M/11):M=M+2-12*W
920  Y=100*(R-49)+Y+W
930  A$=STR$(M):W=LEN(A$)-1
940  C$=MID$(A$,2,W)+"/"
950  A$=STR$(D):W=LEN(A$)-1
960  C$=C$+MID$(A$,2,W)+"/"
970  A$=STR$(Y):W=LEN(A$)-1
980  C$=C$+MID$(A$,W,2)
990  RETURN
1000 U$=STRING$((T+T+1),176):RETURN
```

EASY CHANGES

1. Want to see the number of days between any two dates? Insert this line:

335 PRINT "DAYS = ";N: END

Then enter the earlier date as the birth date, and the later date as the start date for the chart. This will cause the program to display the difference in days and then end.

2. To alter the number of days of the chart shown on each screen, alter the 18 in line 390.

3. As written the program requires an 80 column video display. To use a 40 column display, change T in line 150 from 33 to 14, and change WIDTH 80 in line 160 to WIDTH 40.

4. To get black characters on a white background, you can change COLOR 7,0 in line 160 to COLOR 0,7.

MAIN ROUTINES

140- 180   Initializes variables. Displays titles.
190- 220   Asks for birth date and converts to Julian date format (i.e., the number of days since January 1, 4713 B.C.)
230- 260   Asks for start date for chart and converts to Julian date format.

270- 300	Checks that chart date is not sooner than birth date.
310	Delays about one second before displaying chart.
320	Displays heading at top of screen.
330	Determines number of days between birth date and current chart date.
340- 360	Plots points in L$ string for each of the three cycles.
370	Converts Julian date back into month/day/year format.
380	Displays one line on the chart.
390- 440	Adds one to chart date. Checks to see if the screen is full.
450- 540	Subroutine to ask operator for month, day, and year. Edits replies.
550- 620	Subroutine to convert month, day, and year into Julian date format.
630- 680	Subroutine to clear screen and display headings.
690- 820	Subroutine to calculate remainder R of N/V, and plot a point in L$ based on V and R.
830- 990	Subroutine to convert Julian date JC back into month/day/year format.
1000	Subroutine to create U$.

MAIN VARIABLES

L	Counter of number of lines on screen.
T	Number of characters on one side of the center of the chart.
P	Pi.
JB	Birth date in Julian format.
JD	Julian date calculated in subroutine.
JC	Chart start date in Julian format.
K	Loop and work variable.
N	Number of days between birth and current chart date.
V	Number of days in present biorhythm cycle (23, 28, or 33).
C$	String with date in month/day/year format.
L$	String with one line of the biorhythm chart.
R$	Reply from operator after screen fills up.
M	Month (1-12)
D	Day (1-31)
Y	Year (100 or greater)

W, B   Work variables.
R   Remainder of N/V (number of days into cycle).
A$ Work variable.
U$ String of 67 "block" characters for the top of the
                chart.

SUGGESTED PROJECTS

1. Investigate the biorhythms of some famous historical or ath-
   letic personalities. For example, are track and field athletes
   usually in the positive side of the physical cycle on the days
   that they set world records? Where was Lincoln in his emotional and intellectual cycles when he wrote "The Gettysburg
   Address"? Do a significant percentage of accidents befall
   people on critical days?
2. Modify the program to print the chart on a line printer. (Be
   sure to print the name and/or birthdate on the chart, too.)

   To start, change each **PRINT** to **LPRINT** in lines 380, 640,
   650, 660, and 670.

CHECKBOOK

PURPOSE

Many people consider the monthly ritual of balancing the checkbook to be an irritating and error-prone activity. Some people get confused and simply give up after the first try, while others give up the first time they cannot reconcile the bank statement with the checkbook. Fortunately, you have an advantage—your computer. This program takes you through the necessary steps to balance your checkbook, doing the arithmetic for you, of course.

HOW TO USE IT

The program starts off by giving you instructions to verify that the amount of each check and deposit are the same on the statement as they are in your checkbook. Sometimes the bank will make an error in reading the amount that you wrote on a check (especially if your handwriting is not too clear), and sometimes you will copy the amount incorrectly into your checkbook. While you are comparing these figures, make a check mark in your checkbook next to each check and deposit listed on the statement. A good system is to alternate the marks you use each month (maybe an "x" one month and a check mark the next) so you can easily see which checks and deposits came through on which statement.

Next, the program asks for the ending balance shown on the bank statement. You are then asked for the *check number* (not the amount) of the most recent check shown on the statement. This will generally be the highest numbered check the bank has processed, unless you like to write checks out of sequence. Your account balance after this most recent check will be reconciled with the statement balance, so that is what the program asks for next — your checkbook balance after the most recent check.

The program must compensate for any differences between what your checkbook has in it prior to the most recent check and what the statement has on it. First, if you have any deposits that are not shown on the statement before the most recent check, you must enter them. Generally, there are none, so you just enter END.

Next you have to enter the amounts of any checks that have not yet cleared the bank and that are prior to the most recent check. Look in your checkbook for any checks that do not have your check mark next to them. Remember that some of these could be several months old.

Next you enter the amount of any service charges or debit memos that are on the statement, but which have not been shown in your checkbook prior to the most recent check. Typically, this is just a monthly service charge, but there might also be charges for printing new checks for you or some other adjustment that takes money away from you. Credit memos (which give money back to you) are not entered until later. Be sure to make an entry in your checkbook for any of these adjustments so that next month's statement will balance.

Finally, you are asked for any recent deposits or credit memos that were *not* entered in your checkbook prior to the most recent check, but that *are* listed on the bank statement. It is not unusual to have one or two of these, since deposits are generally processed by banks sooner than checks.

Now comes the moment of truth. The program tells you whether or not you are in balance and displays the totals. If so, pack things up until next month's statement arrives.

If not, you have to figure out what is wrong. The best thing to do first is to make sure you entered all the data correctly. Choose from the seven options to verify the accuracy of your data entry. If you find an error, go back to the beginning and try again.

If you entered everything correctly, the most likely cause of the out of balance condition is an arithmetic error in your checkbook. Look for errors in your addition and subtraction, with subtraction being the most likely culprit. This is especially likely if the amount of the error is a nice even number like one dollar or ten cents.

Another common error is accidentally adding the amount of a check in your checkbook instead of subtracting it. If you did this, your error will be twice the amount of the check (which makes it easy to find).

If this still does not explain the error, check to be sure you subtracted *last* month's service charge when you balanced your checkbook with the previous statement. And, of course, if you did not balance your checkbook last month, you cannot expect it to come out right this month.

The program has limitations of how many entries you can make in each category, but these can be changed easily. See "Easy Changes" below.

SAMPLE RUN

The program displays an introduction, and the operator begins providing the necessary information.

The operator continues by entering the checkbook balance, followed by END to indicate no outstanding deposits.

The operator enters the outstanding checks, and prepares to enter service charges.

After the service charges are entered, the operator indicates no late deposits.

```
CONGRATULATIONS!  IT BALANCES.

STATEMENT BALANCE
+ DEPOSITS OUTSTANDING
+ SERVICE CHARGES =       525.16

CHECKBOOK BALANCE
+ CHECKS OUTSTANDING
+ RECENT DEPOSITS =       525.16

DIFFERENCE =       0.00

PRESS ANY KEY TO CONTINUE

NEXT ACTION:
1 - LIST CHECKS OUTSTANDING
2 - LIST DEPOSITS OUTSTANDING
3 - LIST SERVICE CHARGES
4 - START OVER
5 - END PROGRAM
6 - DISPLAY BALANCING INFO
7 - LIST DEPOSITS AFTER LAST CHECK
? _
```

Finally, the program displays balancing information and, after a key is pressed, displays the seven options.

PROGRAM LISTING

```
100 REM: CHECKBOOK
110 REM: A checkbook balancing program.
120 REM: COPYRIGHT 1982 Tom Rugg and Phil Feldman.
130 REM: Any BASIC, any CRT.
140 KEY OFF:SCREEN 0,0:WIDTH 40:COLOR 7,0:CLS
150 DEFDBL C,D,R,S,T,W:I=1
160 PRINT"CHECKBOOK ANALYZER"
170 PRINT:PRINT
180 MC=50:MD=10:MS=10:MR=10
190 L$="NO MORE ROOM"
200 DIM C(MC),D(MD),S(MS),R(MR)
210 TC=0:TD=0:TS=0:TR=0:NC=0:ND=0:NS=0:NR=0
220 E$="ERROR. RE-ENTER, PLEASE."
230 U$="######.##-"
240 PRINT"FIRST, COMPARE THE BANK STATEMENT"
250 PRINT"WITH YOUR CHECKBOOK."
260 PRINT
270 PRINT"MAKE SURE THE STATEMENT AND THE"
280 PRINT"CHECKBOOK SHOW THE SAME FIGURES"
290 PRINT"FOR EACH CHECK AND DEPOSIT."
300 PRINT:
    PRINT"MAKE A MARK IN THE CHECKBOOK NEXT TO"
310 PRINT"EACH CHECK AND DEPOSIT LISTED"
320 PRINT"ON THE STATEMENT."
330 PRINT:PRINT"WHAT'S THE ENDING BALANCE SHOWN"
340 PRINT"ON THE STATEMENT?":INPUT SB
350 PRINT:
    PRINT"NOW FIND THE MOST RECENT CHECK THAT"
360 PRINT"IS SHOWN ON THE BANK STATEMENT."
370 PRINT
380 PRINT"WHAT IS THE CHECK NUMBER OF"
390 PRINT"THIS CHECK?":INPUT LC
400 IF LC=INT(LC) THEN 430
410 BEEP:PRINT"NO, NOT THE AMOUNT OF THE CHECK."
420 GOTO 350
430 PRINT
440 PRINT"WHAT BALANCE DOES YOUR CHECKBOOK"
450 PRINT"SHOW AFTER CHECK NO. ";LC
460 INPUT CB
470 PRINT:PRINT
480 PRINT"ENTER THE AMOUNT OF EACH DEPOSIT"
490 PRINT"THAT IS SHOWN IN YOUR CHECKBOOK"
500 PRINT"PRIOR TO CHECK NO. ";LC
510 PRINT"BUT IS NOT ON THE STATEMENT."
520 A$="WHEN NO MORE, SAY 'END'":PRINT:PRINT A$
530 INPUT R$
540 IF R$="END" OR R$="end" THEN 600
550 IF VAL(R$)>0 THEN 570
560 BEEP:PRINT:PRINT E$:GOTO 520
570 ND=ND+1:D(ND)=VAL(R$):TD=TD+D(ND)
```

```
580 IF ND<MD THEN 530
590 PRINT:PRINT L$
600 PRINT:PRINT"TOTAL = ";:PRINT USING U$;TD:PRINT
610 PRINT"NOW ENTER THE AMOUNTS OF ANY CHECKS"
620 PRINT"THAT ARE IN THE CHECKBOOK PRIOR"
630 PRINT"TO CHECK ";LC;" BUT THAT"
640 PRINT"HAVE NOT BEEN SHOWN ON A BANK"
650 PRINT"STATEMENT YET."
660 PRINT:PRINT A$
670 INPUT R$
680 IF R$="END" OR R$="end" THEN 750
690 IF VAL(R$)>0 THEN 720
700 BEEP:PRINT:PRINT E$
710 GOTO 660
720 NC=NC+1:C(NC)=VAL(R$):TC=TC+C(NC)
730 IF NC<MC THEN 670
740 PRINT:PRINT L$
750 PRINT:PRINT"TOTAL = ";:PRINT USING U$;TC:PRINT
760 PRINT"NOW ENTER THE AMOUNTS OF ANY"
770 PRINT"SERVICE CHARGES OR DEBIT MEMOS."
780 PRINT:PRINT A$
790 INPUT R$
800 IF R$="END" OR R$="end" THEN 860
810 IF VAL(R$)>0 THEN 830
820 BEEP:PRINT:PRINT E$:GOTO 780
830 NS=NS+1:S(NS)=VAL(R$):TS=TS+S(NS)
840 IF NS<MS THEN 790
850 PRINT:PRINT L$
860 PRINT:PRINT"TOTAL =";:PRINT USING U$;TS:PRINT
870 GOSUB 1370
880 W=SB+TD+TS-CB-TC-TR:W=ABS(W)
890 IF W<.001 THEN W=0
900 IF W<>0 THEN 930
910 PRINT:PRINT"CONGRATULATIONS!  IT BALANCES."
920 GOTO 940
930 BEEP:PRINT:PRINT"SORRY, IT'S OUT OF BALANCE."
940 PRINT
950 PRINT"STATEMENT BALANCE"
960 PRINT"+ DEPOSITS OUTSTANDING"
970 PRINT"+ SERVICE CHARGES = ";
980 PRINT USING U$;SB+TD+TS:PRINT
990 PRINT"CHECKBOOK BALANCE"
1000 PRINT"+ CHECKS OUTSTANDING"
1010 PRINT"+ RECENT DEPOSITS = ";
1020 PRINT USING U$;CB+TC+TR:PRINT
1030 PRINT"DIFFERENCE = ";:PRINT USING U$;W
1040 PRINT:PRINT"PRESS ANY KEY TO CONTINUE"
1050 R$=INKEY$:IF LEN(R$)=0 THEN 1050
1060 PRINT
1070 PRINT"NEXT ACTION:"
1080 PRINT" 1 - LIST CHECKS OUTSTANDING"
1090 PRINT" 2 - LIST DEPOSITS OUTSTANDING"
```

```
1100 PRINT" 3 - LIST SERVICE CHARGES"
1110 PRINT" 4 - START OVER"
1120 PRINT" 5 - END PROGRAM"
1130 PRINT" 6 - DISPLAY BALANCING INFO"
1140 PRINT" 7 - LIST DEPOSITS AFTER LAST CHECK"
1150 INPUT R$:R=VAL(R$)
1160 IF R<1 OR R>7 THEN 1180
1170 ON R GOTO 1190,1230,1270,1310,1320,940,1330
1180 PRINT:PRINT E$:GOTO 1060
1190 PRINT:PRINT"CHECKS OUTSTANDING"
1200 FOR J=1 TO NC
1210 PRINT USING U$;C(J):NEXT
1220 GOTO 1040
1230 PRINT:PRINT"DEPOSITS OUTSTANDING"
1240 FOR J=1 TO ND
1250 PRINT USING U$;D(J):NEXT
1260 GOTO 1040
1270 PRINT:PRINT"SERVICE CHARGES"
1280 FOR J=1 TO NS
1290 PRINT USING U$;S(J):NEXT
1300 GOTO 1040
1310 CLEAR:GOTO 140
1320 END
1330 PRINT:PRINT"RECENT DEPOSITS"
1340 FOR J=1 TO NR
1350 PRINT USING U$;R(J):NEXT
1360 GOTO 1040
1370 PRINT
1380 PRINT"ENTER THE AMOUNT OF EACH DEPOSIT"
1390 PRINT"THAT IS SHOWN IN YOUR CHECKBOOK"
1400 PRINT"AFTER CHECK NO. ";LC;" THAT IS"
1410 PRINT"ALSO LISTED IN THE STATEMENT."
1420 PRINT:PRINT A$
1430 INPUT R$
1440 IF R$="END" OR R$="end" THEN 1500
1450 IF VAL(R$)>0 THEN 1470
1460 BEEP:PRINT:PRINT E$:GOTO 1420
1470 NR=NR+1:R(NR)=VAL(R$):TR=TR+R(NR)
1480 IF NR<MR THEN 1430
1490 PRINT:PRINT L$
1500 PRINT:PRINT"TOTAL = ";:PRINT USING U$;TR:
     PRINT
1510 RETURN
```

EASY CHANGES

Change the limitations of how many entries you can make in each category. Line 180 establishes these limits. If you have more than 50 checks outstanding at some time, change the value of MC to 100, for example. See the "Main Variables" section for an explanation of each limit.

MAIN ROUTINES

140- 340	Initializes variables and displays first instructions.
350- 420	Gets most recent check number.
440- 460	Gets checkbook balance after most recent check number.
470- 600	Gets outstanding deposits.
610- 750	Gets outstanding checks.
760- 860	Gets service charges and debit memos.
870	Gets recent deposits and credit memos.
880-1050	Does balancing calculation. Displays it. Ends program.
1060-1180	Shows seven actions to choose from.
1190-1220	Subroutine to display checks outstanding.
1230-1260	Subroutine to display deposits outstanding.
1270-1300	Subroutine to display service charges.
1310	Starts program over.
1320	Ends program.
1330-1360	Subroutine to display recent deposits.
1370-1510	Subroutine to get recent deposits.

MAIN VARIABLES

MC	Maximum number of checks outstanding.
MD	Maximum number of deposits outstanding.
MS	Maximum number of service charges, debit memos.
MR	Maximum number of recent deposits, credit memos.
C	Array for checks outstanding.
D	Array for deposits outstanding.
S	Array for service charges.
R	Array for recent deposits.
TC	Total of checks outstanding.
TD	Total of deposits outstanding.
TS	Total of service charges and debit memos.
TR	Total of recent deposits and credit memos.
NC	Number of checks outstanding.
ND	Number of deposits outstanding.
NS	Number of service charges and debit memos.

NR	Number of recent deposits and credit memos.
E$	Error message.
SB	Statement balance.
LC	Number of last check on statement.
CB	Checkbook balance after last check on statement.
R$	Reply from operator.
W	Amount by which checkbook is out of balance.
A$	Message showing how to indicate no more data.
L$	Message indicating no more room for data.
R	Numeric value of reply for next action.
J	Loop variable.
U$	String for editing numeric amounts when displayed.

SUGGESTED PROJECTS

1. Add more informative messages and a more complete introduction to make the program a tutorial for someone who
   has never balanced a checkbook before.
2. Save all entries from the operator and allow any of them to
   be reviewed and/or modified if found to be incorrect.
3. If the checkbook is out of balance, have the program do an
   analysis (as suggested in the "How To Use It" section) and
   suggest the most likely errors that might have caused the
   condition.
4. Allow the operator to find arithmetic errors in the checkbook. Ask for the starting balance, then ask for each check
   or deposit amount. Add or subtract, depending on which
   type the operator indicates. Display the new balance after
   each entry so the operator can compare with the checkbook
   entry.

DECIDE

PURPOSE

"Decisions, decisions!" How many times have you uttered this lament when confronted by a difficult choice? Wouldn't a trusty advisor be helpful on such occasions? Well, you now have one—your IBM Personal Computer of course.

This program can help you make decisions involving the selection of one alternative from several choices. It works by prying relevant information from you and then organizing it in a meaningful, quantitative manner. Your best choice will be indicated and all of the possibilities given a relative rating.

You can use the program for a wide variety of decisions. It can help with things like choosing the best stereo system, saying yes or no to a job or business offer, or selecting the best course of action for the future. Everything is personalized to your individual decision.

HOW TO USE IT

The first thing the program does is ask you to categorize the decision at hand into one of these three categories:

1) Choosing an item (or thing),
2) Choosing a course of action, or
3) Making a yes or no decision.

You simply press 1, 2, or 3 followed by the **ENTER** key to indicate which type of decision is facing you. If you are choosing an item, you will be asked what type of item it is.

If the decision is either of the first two types, you must next
enter a list of all the possibilities under consideration. A question mark will prompt you for each one. When the list is complete, type "END" in response to the last question mark. (N.B.
This must be typed with all capital letters, i.e., "END", not
"end".) You must, of course, enter at least two possibilities. (We
hope you don't have trouble making decisions from only one
possibility!) After the list is finished, it will be re-displayed so
that you can verify that it is correct. If not, you must re-enter it.

Now you must think of the different factors that are important to you in making your decision. For example, location,
cost, and quality of education might govern the decision of
which college to attend. For a refrigerator purchase, the factors
might be things like price, size, reliability, and warranty. In any
case, you will be prompted for your list with a succession of
question marks. Each factor is to be entered one at a time with
the word "END" used to terminate the list. When complete, the
list will be re-displayed. You must now decide which single factor is the most important and input its number. (You can enter 0
if you wish to change the list of factors.)

The program now asks you to rate the importance of each of
the other factors relative to the most important one. This is done
by first assigning a value of 10 to the main factor. Then you
must assign a value from 0-10 to each of the other factors. These
numbers reflect your assessment of each factor's relative importance as compared to the main one. A value of 10 means it is just
as important; lesser values indicate how much less importance
you place on it.

Now you must rate the decision possibilities with respect to
each of the importance factors. Each importance factor will be
treated separately. Considering *only* that importance factor, you
must rate how each decision possibility stacks up. The program
first assigns a value of 10 to one of the decision possibilities.
Then you must assign a relative number (lower, higher, or equal
to 10) to each of the other decision possibilities.

An example might alleviate possible confusion here. Suppose
you are trying to decide whether to get a dog, cat, or canary for a
pet. Affection is one of your importance factors. The program
assigns a value of 10 to the cat. Considering *only* affection, you
might assign a value of 20 to the dog and 6.5 to the canary. This
means *you* consider a dog twice as affectionate as a cat but a

canary only about two thirds as affectionate as a cat. (No slighting of bird lovers is intended here, of course. Your actual ratings may be entirely different.)

Armed with all this information, the program will now determine which choice seems best for you. The various possibilities are listed in order of ranking. Alongside each one is a relative rating with the best choice being normalized to a value of 100.

Of course, DECIDE should not be used as a substitute for good, clear thinking. However, it can often provide valuable insights. You might find one alternative coming out surprisingly low or high. A trend may become obvious when the program is re-run with improved data. At least, it may help you think about decisions systematically and honestly.

SAMPLE RUN

DECIDE

I CAN HELP YOU MAKE A DECISION. ALL I NEED TO DO IS ASK SOME QUESTIONS AND THEN ANALYZE THE INFORMATION YOU GIVE.

WHICH OF THESE BEST DESCRIBES THE TYPE OF DECISION FACING YOU?

   1) CHOOSING AN ITEM FROM VARIOUS
      ALTERNATIVES.
   2) CHOOSING A COURSE OF ACTION FROM VARIOUS
      ALTERNATIVES.
   3) MAKING A 'YES' OR 'NO' DECISION.

WHICH ONE (1, 2, OR 3)? **1**

WHAT TYPE OF ITEM MUST YOU DECIDE UPON?
VACATION

I NEED TO HAVE A LIST OF EACH VACATION UNDER CONSIDERATION.

INPUT THEM ONE AT A TIME IN RESPONSE TO EACH QUESTION MARK.

THE ORDER IN WHICH YOU INPUT THEM HAS NO
PARTICULAR SIGNIFICANCE.

TYPE THE WORD 'END' TO INDICATE THAT THE WHOLE
LIST HAS BEEN ENTERED.

? CAMPING
? SAFARI
? TRIP TO WASHINGTON D.C.
? END

O.K. HERE'S THE LIST YOU'VE GIVEN ME:

1) CAMPING
2) SAFARI
3) TRIP TO WASHINGTON D.C.

IS THIS LIST CORRECT (Y OR N)? **Y**

NOW, THINK OF THE DIFFERENT FACTORS THAT ARE
IMPORTANT TO YOU IN CHOOSING THE BEST VACATION.

INPUT THEM ONE AT A TIME IN RESPONSE TO EACH
QUESTION MARK.

TYPE THE WORD 'END' TO TERMINATE THE LIST.

? RELAXATION
? AFFORDABILITY
? CHANGE OF PACE
? END

HERE'S THE LIST OF FACTORS YOU GAVE ME:

1) RELAXATION
2) AFFORDABILITY
3) CHANGE OF PACE

DECIDE WHICH FACTOR ON THE LIST IS THE MOST
IMPORTANT AND INPUT ITS NUMBER.

(TYPE 0 IF THE LIST NEEDS CHANGING.)

? **2**

NOW LET'S SUPPOSE WE HAVE A SCALE OF IMPORTANCE RANGING FROM 0-10.

WE'LL GIVE AFFORDABILITY A VALUE OF 10 SINCE AFFORDABILITY WAS RATED THE MOST IMPORTANT.

ON THIS SCALE, WHAT VALUE OF IMPORTANCE WOULD THE OTHER FACTORS HAVE?

RELAXATION
? **5.5**

CHANGE OF PACE
? **9**

EACH VACATION MUST NOW BE COMPARED WITH RESPECT TO EACH IMPORTANCE FACTOR.

WE'LL CONSIDER EACH FACTOR SEPARATELY AND THEN RATE EACH VACATION IN TERMS OF THAT FACTOR ONLY.

LET'S GIVE CAMPING A VALUE OF 10 ON EVERY SCALE.

THEN EVERY OTHER VACATION WILL BE ASSIGNED A VALUE HIGHER OR LOWER THAN 10. THIS VALUE DEPENDS ON HOW MUCH YOU THINK IT IS BETTER OR WORSE THAN CAMPING.

CONSIDERING ONLY RELAXATION AND ASSIGNING 10 TO CAMPING; WHAT VALUE WOULD YOU ASSIGN TO

SAFARI? **3**

TRIP TO WASHINGTON D.C.? **9**

CONSIDERING ONLY AFFORDABILITY AND ASSIGNING 10 TO CAMPING; WHAT VALUE WOULD YOU ASSIGN TO

SAFARI? <u>1</u>

TRIP TO WASHINGTON D.C.? <u>8</u>

   CONSIDERING ONLY CHANGE OF PACE AND
ASSIGNING 10 TO CAMPING; WHAT VALUE WOULD YOU
ASSIGN TO

SAFARI? **60**

TRIP TO WASHINGTON D.C.? **25**

TRIP TO WASHINGTON D.C. COMES OUT BEST BUT IT'S
VERY CLOSE.

HERE IS THE FINAL LIST IN ORDER.

TRIP TO WASHINGTON D.C. HAS BEEN GIVEN A VALUE
OF 100 AND THE OTHERS RATED ACCORDINGLY.

100	TRIP TO WASHINGTON D.C.
98.65871	CAMPING
78.83755	SAFARI
OK	

PROGRAM LISTING

```
100 REM: DECIDE
110 REM: Guide you through decision making.
120 REM: COPYRIGHT 1982 Phil Feldman and Tom Rugg.
130 REM: Any BASIC, any CRT.
140 KEY OFF:SCREEN 0,0,0,0:WIDTH 40:COLOR 7,0,0
150 CLEAR
160 MD=10
170 DIM L$(MD),F$(MD),V(MD),C(MD,MD),D(MD),Z(MD)
180 E$="END"
190 GOSUB 1510
200 PRINT"   I can help you make a decision   All"
210 PRINT"I need to do is ask some questions and"
220 PRINT
    "then analyze the information you give.":PRINT
```

```
230 PRINT SPC(5);STRING$(28,45):PRINT
240 PRINT"Which of these best describes the type"
250 PRINT"of decision facing you?":PRINT
260 PRINT"  1) Choosing an item from various"
270 PRINT"     alternatives.":PRINT
280 PRINT"  2) Choosing a course of action from"
290 PRINT"     various alternatives.":PRINT
300 PRINT
    "  3) making a 'Yes' or 'No' decision.":PRINT
310 INPUT"Which one (1, 2, or 3)";R$
320 T=INT(VAL(R$)):IF T<1 OR T>3 THEN BEEP:
    GOTO 310
330 GOSUB 1510
340 ON T GOTO 350,370,380
350 PRINT"What type of item must you decide upon"
360 INPUT T$:GOTO 410
370 T$="course of action":GOTO 410
380 T$="'Yes' or 'No'"

390 NI=2:L$(1)="deciding Yes":L$(2)="deciding No"
400 GOTO 640
410 GOSUB 1510:NI=0
420 PRINT"   I need to have a list of each"
430 PRINT T$;" under consideration.":PRINT
440 PRINT"    Input them one at a time"
450 PRINT"in response to each question mark.":
    PRINT
460 PRINT"    The order in which you input them"
470 PRINT"has no particular significance.":PRINT
480 PRINT"    Type the word '";E$;"' to indicate"
490 PRINT
    "that the whole list has been entered.":PRINT
500 NI=NI+1:INPUT L$(NI)
510 IF L$(NI)<> E$ THEN 500
520 NI=NI-1
530 IF NI>=2 THEN 560
540 PRINT:PRINT
    "You must have at least 2 choices":BEEP:PRINT
550 PRINT"Try again":GOSUB 1530:GOTO 410
560 GOSUB 1510:PRINT
    "O.K. Here's the list you've given me:":PRINT
570 FOR J=1 TO NI:
    PRINT SPC(3);J;")";SPC(1);L$(J):NEXT:PRINT
580 PRINT"Is this list correct (Y or N)";
590 INPUT R$:R$=LEFT$(R$,1)
600 IF R$="Y" OR R$="y" THEN 640
610 IF R$="N" OR R$="n" THEN  PRINT:
    PRINT"The list must be re-entered"
620 IF R$="N" OR R$="n" THEN  GOSUB 1530:GOSUB 410
630 BEEP:GOTO 580
640 GOSUB 1510
650 PRINT"   Now, think of the different factors"
```

```
660 IF T<3 THEN PRINT
    "that are important to you in choosing"
670 IF T<3 THEN PRINT"the best ";T$;"."
680 IF T=3 THEN PRINT"that are important to you
    in deciding":PRINT"Yes or No"
690 PRINT:
    PRINT"    Input them one at a time in response"
700 PRINT"to each question mark.":PRINT
710 PRINT"    Type the word '";E$;"' to terminate"
720 PRINT"the list.":PRINT:NF = 0
730 NF=NF+1:INPUT F$(NF)
740 IF F$(NF)<> E$ THEN 730
750 NF=NF-1:PRINT
760 IF NF<1 THEN PRINT
    "You must have at least one! - redo it":BEEP
770 IF NF<1 THEN GOSUB 1530:GOTO 640
780 GOSUB 1510:PRINT"Here's the list of factors
    you gave me:":PRINT
790 FOR J=1 TO NF:
    PRINT SPC(3);J;")";SPC(1);F$(J):NEXT:PRINT
800 PRINT"    Decide which factor on the list is"
810 PRINT
    "the most important and input its number."
820 PRINT"(Type 0 if the list needs changing.)":
    PRINT
830 INPUT A:A=INT(A):IF A=0 THEN 640
840 IF A<0 OR A>NF THEN 780
850 GOSUB 1510:IF NF=1 THEN 980
860 PRINT"    Now let's suppose we have a scale of"
870 PRINT"importance ranging from 0-10.":PRINT
880 PRINT"    We'll give ";F$(A);" a"
890 PRINT"value of 10 since ";F$(A)
900 PRINT"was rated the most important.":PRINT
910 PRINT"    On this scale, what value of"
920 PRINT
    "importance would the other factors have?"
930 FOR J=1 TO NF:Q=A:IF J=Q THEN 970
940 PRINT:PRINT F$(J):INPUT V(J)
950 IF V(J)>=0 AND V(J)<=10 THEN 970
960 PRINT" Impossible value - try again":BEEP:
    GOTO 940
970 NEXT
980 V(A)=10:Q=0:FOR J=1 TO NF:Q=Q+V(J):NEXT:
    FOR J=1 TO NF
990 V(J)=V(J)/Q:NEXT:GOSUB 1510
1000 IF T<> 3 THEN PRINT"    Each ";T$
1010 IF T=3 THEN PRINT
    "    deciding Yes or deciding No"
1020 PRINT"must now be compared with respect to"
1030 PRINT"each importance factor.":PRINT
1040 PRINT"    We'll consider each factor"
```

```
1050 PRINT"separately and then rate"
1060 IF T<> 3 THEN PRINT"each ";T$;" in terms"
1070 IF T=3 THEN PRINT
     "deciding Yes or deciding No in terms"
1080 PRINT"of that factor only.":PRINT
1090 PRINT"   Let's give ";L$(1)
1100 PRINT"a value of 10 on every scale.":PRINT
1110 IF T<> 3 THEN PRINT"   Then every other ";T$
1120 IF T=3 THEN PRINT"   Then deciding No"
1130 PRINT"will be assigned a value higher or"
1140 PRINT"lower than 10.  This value depends on"
1150 PRINT"how much you think it is better or"
1160 PRINT"worse than ";L$(1);"."
1170 PRINT:FOR J=1 TO NF
1180 PRINT SPC(3);STRING$(18,45)
1190 PRINT"   Considering only ";F$(J);" and"
1200 PRINT"assigning 10 to ";L$(1);";"
1210 PRINT"what value would you assign to"
1220 PRINT:FOR K=2 TO NI
1230 PRINT L$(K);:INPUT C(K,J):PRINT:
     IF C(K,J)>=0 THEN 1250
1240 PRINT"  -- Negative values not legal --":
     BEEP:GOTO 1230
1250 NEXT:C(1,J)=10:NEXT
1260 FOR J=1 TO NF:Q=0:FOR K=1 TO NI
1270 Q=Q+C(K,J):NEXT:FOR K=1 TO NI
1280 C(K,J)=C(K,J)/Q:NEXT:NEXT
1290 FOR K=1 TO NI:D(K)=0:FOR J=1 TO NF
1300 D(K)=D(K)+C(K,J)*V(J):NEXT:NEXT
1310 MX=0:FOR K=1 TO NI
1320 IF D(K)>MX THEN MX=D(K)
1330 NEXT:FOR K=1 TO NI:D(K)=D(K)*100/MX:NEXT
1340 FOR K=1 TO NI:Z(K)=K:NEXT:NM=NI-1
1350 FOR K=1 TO NI:FOR J=1 TO NM:N1=Z(J):
     N2=Z(J+1):IF D(N1)>D(N2) THEN 1370
1360 Z(J+1)=N1:Z(J)=N2
1370 NEXT:NEXT:J1=Z(1):J2=Z(2):DF=D(J1)-D(J2):
     GOSUB 1510
1380 PRINT L$(J1);
1390 PRINT" comes out best"
1400 IF DF<5 THEN PRINT"but it's very close.":
     GOTO 1440
1410 IF DF<10 THEN PRINT
     "but it's fairly close.":GOTO 1440
1420 IF DF<20 THEN PRINT"by a fair amount.":
     GOTO 1440
1430 PRINT"quite decisively."
1440 PRINT:
     PRINT"Here is the final list in order.":PRINT
1450 PRINT L$(J1);" has been"
1460 PRINT"given a value of 100 and the others"
```

```
1470 PRINT"rated accordingly.":PRINT
1480 PRINT STRING$(20,45):PRINT
1490 FOR J=1 TO NI:Q=Z(J):
     PRINT D(Q);TAB(16);L$(Q):NEXT
1500 END
1510 FOR J=1 TO 500:NEXT
1520 CLS:PRINT TAB(16);"DECIDE":PRINT:RETURN
1530 FOR J=1 TO 3000:NEXT:RETURN
```

EASY CHANGES

1. The word END (in all capital letters) is used to flag the ter-
    mination of various input lists. If you wish to use something
    else (because of conflicts with items on the list or to use
    lowercase letters for convenience), change the definition of
    E$ in line 180. For example, to use the word "done", change
    line 180 to

    180 E$ = "done"

2. Line 1530 contains a timing delay used regularly in the pro-
    gram. If things seem to change too fast, you can make the
    number 3000 larger. Try

    1530 FOR J = 1 TO 5000:NEXT: RETURN

3. The program can currently accept up to ten decision alterna-
    tives and/or ten importance factors. If you need more, in-
    crease the value of MD in line 160. Thus, to use 15 values,
    line 160 should be

    160 MD = 15

MAIN ROUTINES

150- 180	Initializes and dimensions variables.
190- 330	Determines category of decision.
340- 400	Gets or sets T$.
410- 630	Gets list of possible alternatives from user.
640- 840	Gets list of importance factors from user.
850- 970	User rates each importance factor.
980-1250	User rates the decision alternatives with respect to each importance factor.
1260-1330	Evaluates the various alternatives.
1340-1370	Sorts alternatives into their relative ranking.
1380-1500	Displays results.
1510-1520	Subroutine to clear screen and display header.
1530	Time wasting subroutine.

MAIN VARIABLES

MD	Maximum number of decision alternatives.
NI	Number of decision alternatives.
L$	String array of the decision alternatives.
NF	Number of importance factors.
F$	String array of the importance factors.
V	Array of the relative values of each importance factor.
A	Index number of most important factor.
C	Array of relative values of each alternative with respect to each importance factor.
T	Decision category ($1 = $ item, $2 = $ course of action, $3 = $ yes or no).
T$	String name of decision category.
E$	String to signal the end of an input data list.
J,K	Loop indices.
R$	User reply string.
Q,N1,N2	Work variables.
D	Array of each alternative's value.
MX	Maximum value of all alternatives.
DF	Rating difference between best two alternatives.
Z	Array of the relative rankings of each alternative.

SUGGESTED PROJECTS

1. Allow the user to review his numerical input and modify it if desired.
2. Insights into a decision can often be gained by a sensitivity analysis. This involves running the program a number of times for the same decision. Each time, one input value is changed (usually the one you are least confident about). By seeing how the results change, you can determine which factors are the most important. Currently, this requires a complete rerunning of the program each time. Modify the program to allow a change of input after the regular output is produced. Then recalculate the results based on the new values. (Note that many input arrays are clobbered once all the input is given. This modification will require saving the original input in new arrays so that it can be reviewed later.)

LOAN

PURPOSE

One of the most frustrating things about borrowing money from a bank (or credit union or savings and loan institution) is that it's not easy to fully evaluate your options. When you are borrowing from a credit union to buy a new car, you might have the choice of a thirty-six or a forty-eight month repayment period. When buying a house, you can sometimes get a slightly lower interest rate for your loan if you can come up with a larger down payment. Which option is best for you? How will the monthly payment be affected? Will there be much difference in how fast the principal of the loan decreases? How much of each payment will be for interest, which is tax deductible?

You need to know the answers to all these questions to make the best decision. This program gives you the information you need.

HOW TO USE IT

The program first asks you the size of the loan you are considering. Only whole dollar amounts are allowed — no pennies. Loans of ten million dollars or more are rejected (you can afford to hire an investment counselor if you want to borrow that much). Then you are asked the yearly interest rate for the loan. Enter this number as a percentage, such as 10.8. Next, you are asked to give the period of the loan in months. For a five year loan, enter 60. For a thirty year mortgage, enter 360. The program then displays this information for you and calculates the

monthly payment that will cause the loan to be paid off with
equal payments each month over the life of the loan.

At this point you have four options. First, you can show a
monthly analysis. This displays a month-by-month breakdown,
showing the state of the loan after each payment. The six columns of data shown for each month are the payment number (or
month number) of the loan, the remaining balance of the loan
after that payment, the amount of that payment that was interest, the accumulated interest paid to date, the amount of the
payment that was principal, and the accumulated principal paid
to date. Eighteen lines of data are displayed on the screen, and
then you can either press the **T** key to get the final totals for the
loan, or any other key except **SHIFT**, etc. to get the data for the
next eighteen months of the loan.

The second option is overriding the monthly payment. It is a
common practice with second mortgage loans to make smaller
monthly payments each month with a large "balloon" payment
as the final payment. You can use this second option to try
various monthly payments to see how they affect that big payment at the end. After overriding the monthly payment, you will
want to use the first option next to get a monthly analysis and
final totals using the new monthly payment.

The third option is to simply start over. You will generally use
this option if you are just comparing what the different monthly
payments would be for different loan possibilities.

The fourth option ends the program.

By the way, there is a chance that the monthly payment
calculated by your lender will differ from the one calculated here
by a penny or two. We like to think that this is because we are
making a more accurate calculation.

NOTE: SEE THE IMPORTANT NOTE IN THE FRONT OF
THIS BOOK

SAMPLE RUN

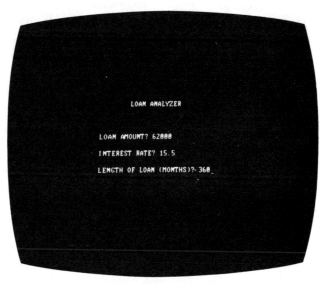

The operator enters the three necessary pieces of information about his or her loan.

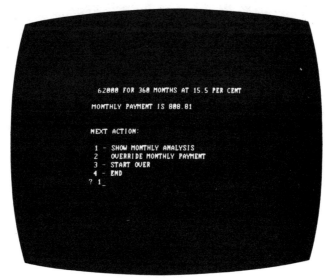

The program responds with the monthly payment that will pay off the loan with equal payments over its life, then asks the operator what to do next. The operator asks for the monthly analysis.

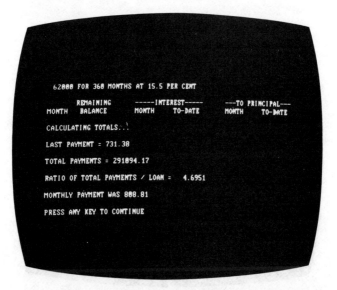

```
 62000 FOR 360 MONTHS AT 15.5 PER CENT

         REMAINING    -----INTEREST-----    ---TO PRINCIPAL---
MONTH    BALANCE      MONTH    TO-DATE       MONTH    TO-DATE
  1      61992.02     800.83   800.83        7.98     7.98
  2      61983.94     800.73   1601.56       8.08     16.06
  3      61975.76     800.63   2402.19       8.18     24.24
  4      61967.47     800.52   3202.71       8.29     32.53
  5      61959.07     800.41   4003.12       8.40     40.93
  6      61950.56     800.30   4803.42       8.51     49.44
  7      61941.94     800.19   5603.61       8.62     58.06
  8      61933.21     800.08   6403.69       8.73     66.79
  9      61924.37     799.97   7203.66       8.84     75.63
 10      61915.42     799.86   8003.52       8.95     84.58
 11      61906.35     799.74   8803.26       9.07     93.65
 12      61897.16     799.62   9602.88       9.19     102.84
 13      61887.85     799.50   10402.38      9.31     112.15
 14      61878.42     799.38   11201.76      9.43     121.58
 15      61868.87     799.26   12001.02      9.55     131.13
 16      61859.20     799.14   12800.16      9.67     140.80
 17      61849.40     799.01   13599.17      9.80     150.60
 18      61839.48     798.89   14398.06      9.92     160.52

PRESS 'T' FOR TOTALS, OR ANY OTHER KEY FOR NEXT SCREEN
```

The program responds with information about the first eighteen months
of the loan, then waits.

```
 62000 FOR 360 MONTHS AT 15.5 PER CENT

         REMAINING    -----INTEREST-----    ---TO PRINCIPAL---
MONTH    BALANCE      MONTH    TO-DATE       MONTH    TO-DATE

CALCULATING TOTALS...

LAST PAYMENT = 731.38

TOTAL PAYMENTS = 291094.17

RATIO OF TOTAL PAYMENTS / LOAN =    4.6951

MONTHLY PAYMENT WAS 800.81

PRESS ANY KEY TO CONTINUE
```

The operator presses "T", and after a few seconds the program displays
totalling information about the loan.

PROGRAM LISTING

```
100 REM: LOAN
110 REM: A loan payment analyzer.
120 REM: COPYRIGHT 1982 Tom Rugg and Phil Feldman.
130 REM: Any BASIC, 80 column CRT.
140 KEY OFF:SCREEN 0,0:WIDTH 80:COLOR 7,0
150 CLEAR:CLS:DEFINT J,L,N:DEFDBL A-F,M,P-Z
160 PRINT TAB(8);"LOAN ANALYZER"
170 PRINT:PRINT:PRINT:I=1
180 INPUT"LOAN AMOUNT";A
190 GOSUB 870:IF A=0 THEN 180
200 PRINT:INPUT"INTEREST RATE";R
210 PRINT:INPUT"LENGTH OF LOAN (MONTHS)";N
220 R=ABS(R):N=INT(N):M=R/1200:PRINT
230 GOSUB 830
240 REM: 'Up arrow' in next line is shifted '6'.
250 W=(1+M)^N
260 P=A*M*W/(W-1)
270 P=INT(P*100+.998):P=P/100
280 PRINT"MONTHLY PAYMENT IS";P
290 FP=P:PRINT:PRINT
300 PRINT"NEXT ACTION:"
310 PRINT
320 PRINT" 1 - SHOW MONTHLY ANALYSIS"
330 PRINT" 2 - OVERRIDE MONTHLY PAYMENT"
340 PRINT" 3 - START OVER"
350 PRINT" 4 - END"
360 INPUT C
370 ON C GOTO 430,410,150,400
380 PRINT"CHOICES ARE 1, 2, 3, AND 4"
390 GOTO 300
400 END
410 PRINT:INPUT"MONTHLY PAYMENT";P
420 GOTO 290
430 GOSUB 440:GOTO 520
440 GOSUB 830
450 PRINT TAB(8);"REMAINING";TAB(23);
460 PRINT"-----INTEREST-----";TAB(47);
470 PRINT"---TO PRINCIPAL---"
480 PRINT"MONTH    BALANCE";TAB(23);
490 PRINT"MONTH       TO-DATE";TAB(47);
500 PRINT"MONTH       TO-DATE"
510 RETURN
520 B=A*100:TT=0:TP=0:L=0:P=P*100:R$=""
530 FOR J=1 TO N
540 T=M*B
550 T=INT(T+.5)
560 IF J=N THEN P=B+T
570 PR=P-T
580 TP=TP+P:B=B-P+T:TT=TT+T:TPR=TPR+PR
```

```
590  IF B<0 THEN GOSUB 910
600  IF R$="T" OR R$="t" THEN 740
610  PB=B/100:PT=T/100:T2=TT/100
620  PPR=PR/100
630  PTPR=TPR/100
640  PRINT J;TAB(6);
650  PRINT USING "########.##-";PB;PT;T2;PPR;PTPR
660  IF B=0 THEN J=N:GOTO 690
670  L=L+1:IF L<18 THEN 740
680  DEF SEG:POKE 106,0
690  PRINT:PRINT"PRESS 'T' FOR TOTALS, OR";
700  PRINT" ANY OTHER KEY FOR NEXT SCREEN";
710  R$=INKEY$:IF LEN(R$)=0 THEN 710
720  DEF SEG:POKE 106,0:L=0:GOSUB 440
730  IF R$="T" OR R$="t" THEN PRINT:
     PRINT"CALCULATING TOTALS...
740  NEXT
750  PRINT:PRINT"LAST PAYMENT =";P/100
760  PRINT:PRINT"TOTAL PAYMENTS =";TP/100
770  PRINT:PRINT"RATIO OF TOTAL PAYMENTS / LOAN =";
780  PRINT USING "####.####";TP/A/100
790  PRINT:PRINT"MONTHLY PAYMENT WAS";FP
800  PRINT:PRINT"PRESS ANY KEY TO CONTINUE"
810  R$=INKEY$:IF LEN(R$)=0 THEN 810
820  P=FP:GOTO 290
830  CLS
840  PRINT A;"FOR";N;"MONTHS AT";R;"PER CENT"
850  PRINT
860  RETURN
870  A=ABS(A):A=INT(A)
880  IF A<10000000# THEN RETURN:REM--Ten million
890  PRINT"TOO LARGE"
900  A=0:RETURN
910  P=P+B:TP=TP+B:B=0
920  RETURN
```

EASY CHANGES

1. The number of lines of data displayed on each screen when
    doing a monthly analysis can be changed by altering the con-
    stant 18 in statement 670. You might prefer seeing 12
    payments on each screen.
2. To print the monthly analysis on your printer, make these
    changes:
    a. Change every **PRINT** to **LPRINT** in lines 450-500,
       640-650, 750-790, and 840-850.

    b. Change line 230 and insert line 702 as follows:

       230 REM
       702 FOR H = 1 TO 14:LPRINT:NEXT

    c. Change the 18 in line 670 to 48.
    This will print 48 months of payments on each page.

3. To include the monthly payment in the heading at the top of each screen of the monthly analysis, change the following line:

850 IF FP < > 0 THEN PRINT"MONTHLY PAYMENT IS";FP

MAIN ROUTINES

140-230	Displays title. Gets loan information.
240-290	Calculates and displays monthly payment.
300-390	Asks for next action. Goes to corresponding routine.
410-420	Gets override for monthly payment.
430-820	Calculates and displays monthly analysis.
830-860	Subroutine to clear screen and display data about the loan at the top.
870-900	Edits loan amount (size and whole dollar).
910-920	Subroutine to handle early payoff of loan.

MAIN VARIABLES

A	Amount of loan.
R	Interest rate (percentage).
N	Length of loan (number of months).
M	Monthly interest rate (not percentage).
W	Work variable.
P	Monthly payment (times 100).
FP	First monthly payment.
C	Choice of next action.
B	Remaining balance of loan (times 100).
TT	Total interest to date (times 100).
TP	Total payments to date.
L	Number of lines of data on screen.
R$	Reply from operator at keyboard.
J	Work variable for loops.
T	Monthly interest.

PR   Amount of payment that goes to principal.
TPR   Running total of PR.
PPR   PR/100 (for displaying PR).
PTPR   TPR/100 (for displaying TPR).

SUGGESTED PROJECTS

1. Add another column of data to the monthly analysis to show the portion (percentage) of the loan that has been paid off so far.
2. Modify the program to show an analysis of resulting monthly payments for a range of interest rates and/or loan lengths near those provided by the operator. For example, if an interest rate of 9.5 percent was entered, display the monthly payments for 8.5, 9, 9.5, 10, and 10.5 percent.

MILEAGE

PURPOSE

For many of us, automobile operating efficiency is a continual concern. This program can help by keeping track of gasoline consumption, miles driven, and fuel mileage for a motor vehicle. It allows reading and writing data files with the disk unit. Thus, a master data file may be retained and updated. The program computes mileage (miles per gallon or MPG) obtained after each gasoline fill-up. A running log of all information is maintained. This enables trends in vehicle operation efficiency to be easily checked.

HOW TO USE IT

The program requests the following data from the operator as a record of each gasoline fill-up: date, odometer reading, and number of gallons purchased. The most useful results will be obtained if entries are chronological and complete, with each entry representing a full gasoline fill-up.

The program operates from a central command mode. The operator requests branching to any one of six available subroutines. When a subroutine completes execution, control returns to the command mode for any additional requests. A description of each subroutine now follows:

1) ENTER DATA FROM THE KEYBOARD

This option allows you to enter data records directly from the terminal. This mode is used when you want to add information to your file of mileage records or to enter data for the first time. The program will prompt you for the required information.

Each input line contains a date, odometer reading, and the number of gallons purchased. These data fields must be separated by commas. You may leave a field blank (resulting in a value of zero or a null string for the date) but each line must contain exactly two commas.

The date can include any keyboard characters except commas or quotation marks. Only the eight characters at the far left will be used if more than eight are entered. We recommend that you use the month/date/year form such as 12/25/82. However, you might want to use other notations such as AUG 2, or WEEK 5, or something else. The odometer reading should be a number between 0 and 999999. The number of gallons should be greater than 0 and less than 99999. A typical input line might be: 99999. A typical input line might be:

10/31/82, 45123.6, 18.2

When your input is complete, enter a ficticious last line containing zero for both the odometer reading and number of gallons purchased. This can be done simply by typing two commas.

2) VERIFY DATA IN MEMORY

Choose this option and the computer will scan the data in memory to report any trouble it may find in your input. Bad dates, bad odometer values, and bad gallon values will be flagged and printed with their data record number. In addition, the first and last dates, and the total number of data records are displayed. After each error, you are requested to hit any key to continue. After all data is processed, you are requested to hit any key to return to command mode.

3) DISPLAY MILEAGE INFORMATION

This subroutine computes mileage (miles per gallon or MPG) from the available data. It formats all information and displays it in tabular form. Numbers are rounded off so that four columns of information can be displayed on one line. When data fills the screen, you are prompted to hit any key to continue the listing. When all data is displayed, pressing any key will put you back into the command mode.

4) READ DATA FROM DISK FILE

This option, and the next, apply only if you have a disk drive(s). This one enables you to read information into the computer that has been saved by this program on a disk file. You will presumably add new data, then save the new file for later recall.

The program will display the files already on the disk before asking you for the *filespec* of the file you want to read. You will want to select the name of a file that already exists. If this file is not on the disk or you change your mind, you can return to the command mode simply by pressing **ENTER** without entering a *filespec*.

A *filespec* is typically a simple one to eight character name for a disk file. However, it can be a complete file specification in the form of "d:filename.ext" as explained in the Disk Operating System (DOS) manual.

After you enter the *filespec* the program will wipe out any data already in memory, read the file, and show you how many data records were found on it. It then returns to the command mode.

5) WRITE DATA TO DISK FILE

This choice enables you to write the data that is in memory to a disk file for later recall as described in the last section. The files currently on the disk will be displayed and you will be prompted for a *filespec*. You can press **ENTER** to immediately return to command mode if you change your mind.

Here, you probably will want to enter a unique *filespec*, otherwise the old file will be replaced by the new one. After the data is written to the disk, the program will display the number of records written to the new file. It then returns to the command mode.

6) END PROGRAM

The program will stop execution and return the computer to BASIC.

SAMPLE RUN

```
                    MILEAGE
+++++++++++++++++++++++++++++++++++++++++++
Command List

1) Enter data from the keyboard.
2) Verify data in memory.
3) Display mileage information.
4) Read data from disk file.
5) Write data to disk file.
6) End program.

Enter command by number? 4_
```

The program's menu is displayed and the operator chooses option #4.
This permits previously stored data on the disk to be read into memory.

```
     Files on disk are:
     MILEAGE .BAS VOLVO    .1
     filespec to read? VOLVO.1
      6 records read from file:VOLVO.1
     +++++++++++++++++++++++++++++++++++++
     Command List

     1) Enter data from the keyboard.
     2) Verify data in memory.
     3) Display mileage information.
     4) Read data from disk file.
     5) Write data to disk file.
     6) End program.

     Enter command by number? 1_
```

The files on the default disk drive are displayed. The operator chooses
to read in the file called VOLVO.1. This file has 6 data records. The
operator then chooses the option to enter additional data from the
keyboard.

```
        Each input line is to be a data
    record consisting of (in order):

     -Date (e.g. 1/1/83)
     -Odometer reading (miles)
     -No. gallons bought

        Separate the three fields by commas.
    Any field may be left blank but each
    line must contain exactly two commas.

        Terminate data entry with an entry
    of zero for both odometer reading
    and gallons bought.  (,,) will do.

    6 records already in memory,
    300 is maximum number allowed.

    Input will begin with record # 7

    7)? _
```

The program explains how to enter additional data and waits for the
newest data record (#7) to be entered.

```
    7)? 11/26/82,52570.8,13.7

    8)? 12/1/82,52842.5,14.6

    9)? 12/9/82,53048.4,11.8

    10)? 12/15/82,53359.7,14.7

    11)? 12/23/82,53601.2,13.3

    12)? ,,
    ++++++++++++++++++++++++++++++++++++
    Command List

    1) Enter data from the keyboard.
    2) Verify data in memory.
    3) Display mileage information.
    4) Read data from disk file.
    5) Write data to disk file.
    6) End program.

    Enter command by number? 3_
```

The operator enters the new data. The input is terminated with a special
string of two commas (,,).

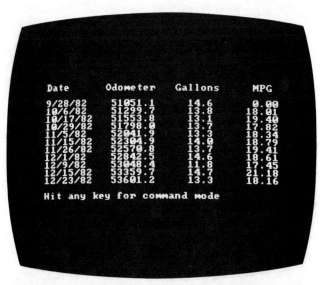

```
Date        Odometer   Gallons     MPG

9/28/82     51051.1     14.6      0.00
10/6/82     51299.7     13.8     18.01
10/17/82    51553.8     13.1     19.40
10/29/82    51798.0     13.7     17.82
11/5/82     52041.9     13.3     18.34
11/15/82    52304.9     14.0     18.79
11/26/82    52570.8     13.7     19.41
12/1/82     52842.5     14.6     18.61
12/9/82     53048.4     11.8     17.45
12/15/82    53359.7     14.7     21.18
12/23/82    53601.2     13.3     18.16

Hit any key for command mode
```

After returning to the command menu, the operator selects option #3 to display the entire set of mileage information.

```
Files now on disk are:

MILEAGE .BAS VOLVO    .1

filespec to write? VOLVO.2

   11 records written to file: VOLVO.2

++++++++++++++++++++++++++++++++++++

Command List

1) Enter data from the keyboard.
2) Verify data in memory.
3) Display mileage information.
4) Read data from disk file.
5) Write data to disk file.
6) End program.

Enter command by number? 6
Ok
```

Next, option #5 is selected to store all the data on a new disk file. This new file is given the name VOLVO.2. Finally the program is terminated with the selection of option #6.

PROGRAM LISTING

```
100 REM: MILEAGE
110 REM: Analyze a car's gasoline usage.
120 REM: COPYRIGHT 1982 Phil Feldman and Tom Rugg.
130 REM: Any BASIC, any CRT.
140 KEY OFF:SCREEN 0,0,0,0:WIDTH 40:COLOR 7,0,0
150 CLEAR:CLS:N=0
160 MW=100
170 MR=300
180 DIM D$(MR),D(MR),G(MR),M(MR)
190 B$=SPACE$(2):X$="\"+B$+B$+B$+"\"+B$
200 X$=X$+"######.#"+B$+"#####.#"+B$+"#####.##"
210 PRINT TAB(14);"MILEAGE"
220 PRINT:PRINT STRING$(33,43):PRINT:R=0:
    PRINT"Command List"
230 PRINT:PRINT"1) Enter data from the keyboard."
240 PRINT"2) Verify data in memory."
250 PRINT"3) Display mileage information."
260 PRINT"4) Read data from disk file."
270 PRINT"5) Write data to disk file."
280 PRINT"6) End program."
290 DEF SEG:POKE 106,0:PRINT:
    INPUT"Enter command by number";R
300 R=INT(R):IF R<1 OR R>6 THEN BEEP:GOTO 220
310 ON R GOTO 320,550,800,940,1050,1160
320 CLS:PRINT"    Each input line is to be a data"
330 PRINT"record consisting of (in order):":PRINT
340 PRINT" -Date (e.g. 1/1/83)"
350 PRINT" -Odometer reading (miles)"
360 PRINT" -No. gallons bought"
370 PRINT:
    PRINT"    Separate the three fields by commas."
380 PRINT"Any field may be left blank but each"
390 PRINT"line must contain exactly two commas."
400 PRINT:
    PRINT"    Terminate data entry with an entry"
410 PRINT"of zero for both odometer reading"
420 PRINT"and gallons bought.  (,,) will do."
430 PRINT:PRINT N;"records already in memory,"
440 PRINT MR;"is maximum number allowed.":PRINT
450 PRINT"Input will begin with record #";N+1
460 N=N+1:IF N<=MR THEN 510
470 PRINT:BEEP:COLOR 23
480 PRINT"    No more input allowed !!"
490 PRINT"Maximum no. records in memory -";MR
500 COLOR 7:N=N-1:GOTO 220
510 PRINT:PRINT N;CHR$(29);")";
520 INPUT D$(N),D(N),G(N)
530 IF D(N)<>0 OR G(N)<>0 THEN 460
540 N=N-1:GOTO 220
550 CLS:IF N>0 THEN 570
```

```
560 COLOR 23:PRINT"No data records!":COLOR 7:
    GOTO 220
570 PRINT"Beginning date: ";D$(1)
580 IF N>1 THEN PRINT SPACE$(5);"Last date:
    ";D$(N)
590 PRINT:PRINT N;"total records":IF N=1 THEN 220
600 FOR J=2 TO N:F=0:IF LEN(D$(J))<=8 THEN 620
610 GOSUB 750:
    PRINT"Date is longer than 8 characters"
620 IF D(J)>=0 AND D(J)<=999999! THEN 640
630 GOSUB 750:PRINT"Odometer value is bad"
640 IF D(J)>D(J-1) THEN 680
650 GOSUB 750
660 PRINT"Odometer <= value of";D(J-1)
670 PRINT SPACE$(4);"at previous date"
680 IF G(J)>0 AND G(J)<=99999! THEN 700
690 GOSUB 750:PRINT"Gallons value is bad"
700 IF F=0 THEN 720
710 PRINT:PRINT"Hit any key to continue":
    GOSUB 1170
720 NEXT:PRINT
730 PRINT"All done - hit any key for command mode"
740 GOSUB 1170:GOTO 220
750 IF J=F THEN RETURN
760 F=J:PRINT STRING$(35,45)
770 PRINT"Error found in data record";J
780 PRINT"-Date:";D$(J):PRINT"-Odometer =";D(J)
790 PRINT"-Gallons bought =";G(J):PRINT:RETURN
800 CLS:IF N>0 THEN 820
810 COLOR 23:PRINT"No data records!":COLOR 7:
    GOTO 220
820 M(1)=0:IF N=1 THEN 870
830 FOR J=2 TO N
840 IF G(J)>0 THEN M(J)=(D(J)-D(J-1))/G(J) ELSE
    M(J)=0
850 IF M(J)<0 THEN M(J)=0
860 NEXT
870 K=-17:L=0
880 CLS:K=K+18:L=L+18:IF L>N THEN L=N
890 PRINT "Date";TAB(11);"Odometer";TAB(22);
    "Gallons";TAB(34);"MPG"
900 PRINT:FOR J=K TO L:
    PRINT USING X$;D$(J);D(J);G(J);M(J):NEXT
910 PRINT:IF L<N THEN 930
920 PRINT"Hit any key for command mode":
    GOSUB 1170:GOTO 220
930 PRINT"Hit any key to continue":GOSUB 1170:
    GOTO 880
940 CLS:PRINT"Files on disk are:":PRINT
950 FILES:PRINT:PRINT:INPUT"filespec to read";F$
960 N=1:IF LEN(F$)=0 THEN 220
970 PRINT:OPEN F$ FOR INPUT AS #1
```

```
980 INPUT#1,D$(N),D(N),G(N)
990 IF EOF(1) THEN 1030
1000 IF N<MR THEN N=N+1:GOTO 980
1010 PRINT N;"records read on file: ";F$
1020 PRINT"   Maximum allowed!":GOTO 1040
1030 PRINT N;"records read from file:";F$
1040 CLOSE#1:GOTO 220
1050 CLS:PRINT"Files now on disk are:":PRINT
1060 FILES:PRINT:PRINT:INPUT"filespec to write";F$
1070 K=1:IF LEN(F$)=0 THEN 220
1080 OPEN F$ FOR OUTPUT AS #1:IF N=0 THEN 1140
1090 PRINT:K=1:IF MW>=N THEN 1120
1100 PRINT
    "Only the last";MW;"records will be written"
1110 PRINT:K=N-MW+1
1120 FOR J=K TO N
1130 WRITE#1,D$(J),D(J),G(J):NEXT
1140 PRINT N-K+1;"records written to file: ";F$
1150 CLOSE#1:GOTO 220
1160 END
1170 DEF SEG:POKE 106,0:Q$=INKEY$:
    IF Q$="" THEN 1170
1180 RETURN
```

EASY CHANGES

1. Changing the value of MR in line 170 alters the maximum
    number of data records that the program allows. You may
    need to make MR larger to accommodate additional data or
    smaller to conserve memory. To adjust MR, simply change
    its value in line 170 from its current value of 300 to whatever
    you choose.

2. Currently, the program will write a maximum of 100 data
    records during the disk write operation. This number can be
    altered by changing the value of MW in line 160 from its
    value of 100 to whatever you choose. Only the most recent
    MW records will be written to disk if MW is less than the
    number of available records when a disk write is issued. If
    the number of available records is less than MW, then all the
    records will be written. The value of MW should not be
    larger than the value of MR.

MAIN ROUTINES

150- 200   Dimensioning and variable initialization.
210- 310   Command mode. Displays available subroutines
           and branches to the operator's choice..

320- 540	Accepts terminal input.
550- 790	Verifies data in memory.
800- 930	Calculates mileage and displays all information.
940-1040	Reads data from disk file.
1050-1150	Writes data to disk file.
1160	Terminates execution.
1170-1180	Waits for user to hit any key.

MAIN VARIABLES

MW	Maximum number of data records to write.
MR	Maximum number of data records in memory.
N	Current number of data records in memory.
D$	Array of dates.
D	Array of odometer readings.
G	Array of gallons per fill-up.
M	Array of mileage per fill-up.
R	Command mode input.
F$	Filespec of disk file to read or write.
F	Data record number of error during verify.
B$,Q$	Temporary string variables.
J	Work variable, loop index.
K,L	Loop bounds.
X$	String format for PRINT USING.

SUGGESTED PROJECTS

1. Calculate and print the average MPG over the whole data file. The total miles driven is $D(N) - D(1)$. The total gallons used is the sum of $G(J)$ for $J = 2$ to N. This calculation can be done at the end of the DISPLAY MILEAGE subroutine. Programming should be done between lines 910 and 920.
2. Allow the user the option to write to disk only the entries since a certain date. Ask which date and search the D$ array for it. Then set MW to the appropriate number of records to write. These changes are to be made at and after line 1050 at the beginning of the subroutine to write to disk.
3. Add an option to modify data in memory. This would be useful in conjunction with the VERIFY DATA subroutine after an error is detected.
4. Add an option to do statistical calculations over a given subset of the data. The operator inputs a beginning and ending

date. He is then shown things like average MPG, total miles driven, total gallons purchased, etc.; all computed only over the range requested.

5. Write a subroutine to graphically display MPG. A bar graph might work well.

6. Add a new parameter in each data record — the cost of each fill-up. Then compute things like the total cost of gasoline, miles/dollar, etc.

QUEST/EXAM

PURPOSE

If you've ever had to analyze the results of a questionnaire, or grade a multiple-choice examination, you know what a tedious and time-consuming process it can be. This is particularly true if you need to accumulate statistics for each question showing how many people responded with each possible answer.

With this program, you provide the data, and the computer does the work.

HOW TO USE IT

First enter the number of questions on the questionnaire or exam paper. The maximum is 75. Then enter the number of choices for each question. This is an integer from 2 to 9. Each answer must be either left blank, or will be a digit from 1 to this number. Next enter the maximum number of entries (exam papers) that you are going to analyze. If unsure, make this number a little large to be safe.

Finally you are asked if you want to provide names for each entry. This is especially useful when grading exams, to enable you to verify that you entered the proper data for each student, when you are finished.

At this point, the program asks you for the answer key. If you are scoring an exam, provide the correct answers. The program displays "guide numbers" to help you keep track of which answers you are providing. If you are analyzing a questionnaire, you have no answer key, so just press the **ENTER** key.

Now the program asks you to begin providing the answers for each entry. Again, guide numbers are displayed above the area where you are to enter the data so you can more easily provide the proper answer for the proper question number. If no answer was given for a particular question, leave a blank space. However, if the first question was left blank, you will have to enclose the entire string of answers within quotation marks. This will cause a small problem in keeping your alignment straight with the guide numbers, but you'll get used to it.

If you make a mistake when entering the data, the program will say so and ask you to re-enter it. This is most commonly caused by either failing to enter the correct number of answers or entering an invalid character instead of an acceptable answer number. Remember that each answer must be either a blank or a number from one to the number of choices allowed per question.

By the way, you can avoid entering blanks for unanswered questions. Suppose you have a maximum of 5 possible answers per question. Simply tell the program there are 6 choices per question. Then, when a question is unanswered, you can enter a 6 instead of leaving it blank.

If you provided an answer key, the program displays the number and percentage correct after each entry before going on to ask for the next one. When you have no more entries, press the **ENTER** key instead of entering a string of answers.

At this point, the program displays five options from which you choose your next action. Here are brief explanations. You can experiment to verify how they work.

Option One lets you analyze each question, to see how many people responded with each answer. The percentage of people who responded with each answer is also shown. In the case of an exam, the correct answer is indicated with the word RIGHT to the right.

Option Two allows you to go back and provide more entries. This allows you to pause after entering part of the data, do some analysis of what you have entered so far, and then go back and continue entering data.

Option Three lets you review what you have entered, including the answer key. This permits you to check for duplicate, omitted, or erroneous entries.

Option Four restarts the program.

Option Five ends the program.

SAMPLE RUN

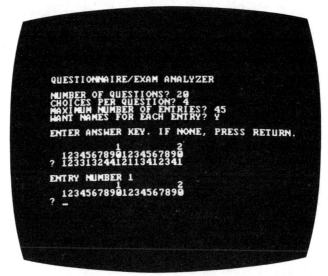

```
QUESTIONNAIRE/EXAM ANALYZER

NUMBER OF QUESTIONS? 20
CHOICES PER QUESTION? 4
MAXIMUM NUMBER OF ENTRIES? 45
WANT NAMES FOR EACH ENTRY? Y

ENTER ANSWER KEY. IF NONE, PRESS RETURN.

           1         2
  12345678901234567890
? 12331324412113412341

ENTRY NUMBER 1
           1         2
  12345678901234567890
? _
```

The operator provides the necessary information and the answer key for the examination being scored. The program waits for the data from the first examination paper.

```
NUMBER OF QUESTIONS? 20
CHOICES PER QUESTION? 4
MAXIMUM NUMBER OF ENTRIES? 45
WANT NAMES FOR EACH ENTRY? Y

ENTER ANSWER KEY. IF NONE, PRESS RETURN.

           1         2
  12345678901234567890
? 12331324412113412341

ENTRY NUMBER 1
           1         2
  12345678901234567890
? 12331324312114412344
NAME FOR ENTRY NUMBER 1
? HANNAH
  17 CORRECT,    85 PERCENT

ENTRY NUMBER 2
           1         2
  12345678901234567890
? _
```

The answers are entered for the first student. The program responds with the number and percentage correct.

```
    14 CORRECT,    70 PERCENT

ENTRY NUMBER 8
            1                   2
   12345678901234567890
?  12331424412113412342
NAME FOR ENTRY NUMBER 8
?  FORDHAM
   18 CORRECT,    90 PERCENT

ENTRY NUMBER 9
            1                   2
   12345678901234567890
?

AVERAGE = 82.5 PERCENT

NEXT ACTION:
    1 - ANALYZE EACH QUESTION
    2 - ADD MORE ENTRIES
    3 - REVIEW DATA ENTERED
    4 - START OVER
    5 - END PROGRAM
?  1
```

Later, instead of providing data for a ninth student, the operator presses the ENTER key, indicating no more entries. The program displays the overall percentage correct, and displays a "menu" of choice of actions. The operator picks number one.

```
     12345678901234567890
?

AVERAGE = 82.5 PERCENT

NEXT ACTION:
    1 - ANALYZE EACH QUESTION
    2 - ADD MORE ENTRIES
    3 - REVIEW DATA ENTERED
    4 - START OVER
    5 - END PROGRAM
?  1


ANALYSIS FOR QUESTION NO. 1
RESPONSE   COUNT    PERCENT
   1         7       87.5         RIGHT
   2         1       12.5
   3         0        0
   4         0        0
BLANK        0        0

PRESS A KEY TO CONTINUE
```

The program provides an analysis of the responses for Question One, then waits for a key to be pressed. Note that seven students answered with number 1, the correct answer.

```
PRESS A KEY TO CONTINUE

NEXT ACTION:
  1 - ANALYZE EACH QUESTION
  2 - ADD MORE ENTRIES
  3 - REVIEW DATA ENTERED
  4 - START OVER
  5 - END PROGRAM
? 3
                  1                   2
       1234567890123456789Ø

       12331324412113412341-ANSWERS
       12331324312114412344-NO. 1 HANNAN
       22331324112134123411-NO. 2 PRESS
       12331324412123412341-NO. 3 ARGO
       12331324412113412341-NO. 4 PRIMO
       12331424413112412344-NO. 5 MAROON
       12331434412112412341-NO. 6 LEMEUR
       13341414413112312341-NO. 7 CLEAVER
       12331424412113412342-NO. 8 FORDHAM
PRESS A KEY TO CONTINUE
```

Later, the operator asks for option number 3, which lists the data
entered for each of the students.

PROGRAM LISTING

```
100 REM: QUEST/EXAM
110 REM: Analyze questionnaires and exam papers.
120 REM: COPYRIGHT 1982 Tom Rugg and Phil Feldman.
130 REM: Any BASIC, any CRT.
140 CLEAR:KEY OFF:SCREEN 0,0:COLOR 7,0:CLS
150 PRINT"QUESTIONNAIRE/EXAM ANALYZER":PRINT
160 E$="** ERROR. RE-ENTER. **":I=1
170 P$="PRESS A KEY TO CONTINUE"
180 INPUT "NUMBER OF QUESTIONS";Q
190 Q=INT(Q):IF Q<1 OR Q>75 THEN PRINT E$:GOTO 180
200 INPUT "CHOICES PER QUESTION";C
210 C=INT(C):IF C<2 OR C>9 THEN PRINT E$:GOTO 200
220 DIM C(C)
230 INPUT "MAXIMUM NUMBER OF ENTRIES";N
240 N=INT(N):IF N<1 THEN PRINT E$:GOTO 230
250 DIM Q$(N+1)
260 INPUT "WANT NAMES FOR EACH ENTRY";R$
270 R$=LEFT$(R$,1):IF R$="N" OR R$="n" THEN 300
280 IF R$<>"Y" AND R$<>"y" THEN PRINT E$:GOTO 260
290 DIM N$(N)
300 PRINT
310 PRINT
        "ENTER ANSWER KEY. IF NONE, PRESS RETURN."
```

```
320 GOSUB 940:C$=RIGHT$(STR$(C),1)
330 INPUT A$:IF LEN(A$)=0 THEN 360
340 IF LEN(A$)<>Q THEN PRINT E$:GOTO 300
350 T$=A$:GOSUB 890:IF T$="B" THEN PRINT E$:
    GOTO 300
360 K=1
370 R=0:PRINT:PRINT"ENTRY NUMBER";K
380 GOSUB 940
390 INPUT Q$(K):W=LEN(Q$(K))
400 IF W=0 THEN 530
410 IF W<>Q THEN PRINT E$:GOTO 370
420 T$=Q$(K):GOSUB 890:IF T$="B" THEN PRINT E$:
    GOTO 370
430 IF R$="N" OR R$="n" THEN 460
440 PRINT"NAME FOR ENTRY NUMBER";K
450 INPUT N$(K)
460 IF LEN(A$)=0 THEN 520
470 FOR J=1 TO Q
480 IF MID$(A$,J,1)=MID$(Q$(K),J,1) THEN R=R+1
490 NEXT
500 TR=TR+R
510 PRINT R;"CORRECT,";TAB(15);R*100/Q;"PERCENT"
520 K=K+1:IF K<=N THEN 370
530 K=K-1:IF LEN(A$)=0 THEN 560
540 IF K=0 THEN 990
550 PRINT:PRINT"AVERAGE =";TR*100/(Q*K);"PERCENT"
560 GOTO 990
570 PRINT:FOR J=1 TO Q
580 R=0:PRINT:PRINT"ANALYSIS FOR QUESTION NO.";J
590 PRINT"RESPONSE   COUNT   PERCENT"
600 FOR L=0 TO C:C(L)=0:NEXT
610 FOR L=1 TO K:T$=MID$(Q$(L),J,1)
620 W=VAL(T$)
630 C(W)=C(W)+1
640 NEXT L
650 IF K=0 THEN 990
660 FOR L=1 TO C
670 PRINT L;TAB(11);C(L);TAB(17);C(L)*100/K;
680 IF LEN(A$)=0 THEN PRINT:GOTO 720
690 T$=RIGHT$(STR$(L),1)
700 IF T$=MID$(A$,J,1) THEN PRINT TAB(29);
    "RIGHT":GOTO 720
710 PRINT
720 NEXT:
    PRINT"BLANK";TAB(11);C(0);TAB(17);C(0)*100/K
730 PRINT:PRINT P$
740 DEF SEG:POKE 106,0
750 T$=INKEY$:IF LEN(T$)=0 THEN 750
760 NEXT J:GOTO 990
770 L=0:GOSUB 940:PRINT:IF LEN(A$)=0 THEN 790
780 PRINT TAB(3);A$;"-ANSWERS"
```

```
790 FOR J=1 TO K
800 PRINT TAB(3);Q$(J);"-NO.";J;
810 IF R$="N" OR R$="n" THEN PRINT:GOTO 830
820 PRINT N$(J)
830 L=L+1:IF L<10 THEN 860
840 L=0:PRINT P$
850 T$=INKEY$:IF LEN(T$)=0 THEN 850
860 NEXT:PRINT P$
870 T$=INKEY$:IF LEN(T$)=0 THEN 870
880 GOTO 990
890 FOR J=1 TO LEN(T$)
900 IF MID$(T$,J,1)=CHR$(32) THEN 920
910 IF MID$(T$,J,1)<
    "1" OR MID$(T$,J,1)>C$ THEN 930
920 NEXT:RETURN
930 T$="B":RETURN
940 W=Q/10:W=INT(W):IF W<1 THEN 960
950 FOR J=1 TO W:PRINT TAB(J*10+1);J;:NEXT:PRINT
960 PRINT TAB(3);
970 FOR J=1 TO Q:PRINT RIGHT$(STR$(J),1);
980 NEXT:PRINT:RETURN
990 PRINT:PRINT"NEXT ACTION: "
1000 PRINT" 1 - ANALYZE EACH QUESTION"
1010 PRINT" 2 - ADD MORE ENTRIES"
1020 PRINT" 3 - REVIEW DATA ENTERED"
1030 PRINT" 4 - START OVER"
1040 PRINT" 5 - END PROGRAM"
1050 INPUT T$:IF T$<"1" OR T$>"5" THEN 1070
1060 ON VAL(T$) GOTO 570,520,770,140,1080
1070 PRINT E$:GOTO 990
1080 END
```

EASY CHANGES

1. 75 is the limit of the number of questions only because it is
    the maximum that will nicely fit onto an 80 column screen.
    If you would like to allow for 100 questions (and have
    enough memory), change the 75 in line 190 to 100.

MAIN ROUTINES

140- 170	Initializes variables.
180- 290	Sets limits for questions, choices, and entries. Allocates arrays.
300- 330	Gets answer key (if any) from operator.
340- 350	Checks legality of answer key.
370- 420	Gets exam data for Kth entry.

430- 510	Scores Kth exam, if applicable.
530- 560	Displays average score, if an exam.
570- 760	Analyzes responses to each question.
770- 880	Displays data entered.
890- 930	Subroutine to check legality of input data.
940- 980	Subroutine to display guide numbers over input data area.
990-1070	Displays choices for next action. Gets response and goes to appropriate routine.

MAIN VARIABLES

I	Constant one.
E$	Error message.
P$	Message about pressing a key to continue.
Q	Number of questions.
C	Number of choices per question.
C	Array for tallying number of people responding with each choice.
N	Maximum number of entries.
Q$	Array of N strings of entries.
N$	Array of names for each entry.
R$	Set to "N" if no names for each entry, or "Y" otherwise.
A$	Answer key string (null if not an exam).
C$	String value of highest legal answer choice.
K	Counter of number of exams scored.
R	Number of questions answered right (if exam).
W	Work variable.
J,L	Loop variables.
TR	Total right for all entries.
T$	Temporary work string variable.

SUGGESTED PROJECTS

1. Add an option to change the answer key after the data for the exams is entered. This would be useful in case a mistake is found when reviewing the data.
2. Add an option to allow the operator to re-score each of the exams after all are entered, in case some were overlooked at the time of entry.
3. Combine some of the capabilities of the STATS program with this one.

SORTLIST

PURPOSE

This program sorts a list of items (words or phrases, or disk records) into alphabetical order. This is a tedious task to do manually, but your computer can do it in seconds. All you need to do is type in the list of items to be sorted, or have them available already on a disk file.

HOW TO USE IT

The program starts by displaying its title and telling you the maximum number of items it can sort. It can take up to 1000 items as currently written, but the "Easy Changes" section shows you how to change that number depending on your computer configuration and needs.

After you press a key to get started, the program displays a list of six options. Pick a number from one to six, and then press the **ENTER** key.

The first option allows you to enter the data you will be sorting directly from the keyboard. The program displays the entry number at the left side of the screen, and you enter the data. Press **ENTER** after each entry. When you have entered all the data, enter the word END (all capitals) to indicate the end of the list. Then you will probably want to use Options Four and Five, to sort the data and display it on the screen.

Each entry can be any kind of data you want to alphabetize, including alphabetic data, numbers, punctuation, and spaces, but remember the following rules. Alphabetizing will be done based on the first characters of each entry. The data is treated as string data; that is, numeric data can be entered but it will not be sorted numerically. For example, if you entered the numbers 1, 2, 13, and 20, they would be sorted into the sequence 1, 13, 2, 20. The number 13 is placed before 2 because the first position gets sorted "alphabetically", and 1 comes ahead of 2.

Spaces are significant. The name JO ANNE will be placed before JOANNE because the space is considered to be ahead of A. Capitalization is also significant. All capital letters will be placed before all lowercase letters. You may want to use either all capitals or all lowercase to avoid this aspect of sorting. To see exactly how each character will be sorted, refer to the "ASCII Character Codes" Appendix in your BASIC manual.

The second and third options apply only if you have a disk drive on your system. Option Two lets you read a disk file into memory, rather than entering data from the keyboard. This could be a file you created earlier using SORTLIST, or a file created some other way, such as by using the EDLIN line editor or a word processing program. Option Three allows you to create a disk file from the data that is currently in memory, whether it has been sorted or not. Options Two and Three both display the files that are already on the disk before asking you for a *filespec*. For Option Two (reading a disk file) you should select the name of a file that already exists. For Option Three (writing a new file), you will probably want to select the name of a file that does *not* exist yet. In either case, you can simply press **ENTER** without entering a filespec if you change your mind and want to go back to the list of options.

A *filespec* is typically a simple one to eight character name for a disk file. However, it can be a complete file specification in the form of "d:filename.ext" as explained in the Disk Operating System (DOS) manual.

Option Four is the essence of this program. It sorts the data that is currently in memory into alphabetical order, as explained earlier. When the data has been sorted, you are shown how many items were sorted and then you can press a key to go back to the main list of options.

Option Five displays on the screen whatever data is currently in memory. On the left side is the entry number, and on the right is the corresponding data. If you have more than 23 items, you will want to us the computer's "pause" capability to make the program temporarily stop while you review the data. This is done by holding down the **CTRL** key and pressing the **NumLock** key. You can let the display continue by pressing another key, such as the space bar. If you don't stop the display fast enough, just ask for Option Five again to get another chance. You may also want to try the Easy Change below that puts more than one item on each line of the display.

Option Six ends the program.

The sorting technique used here is called a *straight selection* sort (see the book by Knuth in the Bibliography). It is simple to program and it executes quickly for small lists (no more than 50 to 100 items). This program typically takes about three to four seconds to sort 25 items, about ten to twelve seconds for 50 items, and about 30 to 50 seconds for 100 items, depending on their length and initial sequence.

SAMPLE RUN

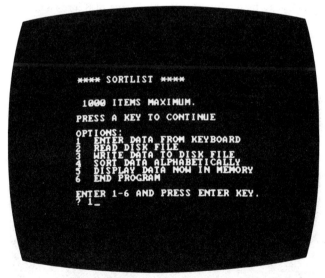

```
**** SORTLIST ****

1000 ITEMS MAXIMUM.

PRESS A KEY TO CONTINUE

OPTIONS:
1   ENTER DATA FROM KEYBOARD
2   READ DISK FILE
3   WRITE DATA TO DISK FILE
4   SORT DATA ALPHABETICALLY
5   DISPLAY DATA NOW IN MEMORY
6   END PROGRAM

ENTER 1-6 AND PRESS ENTER KEY.
? 1_
```

The operator selects option 1 to enter data from the keyboard.

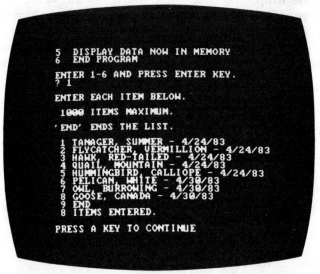

The operator (a nature lover) enters the name of 8 birds and the dates
observed.

The operator selects option 4 to sort the data, and then option 5 to
display the sorted data.

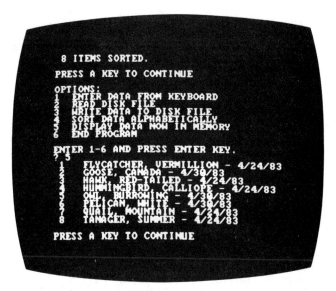

The sorted list is displayed.

PROGRAM LISTING

```
100 REM: SORTLIST
110 REM: Sort a list alphabetically.
120 REM: COPYRIGHT 1982 Tom Rugg and Phil Feldman.
130 REM: Any BASIC, any CRT.
140 N=1000:E$="END"
150 DIM A$(N):I=1:GOTO 390
160 GOSUB 620:K=1
170 IF K>N THEN 210
180 PRINT K;:LINE INPUT R$:IF R$=E$ THEN 210
190 IF LEN(R$)=0 THEN 180
200 A$(K)=R$:K=K+1:GOTO 170
210 K=K-1
220 PRINT K;"ITEMS ENTERED."
230 GOTO 440
240 IF K=1 OR K=0 THEN 320
250 PRINT"SORTING..."
260 FOR J=K TO 2 STEP -1
270 R$=A$(1):F=1
280 FOR L=2 TO J
290 IF A$(L)>R$ THEN R$=A$(L):F=L
300 NEXT:A$(F)=A$(J):A$(J)=R$
```

```
310 NEXT
320 PRINT K;"ITEMS SORTED."
330 GOTO 440
340 IF K=0 THEN PRINT"ZERO DATA ITEMS":GOTO 440
350 FOR J=1 TO K
360 PRINT J;TAB(6);A$(J)
370 NEXT
380 GOTO 440
390 KEY OFF:SCREEN 0,0:COLOR 7,0:CLS
400 PRINT"**** SORTLIST ****"
410 PRINT
420 PRINT
430 PRINT N;"ITEMS MAXIMUM."
440 PRINT
450 PRINT"PRESS A KEY TO CONTINUE";
460 DEF SEG:POKE 106,0
470 R$=INKEY$:IF LEN(R$)=0 THEN 470
480 PRINT:PRINT
490 PRINT"OPTIONS:"
500 PRINT"1   ENTER DATA FROM KEYBOARD"
510 PRINT"2   READ DISK FILE"
520 PRINT"3   WRITE DATA TO DISK FILE"
530 PRINT"4   SORT DATA ALPHABETICALLY"
540 PRINT"5   DISPLAY DATA NOW IN MEMORY"
550 PRINT"6   END PROGRAM"
560 PRINT
570 PRINT"ENTER 1-6 AND PRESS ENTER KEY."
580 INPUT R$:R=VAL(R$)
590 IF R<1 OR R>6 THEN 570
600 ON R GOTO 160,700,880,240,340,1020
610 STOP
620 PRINT
630 PRINT"ENTER EACH ITEM BELOW."
640 PRINT
650 PRINT N;"ITEMS MAXIMUM."
660 PRINT
670 PRINT CHR$(39);E$;CHR$(39);" ENDS THE LIST."
680 PRINT
690 RETURN
700 PRINT
710 PRINT STRING$(40,45)
720 PRINT"FILES ON DISK ARE:"
730 FILES
740 PRINT STRING$(40,45)
750 INPUT"FILESPEC TO READ";F$
760 IF LEN(F$)=0 THEN 440
770 OPEN F$ FOR INPUT AS #1
780 K=1
790 IF K>N THEN CLOSE #1:GOTO 830
800 IF EOF(1) THEN CLOSE #1:GOTO 850
810 LINE INPUT #1,R$
```

```
820 A$(K)=R$:K=K+1:GOTO 790
830 PRINT N;"ITEMS WERE READ -- **MAXIMUM**"
840 BEEP
850 K=K-1
860 PRINT K;"ITEMS READ FROM DISK."
870 GOTO 440
880 PRINT
890 PRINT STRING$(40,45)
900 PRINT"FILES ON DISK ARE:"
910 FILES
920 PRINT STRING$(40,45)
930 INPUT"FILESPEC TO WRITE";F$
940 IF LEN(F$)=0 THEN 440
950 OPEN F$ FOR OUTPUT AS #1
960 IF K=0 THEN 990
970 FOR J=1 TO K
980 PRINT #1,A$(J):NEXT
990 CLOSE #1
1000 PRINT K;"ITEMS WRITTEN TO FILE."
1010 GOTO 440
1020 END
```

EASY CHANGES

1. If you don't have more than about 200 items to sort and you want to allow as much room as possible for long data entries, reduce the maximum number of entries allowed by changing line 140 to:

   140 N = 200:E$ = "END"

2. To eliminate the problem of Option Five displaying only 23 to 25 items on the screen at once, you can try one of these changes:

   360 PRINT J;A$(J);"/";

   or

   360 PRINT A$(J);"/";

   This will print multiple items separated by slashes on each line. The second change will also eliminate the item number from the display. Of course, you can use some character(s) other than slashes if you like.

3. To use some word besides END to indicate the end of the list of items, change line 140. For example, to use DONE:

   140 N = 1000:E$ = "DONE"

4. To slow down the display of items from Option Five, insert:

   365 FOR L = 1 TO 200:NEXT

MAIN ROUTINES

140- 150   Initializes variables; goes to title display.
160- 230   Option 1 processing (gets input from keyboard).
240- 330   Option 4 processing (sorts data in A$ array).
340- 380   Option 5 processing (displays data in memory).
390- 430   Initializes screen; displays title and maximum number of entries.
440- 600   Waits for key to be pressed, then displays main options and processes reply.
620- 690   Subroutine to explain input from keyboard.
700- 870   Option 2 processing (reads disk file into A$).
880-1010   Option 3 processing (writes A$ to disk file).
1020   Option 6 processing (ends program).

MAIN VARIABLES

N   Maximum number of items that can be entered.
E$ Word to end entry of items from keyboard.
A$ Array of items in memory (sorted in place).
I   Constant one.
K   Count of number of items actually entered from keyboard or disk file.
R$ Reply from operator; also a work string variable.
J,L,F,R   Work and subscript variables.
F$ Filespec of disk file to read or write.

SUGGESTED PROJECTS

1. Replace the sorting technique with one that is more efficient for a large number of items. Knuth's and Gruenberger's books (see Bibliography) include discussions of alternatives.
2. Give the program the capability to add, change, or delete items once they are in memory.

Section 2

Educational Programs

Education is one area where computers are certain to have more and more impact. Though a computer cannot completely replace a human teacher, the machine does have certain advantages. It is ready anytime you are, allows you to go at your own pace, handles rote drill effortlessly, and eliminates the possibility of any personality conflicts.

With a good software library, your computer can be a valuable learning center in the school or at home. Here are seven programs to get you started.

Mathematics is certainly a natural subject for computers. NUMBERS is designed for pre-school children. While familiarizing youngsters with computers, it provides an entertaining way for them to learn numbers and elementary counting. ARITHMETIC is aimed at older, grade school students. It provides drill in various kinds of math problems. The child can adjust the difficulty factors, allowing the program to be useful for several years.

By no means is your computer restricted to mathematical disciplines. We include two programs designed to improve your word skills. VOCAB will help you expand your vocabulary. TACHIST turns the computer into a reading clinic, helping you to improve your reading speed.

With the proper programs, the computer can teach you specific subjects. If you've ever wanted to learn International Radio Code, HAMCODE will instruct and then drill you. Many of us feel uncomfortable becoming familiar with the increasingly prevalent metric system. METRIC is the answer to this.

But, what about software that you can customize to help you learn a subject of your choice? FLASHCARD allows you to create your own "computer flashcards." Then you can drill yourself until you get it right.

ARITHMETIC

PURPOSE

ARITHMETIC provides mathematics drills for grade school children. The student can request problems in addition, subtraction, or multiplication from the program. Also, he or she may ask that the problems be easy, medium, or hard. The program should be useful to a child over an extended period of time. He can progress naturally to a harder category of problems when he begins to regularly perform well at one level. The difficulty and types of problems encompass those normally encountered by school children between the ages of six and ten.

The problems are constructed randomly within the constraints imposed by the degree of difficulty selected. This gives the student fresh practice each time the program is used. After entering answers, he is told whether he was right or wrong. The correct answers are also displayed.

HOW TO USE IT

First, in order to initialize its random number generator, the program requests that any key (except **BREAK** or **SHIFT**) be hit.

Next, the student must indicate what type of problem he wishes to do. The program requests an input of **1, 2,** or **3** to indicate addition, subtraction, or multiplication, respectively. It then asks whether easy, medium, or hard problems are desired. Again an input of **1, 2,** or **3** is required.

Now the screen will clear and five problems of the desired type will be displayed. The user now begins to enter his answers to each problem.

A question mark is used to prompt the user for each digit of the answer, one digit at a time. This is done moving right to left, the way arithmetic problems are naturally solved.

To start each problem, the question mark will appear in the spot for the rightmost (or units column) digit of the answer. When the key for a digit from 0-9 is pressed, that digit will replace the question mark on the screen. The question mark moves to the immediate left waiting for a digit for the "tens" column.

Digits are entered in this right to left manner until the complete answer has been input. Then the **ENTER** key must be pressed. This will end the answer to the current problem and move the question mark to begin the answer for the next question.

If the **ENTER** key is pressed to begin a problem, the computer assumes that you have answered zero. No problems created by this program have answers of more than three digits. If a four-digit answer is given, the program will accept the answer, but then go immediately to the next problem. Answers to the problems are never negative.

The program will display the correct answers to the five problems on the screen after the student has entered his five answers. A happy face symbol or the message WRONG! will also be displayed below each problem depending upon whether the student's answer was correct or not. If all five problems are answered correctly, a cheerful high-pitched beeping will be sounded. If any problems are missed, a lower pitched monotone will be generated instead.

Then the message "Hit any key to continue" will be displayed. After a key is pressed, a new set of five problems of the same type will be presented.

This continues until twenty problems have been worked. The program then shows what the student's performance has been. This is expressed as the number of problems solved correctly and also as the percentage of problems solved correctly.

SAMPLE RUN

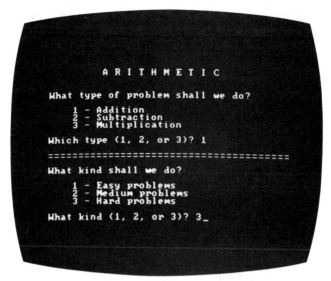

After hitting a key to begin, the operator chooses to do hard addition problems.

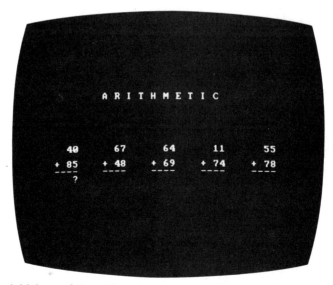

The initial set of 5 problems is presented. With a question mark, the program prompts the operator for the answer to the first problem.

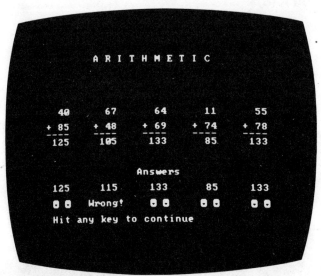

The operator has entered his or her five answers. The program displays the correct answers and indicates whether or not each problem was solved correctly. The program waits for the operator to hit any key in order to continue with the next set of five problems.

PROGRAM LISTING

```
100 REM: ARITHMETIC
110 REM: Math drill for students.
120 REM: COPYRIGHT 1982 Phil Feldman and Tom Rugg.
130 REM: Any BASIC, any CRT.
140 KEY OFF:SCREEN 0,0,0,0:WIDTH 40:COLOR 7,0,0
150 CLEAR:CLS:DEF SEG:POKE 106,0
160 PRINT"Hit any key to begin."
170 R$=INKEY$:K=RND: IF LEN(R$)=0 THEN 170
180 ND=0:DIM A(5),B(5),C(5),G(5)
190 NP=20
200 E$=CHR$(2)+CHR$(32)+CHR$(2)
210 GOSUB 720
220 PRINT:PRINT:
    PRINT"What type of problem shall we do?":PRINT
230 PRINT TAB(5);"1 - Addition"
240 PRINT TAB(5);"2 - Subtraction"
250 PRINT TAB(5);"3 - Multiplication"
260 PRINT:INPUT"Which type (1, 2, or 3)";R$
270 T=INT(VAL(R$)): IF T<1 OR T>3 THEN BEEP:
    GOTO 260
280 PRINT:PRINT STRING$(39,61)
290 PRINT:PRINT"What kind shall we do?"
```

```
300 PRINT:PRINT TAB(5);"1 - Easy problems"
310 PRINT TAB(5);"2 - Medium problems"
320 PRINT TAB(5);"3 - Hard problems"
330 PRINT:INPUT"What kind (1, 2, or 3)";R$
340 D=INT(VAL(R$))
350 IF D<1 OR D>3 THEN BEEP:GOTO 330
360 ON D GOTO 370,380,400
370 GOSUB 750:GOSUB 730:GOSUB 740:GOTO 410
380 GOSUB 750:GOSUB 740:IF T=3 THEN GOSUB 770:
    GOSUB 730:GOTO 410
390 IF T<>3 THEN GOSUB 760:GOSUB 730:GOTO 410
400 GOSUB 760:GOSUB 730:GOSUB 740:
    IF T=3 THEN GOSUB 750:GOSUB 740
410 IF T<>2 THEN 450
420 FOR J=1 TO 5
430 IF B(J)>C(J) THEN SWAP B(J),C(J)
440 NEXT
450 GOSUB 780:GOSUB 720
460 Y=12:FOR J=1 TO 5:X=-4+J*8:GOSUB 820:NEXT
470 FOR K=1 TO 5:X=-3+K*8:GOSUB 620:G(K)=N:NEXT
480 X=17:Y=16:GOSUB 900:PRINT"Answers"
490 Y=18:FOR J=1 TO 5:X=-4+J*8:GOSUB 940:NEXT
500 F=1:Y=20:FOR J=1 TO 5:X=-7+J*8:GOSUB 900
510 IF A(J)<>G(J) THEN COLOR 23:PRINT"Wrong!":
    COLOR 7:F=0:GOTO 530
520 PRINT SPC(2);E$:NR=NR+1
530 NEXT
540 IF F=0 THEN SOUND 40,20:GOTO 560
550 FOR J=1 TO 5:BEEP:FOR K=1 TO 300:NEXT:NEXT
560 PRINT:PRINT"  Hit any key to continue ";
570 R$=INKEY$:IF LEN(R$)=0 THEN 570
580 ND=ND+5
590 IF ND<NP THEN GOSUB 720:GOTO 360
600 GOSUB 990
610 END
620 N=0:M=1
630 COLOR 23:P$="?":GOSUB 710
640 R$=INKEY$:IF LEN(R$)=0 THEN 640
650 A=ASC(R$):IF A=13 AND M=1 THEN P$="0":
    COLOR 7:GOSUB 710:RETURN
660 IF A=13 THEN P$=CHR$(32):COLOR 7:GOSUB 710:
    RETURN
670 IF A<48 OR A>57 THEN 640
680 V=A-48:P$=CHR$(A):COLOR 7:GOSUB 710:N=N+M*V:
    M=M*10
690 IF M>1000 THEN RETURN
700 X=X-1:GOTO 630
710 LOCATE Y,X:PRINT P$;:LOCATE Y,X:RETURN
720 CLS:PRINT TAB(10);"A R I T H M E T I C":RETURN
730 FOR K=1 TO 5:C(K)=INT(RND*(H-L+1))+L:NEXT:
    RETURN
```

```
740 FOR K=1 TO 5:B(K)=INT(RND*(H-L+1))+L:NEXT:
    RETURN
750 H=9:L=0:RETURN
760 H=99:L=0:RETURN
770 H=25:L=1:RETURN
780 ON T GOTO 790,800,810
790 FOR J=1 TO 5:A(J)=B(J)+C(J):NEXT:RETURN
800 FOR J=1 TO 5:A(J)=C(J)-B(J):NEXT:RETURN
810 FOR J=1 TO 5:A(J)=C(J)*B(J):NEXT:RETURN
820 GOSUB 900:CU=5:CL=1:GOSUB 920
830 IF C(J)<10 THEN PRINT CHR$(32);
840 PRINT C(J):GOSUB 900:CU=3:CL=2:GOSUB 920:
    IF T=1 THEN PRINT CHR$(43);
850 IF T=2 THEN PRINT CHR$(45);
860 IF T=3 THEN PRINT CHR$(88);
870 IF B(J)<10 THEN PRINT CHR$(32);
880 PRINT B(J):GOSUB 900:CU=2:CL=2:GOSUB 920:
    PRINT STRING$(4,45)
890 RETURN
900 LOCATE Y,X
910 RETURN
920 FOR K=1 TO CL:PRINT CHR$(29);:NEXT
930 K=CSRLIN:LOCATE K-CU+1:RETURN
940 GOSUB 900:CL=0:IF A(J)>9 THEN CL=1
950 IF A(J)>99 THEN CL=2
960 IF A(J)>999 THEN CL=3
970 FOR K=1 TO CL:PRINT CHR$(29);:NEXT
980 PRINT A(J):RETURN
990 GOSUB 720:PRINT:PRINT
1000 PRINT"You got";NR;"right"
1010 PRINT"out of";NP;"problems."
1020 P=NR/NP*100
1030 PRINT:PRINT"That's";P;"percent correct.":
    RETURN
```

EASY CHANGES

1. The program currently does twenty problems per session.
    You can change this number by altering the variable NP in
    line 190. For example,

    $$190 \text{ NP} = 10$$

    will cause the program to do only ten problems per session.
    The value of NP should be kept a positive multiple of five.

2. Zero is currently allowed as a possible problem operand. If
    you do not wish to allow this, change lines 750 and 760 to
    read as follows:

    $$750 \text{ H} = 9:\text{L} = 1:\text{RETURN}$$
    $$760 \text{ H} = 99:\text{L} = 1:\text{RETURN}$$

MAIN ROUTINES

150- 170	Initializes RND function.
180- 210	Initializes constants, displays header.
220- 350	Asks operator for type of problems desired.
360- 450	Sets A, B, C arrays, clears screen.
460- 610	Mainline routine—displays problems, gets operator's answers, displays correct answers and user's performance.
620- 700	Subroutine to get and display user's answers.
710	Character printing subroutine.
720	Subroutine to clear screen and display title.
730	Subroutine to set C array.
740	Subroutine to set B array.
750- 770	Subroutines to set L, H.
780- 810	Subroutine to calculate array A from arrays B, C.
820- 890	Subroutine to display problems.
900- 910	Subroutine to move cursor to screen position X, Y.
920- 930	Subroutine to move cursor CU lines down and CL spaces left.
940- 980	Subroutine to display the correct answers.
990-1030	Subroutine to display operator's performance.

MAIN VARIABLES

NP	Number of problems to do in the session.
ND	Number of problems done.
NR	Number of correct answers given.
C,B,A	Arrays of top operand, bottom operand, and correct answer to each problem.
N	Operator's answer to current problem.
G	Array of operator's answers.
T	Type of problems requested (1 = addition, 2 = subtraction, 3 = multiplication).
D	Kind of problem requested (1 = easy, 2 = medium, 3 = hard).
H,L	Highest, lowest integers to allow as problem operands.
M	Answer column being worked on.
R$	Operator's input character.
V	Value of R$.
A	ASCII value of R$.
X,Y	Horizontal, vertical position of cursor.

P$ Character to be printed.
E$ Happy Face character string.
J,K   Loop indices and work variables.
P   Percentage of correct answers.
F   Flag on operator's answers (1 = all correct, 0 = some
            wrong).

SUGGESTED PROJECTS

1. Keep track of problems missed and repeat them quickly for
    additional practice.
2. No negative operands or answers are currently allowed. Re-
    write the problem generation routines and the operator's
    answer routines to allow the possibility of negative answers.
3. The answers are now restricted to three-digit numbers.
    However, the program will work fine for four-digit numbers
    if the operands of the problems are allowed to be large
    enough. Dig into the routines at lines 360-450 and 750-770.
    See how they work and then modify them to allow possible
    four-digit answers.
4. The operator cannot currently correct any mistakes he
    makes while typing in his answers. Modify the program to
    allow him to do so.
5. Modify the program to allow problems in division.

FLASHCARD

PURPOSE

There are certain things that the human mind is capable of learning only through repetition. Not many people can remember the multiplication tables after their first exposure, for example. The same applies to learning the vocabulary of a foreign language, the capital cities of the fifty states, or famous dates in history. The best way to learn them is to simply review them over and over until you have them memorized.

A common technique for doing this involves the use of flashcards. You write one half of the two related pieces of information on one side of a card, and the other half on the other side. After creating a set of these cards, you can drill yourself on them over and over until you always remember what's on the other side of each card.

But why waste precious natural resources by using cards? Use your computer instead. This program lets you create flashcards, drill using them, and save them for later review.

HOW TO USE IT

As currently written, the program immediately begins drilling you on Spanish vocabulary words. After explaining how to use the program with this data, we'll show you how to enter your own flashcards (see Easy Changes).

The program flashes one side of one card on the screen for you. Both are chosen at random—the side and the card. Your job is to respond with the other side. If you enter it correctly, the program says, "RIGHT!" If not, it tells you the correct response. In either event, the program continues by picking another side and card at random. This continues until you respond by simply pressing the **ENTER** key, which tells the program you do not want to drill any more. It will then tell you how many you got right out of the number you attempted, as well as the percentage, and then return to command mode.

During the drill sequence, by the way, the program will not repeat a card that was used in the previous four questions (i.e., one less than the minimum number of cards you can enter).

The program tells you to be sure that CAPS LOCK is in effect. This is not really necessary, as long as you are willing to type the exact capitalization that is displayed during the drill.

After ending the drill, you can either drill more or end the program. If you drill more, the percent correct figure will be cumulative.

SAMPLE RUN

```
FLASHCARD PROGRAM

Be sure CAPS LOCK is in effect.
PRESS A KEY TO START

30 FLASHCARDS

TELL ME WHAT'S ON THE OTHER
SIDE OF EACH CARD AS I SHOW IT.

BLANCO
? WHITE
RIGHT!
LEJOS
? _
```

The program begins by displaying one side of a random flashcard. The operator responds with the correct answer, and the next one is displayed.

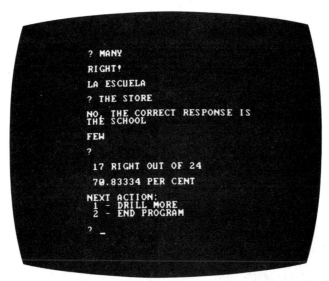

Later, the operator presses **ENTER** without giving an answer to see how many were answered correctly. Then he or she can either continue drilling or end the program.

PROGRAM LISTING

```
100 REM: FLASHCARD
110 REM: Drill on flashcard data.
120 REM: COPYRIGHT 1982 Tom Rugg and Phil Feldman.
130 REM: Any BASIC, any CRT.
140 KEY OFF:SCREEN 0,0:WIDTH 40:CLS
150 L=50:M=5
160 DIM F$(L),B$(L),P(M-1)
170 PRINT"FLASHCARD PROGRAM"
180 PRINT:PRINT
190 PRINT"Be sure CAPS LOCK is in effect."
200 PRINT
210 PRINT"PRESS A KEY TO START"
220 DEF SEG:POKE 106,0
230 R$=INKEY$:R=RND:IF LEN(R$)=0 THEN 230
240 POKE 106,0
250 PRINT:PRINT
260 K=1:C=0:W=0:I=1
270 IF K>L THEN 330
280 READ R$:IF R$="XXX" OR R$="xxx" THEN 340
290 F$(K)=R$
300 READ R$:B$(K)=R$
310 K=K+1
320 GOTO 270
330 PRINT"FLASHCARD ARRAY FULL.":PRINT
```

```
340 K=K-1
350 IF K<M THEN PRINT"NOT ENOUGH FLASHCARDS":END
360 PRINT K;"FLASHCARDS"
370 PRINT:PRINT
380 PRINT"TELL ME WHAT'S ON THE OTHER"
390 PRINT"SIDE OF EACH CARD AS I SHOW IT."
400 PRINT:PRINT
410 R=INT(K*RND)+1
420 FOR J=0 TO M-2
430 IF P(J)=R THEN 410
440 NEXT
450 J=RND:IF J>.5 THEN 480
460 PRINT F$(R):C$=B$(R)
470 GOTO 490
480 PRINT B$(R):C$=F$(R)
490 PRINT:INPUT R$
500 IF LEN(R$)=0 THEN 630
510 PRINT
520 IF R$=C$ THEN 560
530 PRINT"NO, THE CORRECT RESPONSE IS"
540 PRINT C$
550 W=W+1:GOTO 580
560 PRINT"RIGHT!"
570 C=C+1
580 FOR J=1 TO M-2
590 P(J-1)=P(J):NEXT
600 P(M-2)=R
610 PRINT
620 GOTO 410
630 PRINT
640 IF C+W=0 THEN 690
650 PRINT C;"RIGHT OUT OF";C+W
660 PRINT
670 PRINT C*100/(C+W);"PER CENT"
680 PRINT
690 PRINT"NEXT ACTION:"
700 PRINT" 1 - DRILL MORE"
710 PRINT" 2 - END PROGRAM"
720 PRINT
730 INPUT R$
740 IF R$="2" THEN END
750 IF R$="1" THEN 370
760 PRINT"ENTER 1 OR 2 PLEASE."
770 PRINT:GOTO 690
780 REM: Flashcard data follows.
790 DATA THE PEN,LA PLUMA
800 DATA THE DOOR,LA PUERTA
810 DATA THE SCHOOL,LA ESCUELA
820 DATA THE FLOOR,EL SUELO
830 DATA THE STORE,LA TIENDRA
840 DATA THE HAND,LA MANO
```

```
850 DATA THE HOUSE,LA CASA
860 DATA THE FRIEND,EL AMIGO
870 DATA THE DINNER,LA COMIDA
880 DATA THE CHAIR,LA SILLA
890 DATA TO ARRIVE,LLEGAR
900 DATA TO ASK,PREGUNTAR
910 DATA TO BUY,COMPRAR
920 DATA TO BRING,LLEVAR
930 DATA TO COME,VENIR
940 DATA TO EAT,COMER
950 DATA TO FIND,HALLAR
960 DATA TO GO,ANDAR
970 DATA TO HAVE,TENER
980 DATA TO KNOW,SABER
990 DATA BLUE,AZUL
1000 DATA GREEN,VERDE
1010 DATA RED,ROJO
1020 DATA WHITE,BLANCO
1030 DATA YELLOW,AMARILLO
1040 DATA ENOUGH,BASTANTE
1050 DATA FAR,LEJOS
1060 DATA FEW,POCOS
1070 DATA MANY,MUCHOS
1080 DATA NEAR,CERCA
9999 DATA XXX
```

EASY CHANGES

1. Replace the DATA statements with your own flashcards. A comma separates the two sides of each card. Don't use commas, colons, or quotation marks as part of your cards. Use all capital letters. Leave line 9999 as it is to signal the end of the cards. SAVE each version of the program with a different name, such as FLASHSP1 and FLASHSP2 for two sets of Spanish flashcards.

2. Change the limits of the number of flashcards that can be entered by altering line 150. L is the upper limit and M is the minimum. The current upper limit of 50 will fit in a computer with even a minimum amount of memory if each side of each flashcard averages no more than about eight characters in length. If you have 48K or more, you can make L as large as about five hundred for flashcards this size. Do not make M much larger than about ten or so, or you will slow down the program and use more memory than you might want.

3. To cause the program to always display side one of the
    flashcards (and ask you to respond with side two), change
    line 450 to:

                              450 REM

    To cause it to always display side two, change it this way:

                           450 GOTO 480

MAIN ROUTINES

140- 260	Initializes variables. Creates arrays. Displays title and initializes RND.
270- 360	Reads flashcards from DATA statements.
370- 680	Drills operator on flashcards in memory.
690- 770	Displays options and analyzes response. Branches to appropriate routine.
790-9999	DATA statements with flashcard data.

MAIN VARIABLES

L	Upper limit of number of flashcards that can be entered.
M	Minimum number of flashcards that can be entered.
R	Subscript of random flashcard chosen during drill.
K	Number of flashcards entered.
W	Number of wrong responses.
C	Number of correct responses.
I	Constant one.
F$	Array containing front side of flashcards (side 1).
B$	Array containing back side of flashcards (side 2).
P	Array containing subscripts of $M-1$ previous flashcards during drill.
J	Loop and subscript variable.
C$	The correct response during drill.
R$	Response from operator. Also temporary string variable.

SUGGESTED PROJECTS

1. Modify the program for use in a classroom environment.
    Require the operator to drill a fixed number of times (maybe

20 or 50). Don't allow a null response to end the drill. For example, you could make these changes:

```
500 REM
575 IF C = 20 THEN 630
685 END
```

This will cause the program to continue until 20 *correct* answers are given, and then end.

HAMCODE

PURPOSE

At some time in your life you have undoubtedly heard the sound of "Morse Code." The familiar sound of dots and dashes is one that we have nearly all come in contact with at some time or other. Amateur radio operators ("hams") have to learn Morse Code to obtain a license to operate an amateur radio station.

This program helps teach you what is officially called Continental Code, or sometimes referred to (ambiguously) as the International Morse Code, as used for ham radio. This is a little confusing, since the so-called *International* Morse Code, although similar, is *not* the same as the original Morse Code, which is still in use only for some types of land line transmissions. The code that nearly everyone uses anymore is Continental Code, so we picked the name HAMCODE for this chapter to try to be most descriptive of its use.

HOW TO USE IT

The program begins by displaying its title and sounding it in code for you. It then shows you six options to choose from. To learn the code, you will be selecting different options to enable you to learn each character and become proficient at understanding groups of characters.

The first option teaches you each character. All you do is press any key on the computer's keyboard, and the program sounds the code of that character for you. As the code is sounded, the dots and dashes for it are displayed to help you both visualize and hear the code together. The program recognizes only capital letters, so be sure to press CAPS LOCK when you start.

It's up to you to decide which characters you want to learn first. Most people will find it easiest to learn only a few each day (maybe three or four), and drill on them until they can be recognized immediately. Then add a few more characters the next day. Start with the alphabet, then move on to the numbers and punctuation characters. Keeping each session short is a good idea — half an hour is about right. Doing two or three short sessions each day is better than doing one long one.

Some keys on the computer keyboard do not have a code assigned to them. If you press one of the "illegal" keys, a distinctive low beep is sounded to let you know. To end the character-learning option, press the **ESC** key. This causes the six options to be displayed for you again.

After you have learned a few letters of the alphabet, you may want to try listening to groups of letters (words or phrases). This is done with Option Two. Simply enter one or more characters and press the **ENTER** key. The program will respond by sounding the code of the entire phrase at a rate of about 11 words per minute (five characters comprise an average word). Option Five lets you make the speed faster, when you are ready.

If the phrase has multiple words, they are separated by blocks on the video display. As the program is currently written, you should limit the length of your phrases to no more than 255 characters. If you want to include any colons or commas in the phrase, you have to enclose the phrase in quotation marks. To hear a phrase a second time, simply press **ENTER** and it will be repeated.

To end Option Two, enter the word END as your phrase. Once again, this causes the six options to be displayed.

Once you have learned all the characters, you should try Option Three to quiz yourself on them. Option Three randomly picks a character, sounds it for you, and waits for you to press the key of that character. There is no need to press the **ENTER** key. If you press the right key, the program tells you so and picks another random character.

If you press the wrong key, the program tells you what character it was and then sounds it for you again. You have to respond with the right answer before the program will pick a new character. This helps reinforce the correct answers. To end Option Three, press the **ESC** key.

Option Four quizzes you on groups of characters which have been chosen at random. As currently written, groups of five characters are used, but the Easy Changes section shows how to make the program use other lengths.

After the five characters are sounded, enter the corresponding five characters and press the **ENTER** key. As with Option Three, the program tells you if you were right or wrong. If wrong, it tells you the correct answer and sounds the same characters for you again to make you enter them correctly. As with Option Two, if there are any colons or commas included in the group of characters, you must enclose the entire group of characters within quotation marks. And again, if you simply press the **ENTER** key, the phrase will be repeated for you.

The last option, Option Six, ends the program.

A few characters are not included in this program; these will have to be learned through other means. In all cases but two, this is because there are no ASCII characters on the keyboard to correspond with them (e.g., wait, double dash, error). The two exceptions are the quotation mark and the right parenthesis.

As mentioned above, quotation marks are used by BASIC to enclose a string of characters being entered by the operator. Since this would make it very awkward to include the quotation mark character in the program, and because the other characters are more important to learn, it has been omitted.

The right and left parentheses are both supposed to use the same code. To avoid ambiguity in having you figure out whether the program was asking for the left or right parenthesis during the quiz options, we simply decided to treat the right one as an illegal character and thereby allow you to always respond with the left one.

Please be *very* careful when entering this program into your computer, especially for lines 1140 through 1260. If you make a mistake in typing the dots, dashes, commas, and X's, the program either will not work (Out of Data error, most likely), or you will teach yourself the wrong code! Be sure that you compare your results against the Sample Run photos to be sure that your codes look the same as ours.

SAMPLE RUN

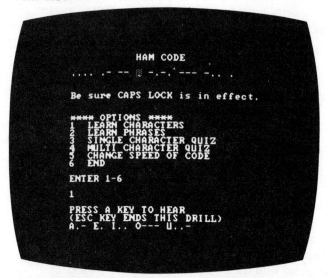

The program displays its title (both alphabetically and in code) and displays its options. The operator picks the first option and begins learning the vowels.

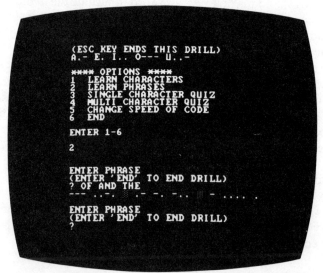

The operator proceeds to option 2, and begins by drilling on some common short words.

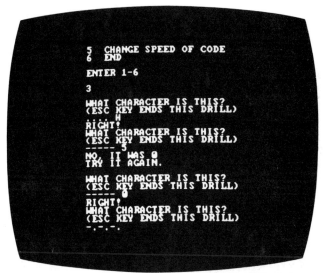

Next the operator tries option 3, to be quizzed on individual characters.
The first response is correct, but the next is not, the program repeats it
to force the operator to respond correctly before going on to the next
character.

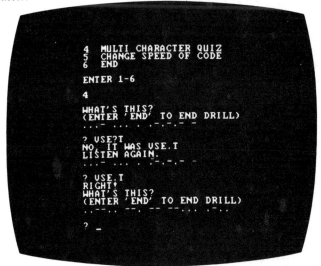

Finally, the operator asks for option 4, to test himself on random five
character groups. After a mistake in his response for the first group, he
replies correctly when it is repeated.

PROGRAM LISTING

```
100 REM: HAMCODE
110 REM: Learn "International Morse" code.
120 REM: COPYRIGHT 1982 Tom Rugg and Phil Feldman.
130 REM: Any BASIC, any CRT.
140 GOTO 840
150 W=ASC(R$)-39:IF W<0 OR W>51 THEN 240
160 T$=C$(W):IF T$>"/" THEN 240
170 FOR J=1 TO LEN(T$):W$=MID$(T$,J,1)
180 D=L:IF W$="." THEN D=S
190 PRINT W$;
200 SOUND P,D
210 SOUND Q,S
220 NEXT:SOUND Q,S+S
230 PRINT CHR$(32);:RETURN
240 SOUND 40,8:RETURN
250 FOR K=1 TO LEN(P$):R$=MID$(P$,K,1)
260 IF ASC(R$)=32 THEN 280
270 GOSUB 150:GOTO 290
280 PRINT CHR$(176);CHR$(32);:SOUND Q,S+S
290 NEXT:PRINT:RETURN
300 PRINT"PRESS A KEY TO HEAR"
310 PRINT"(ESC KEY ENDS THIS DRILL)"
320 R$=INKEY$:IF LEN(R$)=0 THEN 320
330 W=ASC(R$):IF W=27 THEN 950
340 IF W<39 OR W>90 THEN 360
350 IF C$(W-39)<>"X" THEN 370
360 SOUND 40,8:GOTO 320
370 PRINT R$;:GOSUB 150:GOTO 320
380 PRINT:PRINT"ENTER PHRASE"
390 PRINT"(ENTER 'END' TO END DRILL)"
400 INPUT P$
410 IF LEN(P$)=0 THEN P$=L$
420 IF P$="END" THEN 950
430 GOSUB 250:L$=P$
440 GOTO 380
450 GOSUB 800
460 GOSUB 820
470 PRINT"WHAT CHARACTER IS THIS?"
480 PRINT"(ESC KEY ENDS THIS DRILL)"
490 GOSUB 150
500 T$=INKEY$:IF LEN(T$)=0 THEN 500
510 IF ASC(T$)=27 THEN 950
520 IF ASC(T$)=13 THEN 490
530 PRINT T$:IF T$=R$ THEN 570
540 PRINT"NO, IT WAS ";R$
550 PRINT"TRY IT AGAIN.":PRINT
560 GOTO 460
570 PRINT"RIGHT!":GOTO 450
580 PRINT"WHAT'S THIS?"
590 PRINT"(ENTER 'END' TO END DRILL)"
```

```
600 P$="":FOR J=1 TO N
610 GOSUB 800
620 P$=P$+R$:NEXT
630 GOSUB 820:GOSUB 250:PRINT
640 INPUT T$:IF LEN(T$)=0 THEN 630
650 IF T$="END" THEN 950
660 IF T$=P$ THEN PRINT"RIGHT!":GOTO 580
670 PRINT"NO, IT WAS ";P$
680 PRINT"LISTEN AGAIN."
690 GOTO 630
700 PRINT"SELECT SPEED:"
710 PRINT"1   SLOW (11 WPM)"
720 PRINT"2   FAST (22 WPM)"
730 PRINT:PRINT"ENTER 1-2"
740 DEF SEG:POKE 106,0
750 R$=INKEY$:IF LEN(R$)=0 THEN 750
760 R=VAL(R$):IF R<1 OR R>2 THEN 750
770 PRINT R$:PRINT
780 R=3-R:S=R:L=R+R+R
790 GOTO 950
800 R=INT(52*RND):IF C$(R)="X" THEN 800
810 R$=CHR$(R+39):RETURN
820 FOR J=1 TO 800:NEXT:RETURN
830 END
840 KEY OFF:SCREEN 0,0:WIDTH 40:COLOR 7,0:CLS
850 DIM C$(51):I=1
860 FOR J=0 TO 51:READ C$(J):NEXT
870 P=528
880 S=2:L=6:Q=32767
890 P$="HAM CODE"
900 PRINT TAB(12);P$:PRINT
910 GOSUB 250
920 N=5:L$=CHR$(32)
930 PRINT:PRINT
940 PRINT"Be sure CAPS LOCK is in effect."
950 PRINT:PRINT
960 PRINT"**** OPTIONS ****"
970 PRINT"1   LEARN CHARACTERS"
980 PRINT"2   LEARN PHRASES"
990 PRINT"3   SINGLE CHARACTER QUIZ"
1000 PRINT"4   MULTI CHARACTER QUIZ"
1010 PRINT"5   CHANGE SPEED OF CODE"
1020 PRINT"6   END"
1030 PRINT
1040 PRINT"ENTER 1-6"
1050 PRINT
1060 DEF SEG:POKE 106,0
1070 R$=INKEY$:R=RND
1080 IF LEN(R$)=0 THEN 1070
1090 R=VAL(R$):IF R<1 OR R>6 THEN 1070
1100 PRINT R$:PRINT
1110 ON R GOTO 300,380,450,580,700,830
```

```
1120 REM: Enter data below VERY carefully.
1130 REM: Note that X's are capitals.
1140 DATA .----.,-.--.-,X,X,X
1150 DATA --..--,-....-,.-.-.-
1160 DATA -..-.,-----,.----
1170 DATA ..---,...--,....-
1180 DATA .....,-....,--...
1190 DATA ---..,----.,---...
1200 DATA -.-.-.,X,X,X,..--..,X
1210 DATA .-,-...,-.-.,-..,.
1220 DATA ..-.,--.,....,..,.---
1230 DATA -.-,.-..,--,-.,---
1240 DATA .--.,--.-,.-.,...,-
1250 DATA ..-,...-,.--,-..-
1260 DATA -.--,--..
```

EASY CHANGES

1. Change the number of characters in the multi-character quiz
   (option 4) by changing the value of N in line 920.
2. Many experts stress that code is a language of *sound*, not
   sight, and should be learned that way. If you like, you can
   eliminate the displaying of dots and dashes on the screen by
   deleting line 190 and changing these lines:

   230 RETURN

   280 SOUND Q,S+S

3. Eliminate the sounding of HAM CODE at the start of the
   program by deleting line 910.
4. To drill on only alphabetic characters during options three
   and four, make this change:

   800 R = INT(26*RND) + 26:IF C$(R) = "X" THEN 800

5 . A short delay is built into the program at several points. To
   lengthen it, replace the 800 in line 820 with 2000. To
   eliminate the delay, replace the 800 with 1.

MAIN ROUTINES

150- 240 Subroutine to sound and display character R$.
250- 290 Subroutine to sound and display phrase P$.
300- 370 Teaches characters by echoing keys until ESC is
          pressed.
380- 440 Teaches phrases by echoing entries until END is
          entered.
450- 570 Quizzes individual characters until ESC is pressed.

580- 690	Quizzes random N character phrases until END is entered.
700- 790	Changes code speed.
800- 810	Subroutine to pick random character R$.
820	Time delay subroutine.
840- 880	Initializes variables. Stores codes in C$ array.
890- 940	Displays and sounds title. Initializes more variables.
950-1110	Displays options. Gets response. Initializes RND. Goes to option entered.
1140-1260	DATA statements with codes for ASCII 39 (apostrophe) through 90 (Z). X value is illegal code. A through Z are in 1210 through 1260.

MAIN VARIABLES

W	Work variable and subscript.
R$	Character to be sounded; work character.
T$	Work string.
C$	Array of code strings.
J,K	Loop and work variables.
W$	Element (dot or dash) of code to be sounded.
D	Duration of sound to be made (dash = 3 times dot). Also loop variable.
P	Pitch of sound to be made.
P$	Phrase of characters to be sounded.
L$	Last phrase entered.
N	Number of characters in multi-character quiz.
R	Random number for character selection; work variable.
S	Duration of short sound (dot).
L	Duration of long sound (dash).
Q	32767 (for "quiet" sound).

SUGGESTED PROJECTS

1. Add another option to randomly quiz the operator on a series of common words and/or phrases that have been stored in DATA statements.
2. Program some "intelligence" into the learning phase of the program. Have the program teach 3 or 4 common letters until the operator has mastered them, then begin teaching 3 or 4 more, etc.

3. Determine how to interface your computer with amateur radio equipment so you can use the program to actually send code automatically under program control.

4. Now try the reverse of Project 3 — have the computer figure out how to decode a transmission that has been received over the radio, converting it into text. This will almost undoubtedly require some or all of the program to be in assembly language in order to run fast enough to handle this job in real time.

METRIC

PURPOSE

In case you don't realize it, we live in a metric world. The United States is one of the last holdouts, but that is changing rapidly. So if you're still inching along or watching those pounds, it's time to convert.

METRIC is an instructional program designed to familiarize you with the metric system. It operates in a quiz format; the program randomly forms questions from its data resources. You are then asked to compare two quantities—one in our old English units and one in the corresponding metric units. When you are wrong, the exact conversion and the rule governing it are given.

The two quantities to compare are usually within 50% of each other. Thus, you are constantly comparing an "English" quantity and a metric one which are in the same ball park. This has the effect of providing you some insight by sheer familiarity with the questions.

HOW TO USE IT

The program first requests that you hit a key to begin. When this is done, it asks how many questions you would like to do for the session. Any value of one or higher is acceptable.

The sample run shows how each question is formulated. A quantity in English units is compared with one in metric units. Either one may appear first in the question. Each quantity will have an integral value. The relating word ("longer," "hotter," "heavier," etc.) indicates what type of quantities are being compared.

There are three possible replies to each question. Pressing **Y** (or **y**) means that you think the answer is yes. Pressing **N** (or **n**) means that you think the answer is no. Pressing any other key indicates that you have no idea as to the correct answer.

If you answer the question correctly, you will be duly congratulated and the program will proceed to the next question. A wrong answer or a response of "no idea," however, will generate some diagnostic information. The first value used in the question will be shown converted to its exact equivalent in the corresponding units. Also, the rule governing the situation will be displayed. At the end of any question, the program will request that you hit any key to proceed to the next question.

The program will continue generating the requested number of questions. Before ending, it will show you how many correct answers you gave and your percentage correct.

SAMPLE RUN

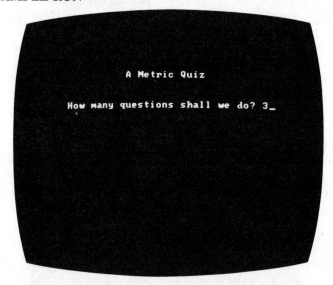

After hitting a key to begin the program, the operator requests a three question quiz.

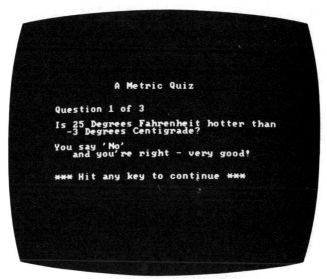

The first question is correctly answered "no." The program waits for a key to be pressed before continuing the quiz.

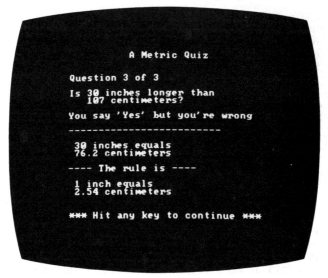

Later, the third question is incorrectly answered with "yes." The correct conversion and governing rule are then displayed.

The program shows the number and percentage of correctly answered questions.

PROGRAM LISTING

```
100 REM: METRIC
110 REM: A metric system teaching quiz.
120 REM: COPYRIGHT 1982 Phil Feldman and Tom Rugg.
130 REM: Any BASIC, any CRT.
140 KEY OFF:SCREEN 0,0,0,0:WIDTH 40:COLOR 7,0,0
150 CLEAR:CLS:DEF SEG:POKE 106,0
160 PRINT"  Hit any key to begin."
170 Q$=INKEY$:Q=RND:IF LEN(Q$)=0 THEN 170
180 DIM ES$(30),MS$(30),R$(30),C(30),EP$(30),
    MP$(30)
190 B$=CHR$(32):CLS
200 GOSUB 260:GOSUB 300
210 PRINT:INPUT"How many questions shall we do";
    NQ:NQ=INT(NQ):IF NQ<1 THEN 210
220 FOR J=1 TO NQ:GOSUB 310:GOSUB 550:NEXT
230 GOSUB 300:PRINT"You got";NR;"right out of";
    NQ;"questions":PRINT
240 P=100*NR/NQ:PRINT"Percentage correct =";P
250 PRINT:END
260 RESTORE:ND=0
270 ND=ND+1:READ ES$(ND),MS$(ND),R$(ND),C(ND),
    EP$(ND),MP$(ND)
280 IF ES$(ND)<> "XXX" THEN 270
290 ND=ND-1:RETURN
```

```
300 CLS:PRINT TAB(11);"A Metric Quiz":PRINT:
    PRINT:RETURN
310 N=INT(ND*RND)+1
320 F=0:IF RND>.5 THEN F=1
330 V1=INT(RND*99)+2:V3=V1*C(N):
    IF F=1 THEN V3=V1/C(N)
340 IF N=1 THEN V3=(V1-32)/1.8:
    IF F=1 THEN V3=(V1*1.8)+32
350 V2=V3*(.5+RND):V2=INT(V2+.5):T=0:
    IF V2<V3 THEN T=1
360 GOSUB 300:PRINT"Question";J;"of";NQ:PRINT
370 IF F=0 THEN PRINT"Is";V1;EP$(N);B$;R$(N);
    SPC(1);"than":PRINT SPC(2);V2;MP$(N);"?"
380 IF F=1 THEN PRINT"Is";V1;MP$(N);B$;R$(N);
    SPC(1);"than":PRINT SPC(2);V2;EP$(N);"?"
390 Q$=INKEY$:IF LEN(Q$)=0 THEN 390
400 IF Q$="Y" OR Q$="y" THEN PRINT:
    PRINT"You say 'Yes' ";:R=1:GOTO 430
410 IF Q$="N" OR Q$="n" THEN PRINT:
    PRINT"You say 'No' ";:R=0:GOTO 430
420 PRINT:PRINT"You have no idea":R=2
430 X=T-R:IF R=2 THEN GOSUB 470:GOTO 460
440 IF X=0 THEN PRINT:PRINT"   and you're right
    - very good!":NR=NR+1:GOTO 460
450 PRINT"but you're wrong":GOSUB 470
460 RETURN
470 PRINT:PRINT STRING$(25,45):PRINT
480 IF F=0 THEN PRINT V1;EP$(N);B$;"equals":
    PRINT V3;MP$(N)
490 IF F=1 THEN PRINT V1;MP$(N);B$;"equals":
    PRINT V3;EP$(N)
500 PRINT:PRINT"---- The rule is ----":PRINT
510 IF N=1 AND F=0 THEN PRINT
    " Deg.C = (Deg.F - 32)/1.8": RETURN
520 IF N=1 AND F=1 THEN PRINT
    " Deg.F = (Deg.C * 1.8) + 32": RETURN
530 IF F=0 THEN PRINT SPC(1);"1";SPC(1);ES$(N);
    SPC(1);"equals":PRINT C(N);MP$(N):RETURN
540 Q=INT(100000!/C(N))/100000!:PRINT SPC(1);"1"
    ;SPC(1);MS$(N);SPC(1);"equals":PRINT Q;EP$
    (N):RETURN
550 DEF SEG:POKE 106,0:PRINT:PRINT:
    PRINT"*** Hit any key to continue ***"
560 Q$=INKEY$:IF LEN(Q$)=0 THEN 560
570 RETURN
580 DATA Degree Fahrenheit,Degree Centigrade,
    hotter,0.5
590 DATA Degrees Fahrenheit,Degrees Centigrade
600 DATA mile per hour,kilometer per hour,
    faster,1.60935
610 DATA miles per hour,kilometers per hour
```

```
620 DATA foot,meter,longer,0.3048
630 DATA feet,meters
640 DATA mile,kilometer,longer,1.60935
650 DATA miles,kilometers
660 DATA inch,centimeter,longer,2.54
670 DATA inches,centimeters
680 DATA gallon,litre,more,3.78533
690 DATA gallons,litres
700 DATA pound,kilogram,heavier,0.45359
710 DATA pounds,kilograms
999 DATA XXX,XXX,XXX,0,XXX,XXX
```

EASY CHANGES

1. To have the program always ask a fixed number of questions, change line 210 to set NQ to the desired value. For example:

    $$210 \ NQ = 10$$

    will cause the program to do 10 questions.

2. There are currently seven conversions built into the program:

N	Type	English Unit	Metric Unit
1	temperature	degrees F.	degrees C.
2	speed	miles/hour	kilometers/hour
3	length	feet	meters
4	length	miles	kilometers
5	length	inches	centimeters
6	volume	gallons	litres
7	weight	pounds	kilograms

    If you wish to be quizzed on only one type of question, set N to this value in line 310. Thus,

    $$310 \ N = 4$$

    will cause the program to only produce questions comparing miles and kilometers. To add additional data to the program, see the first suggested project.

3. You can easily have the questions posed in one "direction" only. To go only from English to metric units use

    $$320 \ F = 0$$

    while to go from metric to English units use

    $$320 \ F = 1$$

4.   You might want the converted value and governing rule to be displayed even when the correct answer is given. This is accomplished by changing line 460 and adding line 465 as follows:

460 IF X = 0 THEN GOSUB 470
465 RETURN

MAIN ROUTINES

160-170	Prompts user to hit any key to begin.
180-190	Dimensions and initializes variables.
200-250	Mainline routine, drives other routines.
260-290	Reads and initializes data.
300	Displays header.
310-460	Forms and asks questions. Processes user's reply.
470-540	Displays exact conversion and governing rule.
550	Requests the user to hit any key.
560-570	Waits for user to hit any key.
580-999	Data statements.

MAIN VARIABLES

ND	Number of conversions in the data.
ES$,EP$	String arrays of English units' names (singular, plural).
MS$,MP$	String arrays of metric units' names (singular, plural).
R$	String array of the relation descriptors.
C	Array of the conversion factors.
Q	Work variable.
B$	String constant of one blank character.
J	Current question number.
NR	Number of questions answered right.
P	Percentage answered right.
NQ	Number of questions in session.
N	Index number of current question in the data list.
F	Flag on question "direction" (0 = English to metric; 1 = metric to English).
V1,V2	Numeric values on left, right sides of the question.
V3	The correct value of the right hand side.
T	Flag on the question's correct answer (1 = true; 0 = false).

Q$ User reply string.
R   User reply flag (0 = no; 1 = yes; 2 = no idea).
X   User's result (0 if correct answer was given).

SUGGESTED PROJECTS

1. Each built-in conversion requires six elements of data in this
    order:

    Element   *Data Description*
        1   English unit (singular)
        2   Metric unit (singular)
        3   Relation descriptor (e.g., "hotter," "faster," etc.)
        4   Conversion factor (from English to metric)
        5   English unit (plural)
        6   Metric unit (plural)

    Each of these elements, except the fourth, is a string. The
    data statements in the listing should make clear how the in-
    formation is to be provided. You can add new data to the
    program with appropriate data statements in this format.
    New data should be added after the current data, i.e., just
    before line 999. Line 999 is a special data statement to trig-
    ger the end of all data to the program. The program is
    dimensioned up to thirty entries while only seven are cur-
    rently used. (Note: this format allows only conversions
    where one unit is a direct multiple of the other.
    Temperature, which does not fit this rule, is handled as a
    special case throughout the program.)

2. Convert the program to handle units conversion questions
    of any type.

3. Keep track of the questions asked and which ones were
    missed. Then do not ask the same questions too soon if they
    have been answered correctly. However, do repeat those
    questions missed to provide additional practice.

NUMBERS

PURPOSE

This is an educational program for pre-school children. After a few weeks of watching "Sesame Street" on television, most three and four year old children will learn how to count from one to ten. The NUMBERS program allows these children to practice their numbers and have fun at the same time.

HOW TO USE IT

We know a child who learned how to type LOAD and RUN to get this program started before she turned three, but you'll probably have to help your child with this for a while. The program asks the question, "WHAT NUMBER COMES AFTER n?", where n is a number from one to eight. Even if the child can't read yet, he or she will soon learn to look for the number at the end of the line. The child should respond with the appropriate number, and then press the **ENTER** key.

If the answer is correct, the program displays the message "THAT'S RIGHT!", pauses for a couple of seconds, and then clears the screen and displays three geometric shapes. In the upper left of the screen a square is drawn. In the lower center, a triangle is drawn. Then an asterisk (or a snowflake, perhaps?) is drawn in the upper right portion of the screen. After a few seconds delay, the program clears the screen and asks another question. The same number is never asked twice in a row. The size of the three figures is chosen at random each time. If the child provides the wrong answer, a message indicates the error and the same question is asked again.

The program keeps on going until you enter "E" (for end). Remember that most children have a pretty short attention span, so please do not force your child to continue after his or her interest diminishes. Keep each session short and fun. This way, it will always be a treat to "play" with the computer.

SAMPLE RUN

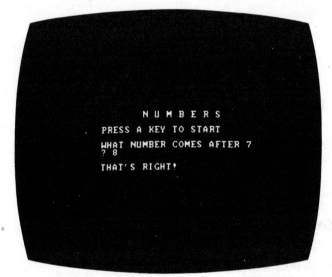

```
                    N U M B E R S
         PRESS A KEY TO START
         WHAT NUMBER COMES AFTER 7
         ? 8

         THAT'S RIGHT!
```

The program asks what number comes after 7, and waits for a response. The operator says "8", and the program acknowledges that the answer is correct.

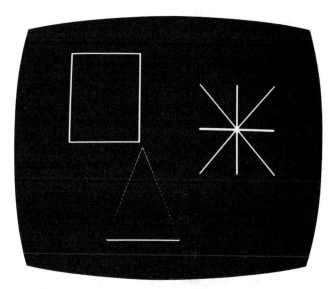

Because of the correct response, the program draws three geometric
figures.

PROGRAM LISTING

```
100 REM: NUMBERS
110 REM: Number practice for children.
120 REM: COPYRIGHT 1982 Tom Rugg and Phil Feldman.
130 REM: Any BASIC, graphics interface card.
140 KEY OFF:SCREEN 1,0:COLOR 0,1:WIDTH 40:CLS
150 M=8
160 X=220:Y=80:TS=100:CLS:I=1
170 PRINT
180 PRINT TAB(8);"N U M  B E R S"
190 PRINT:PRINT"PRESS A KEY TO START"
200 DEF SEG:POKE 106,0
210 R$=INKEY$:E=RND:IF LEN(R$)=0 THEN 210
220 E=RND(-E)
230 R=INT(M*RND)+1:IF R=P THEN 230
240 PRINT
250 PRINT"WHAT NUMBER COMES AFTER";R
260 INPUT R$
270 PRINT:IF R$="E" OR R$="e" THEN END
280 IF VAL(R$)=R+1 THEN 310
290 PRINT"NO, THAT'S NOT IT.   TRY AGAIN."
300 GOTO 240
```

```
310 PRINT"THAT'S RIGHT!"
320 FOR J=1 TO 1500:NEXT
330 CLS:P=R
340 E=INT(80*RND)+20
350 C=INT(3*RND)+1
360 IF RND>.5 THEN 390
370 LINE (1,1)-(E,E),C,BF
380 GOTO 400
390 LINE (1,1)-(E,E),C,B:LINE (2,1)-(E+1,E),C,B
400 C=INT(3*RND)+1
410 B=INT(E/2)
420 LINE (TS,TS)-(TS+B,TS+E),C
430 LINE -(TS-B,TS+E),C
440 LINE -(TS,TS),C
450 C=INT(3*RND)+1
460 LINE (X,Y)-(X,Y-B),C:LINE (X+1,Y)-(X+1,Y-B),C
470 LINE (X,Y)-(X+B,Y-B),C:
    LINE (X+1,Y)-(X+B+1,Y-B),C
480 LINE (X,Y)-(X+B,Y),C:LINE (X,Y+1)-(X+B,Y+1),C
490 LINE (X,Y)-(X+B,Y+B),C:
    LINE (X+1,Y)-(X+B+1,Y+B),C
500 LINE (X,Y)-(X,Y+B),C:LINE (X+1,Y)-(X+1,Y+B),C
510 LINE (X,Y)-(X-B,Y+B),C:
    LINE (X+1,Y)-(X-B+1,Y+B),C
520 LINE (X,Y)-(X-B,Y),C:LINE (X,Y+1)-(X-B,Y+1),C
530 LINE (X,Y)-(X-B,Y-B),C:
    LINE (X+1,Y)-(X-B+1,Y-B),C
540 FOR J=1 TO 6000:NEXT
550 CLS
560 GOTO 230
```

EASY CHANGES

1. Change the range of numbers that the program asks by altering the value of M in line 150. For a beginner, use a value of 3 for M instead of 8. Later, increase the value of M to 5, and then 8.

2. Alter the delay after "THAT'S RIGHT!" is displayed by altering the value of 1500 in statement 320. Double it to double the time delay, etc. The same can be done with the 6000 in line 540 to alter the delay after the figures are drawn.

3. To avoid randomness in the size of the figures that are drawn, replace line 340 with

$$340 \ E = 50$$

Instead of 50, you can use any integer from 5 to 99.

4. To slowly increase the size of the figures from small to large

as correct answers are given (and the reverse for incorrect answers), do the following:

a. Insert these lines:

$$165 \ E = 5$$
$$285 \ E = E - 5 : IF \ E < 5 \ THEN \ E = 5$$

b. Replace line 340 with:

$$340 \ E = E + 5 :$$
$$IF \ E > 95 \ THEN \ E = 95$$

MAIN ROUTINES

140-220	Initializes variables. Clears screen. Initializes RND.
230	Picks random integer from 1 to M.
240-300	Asks question. Gets answer. Determines if right or wrong.
320	Delays about 1.5 seconds.
330-390	Draws a square (filled or open at random).
400-440	Draws a triangle.
450-530	Draws an asterisk.
540	Delays about 5 seconds.
550-560	Clears screen. Goes back to ask next question.

MAIN VARIABLES

M	Maximum number that will be asked.
E	Edge length of geometric figures.
R	Random integer in range from 1 to M.
P	Previous number that was asked.
R$	Reply given by operator.
X,Y	Coordinates of center of asterisk.
TS	Triangle's starting location (top).
B	Half of base of triangle.
J	Subscript variable.
C	Color of geometric shape.

SUGGESTED PROJECTS

1. Modify the program to ask the next letter of the alphabet. Use the ASC and CHR$ functions in picking a random letter from A to Y, and to check whether the response is correct or not.

2. Ask each number from 1 to M once (in a random sequence). At the end of the sequence, repeat those that were missed.
3. Add different shapes to the graphics display that is done after a correct answer. Try an octagon, a diamond, and a rectangle. Or, combine this program with one of the graphics display programs.

TACHIST

PURPOSE

This program turns your computer into a tachistoscope (tah-KISS-tah-scope). A tachistoscope is used in reading classes to improve reading habits and, as a result, improve reading speed. The program displays a word or phrase on the screen for a fraction of a second, then asks you what it was. With a little practice, you will find that you can read phrases that are displayed for shorter and shorter time periods.

HOW TO USE IT

The program starts off by displaying a brief introduction and waiting for you to press any key (except the special keys like **Num Lock** and **SHIFT**, of course). After you press a key, the screen is blanked out except for two horizontal dash lines in the upper left-hand corner. After one and a half seconds, the phrase is flashed on the screen between the two lines. Then the screen is blanked again, and you are asked what the phrase was.

If you respond correctly, the next phrase is displayed for a shorter time period (half as long). If you respond incorrectly, the program shows you the correct phrase, and the next phrase is displayed for a longer period of time (twice as long).

Pressing the **ESC** key ends the program.

The fastest the computer can display a phrase and erase it is about .02 seconds (one-fiftieth). See if you can reach the top speed and still continue to read the phrases correctly.

A great deal of research has been done to determine how people read and what they should do to read both faster and with better comprehension. We will not try to explain it all (see the Bibliography), but a couple of things are worth mentioning.

To read fast, you should not read one word at a time. Instead, you should learn to quickly read an entire phrase at once. By looking at a point in the center of the phrase (and slightly above it), your eyes can see the whole phrase *without* the necessity of scanning it from left to right, word by word. Because the tachistoscope flashes an entire phrase on the screen for such a short time, it forces you to look at a single point and absorb the whole phrase, rather than scanning left to right, word by word.

If you can incorporate this technique into your reading and increase the width of the phrases you absorb, your reading speed can increase dramatically.

SAMPLE RUN

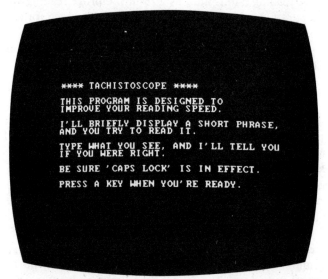

The program displays an introduction, then waits.

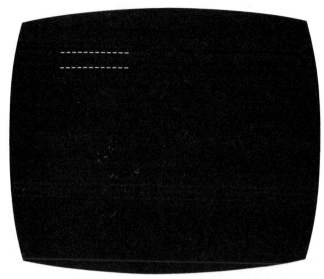

The program clears the screen and displays two parallel lines in the upper left corner of the screen for a couple of seconds.

The program flashes a short phrase (chosen at random) between the two lines for a fraction of a second, then clears the screen.

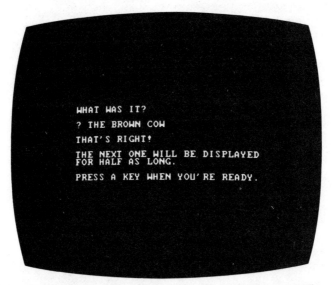

```
WHAT WAS IT?
? THE BROWN COW
THAT'S RIGHT!
THE NEXT ONE WILL BE DISPLAYED
FOR HALF AS LONG.
PRESS A KEY WHEN YOU'RE READY.
```

The program asks what the phrase was. The operator responds correctly. The program acknowledges the correct response, and indicates that the next phrase will be shown for half as long.

PROGRAM LISTING

```
100 REM: TACHIST
110 REM: A tachistoscope for reading improvement.
120 REM: COPYRIGHT 1982 Tom Rugg and Phil Feldman.
130 REM: Any BASIC, any CRT.
140 KEY OFF:SCREEN 0,0:WIDTH 40:COLOR 7,0
150 T=256
160 L=50
170 DIM T$(L)
180 C=0:I=1
190 READ R$
200 IF R$="XXX" OR R$="xxx" THEN 250
210 C=C+1
220 IF C>L THEN PRINT"TOO MANY DATA STATEMENTS":
    END
230 T$(C)=R$
240 GOTO 190
250 CLS
260 PRINT"**** TACHISTOSCOPE ****"
270 PRINT
```

```
280 PRINT"THIS PROGRAM IS DESIGNED TO"
290 PRINT"IMPROVE YOUR READING SPEED."
300 PRINT
310 PRINT"I'LL BRIEFLY DISPLAY A SHORT PHRASE,"
320 PRINT"AND YOU TRY TO READ IT."
330 PRINT
340 PRINT"TYPE WHAT YOU SEE, AND I'LL TELL YOU"
350 PRINT"IF YOU WERE RIGHT."
360 PRINT
370 PRINT"BE SURE 'CAPS LOCK' IS IN EFFECT."
380 PRINT
390 DEF SEG:POKE 106,0
400 PRINT"PRESS A KEY WHEN YOU'RE READY."
410 R$=INKEY$:R=RND:IF LEN(R$)=0 THEN 410
420 IF ASC(R$)=27 THEN END
430 DEF SEG:POKE 106,0
440 R=INT(C*RND)+1
450 IF R=P1 OR R=P2 OR R=P3 THEN 440
460 IF R=P4 OR R=P5 THEN 440
470 GOSUB 680:FOR K=1 TO 1500:NEXT
480 LOCATE 2,1:PRINT T$(R)
490 FOR J=1 TO T:NEXT
500 CLS:FOR K=1 TO 500:NEXT
510 PRINT:PRINT:PRINT
520 PRINT"WHAT WAS IT?"
530 PRINT:INPUT R$
540 IF R$<>T$(R) THEN 630
550 PRINT:PRINT"THAT'S RIGHT!"
560 T=T/2
570 R$="FOR HALF AS LONG."
580 P1=P2:P2=P3:P3=P4:P4=P5:P5=R
590 PRINT
600 IF T<=16 THEN T=16:R$="AT MAXIMUM SPEED."
610 PRINT"THE NEXT ONE WILL BE DISPLAYED":PRINT R$
620 PRINT:GOTO 400
630 PRINT"NO, THAT'S NOT IT.  IT WAS"
640 PRINT:PRINT CHR$(34);T$(R);CHR$(34)
650 T=T*2
660 IF T>2048 THEN T=2048:
    R$="AT THE SAME SPEED.":GOTO 580
670 R$="FOR TWICE AS LONG.":GOTO 580
680 CLS:PRINT"------------"
690 PRINT
700 PRINT"------------"
710 RETURN
720 DATA AT THE TIME
730 DATA THE BROWN COW
740 DATA LOOK AT THAT
750 DATA IN THE HOUSE
760 DATA THIS IS MINE
770 DATA SHE SAID SO
780 DATA THE BABY CRIED
```

```
790 DATA TO THE STORE
800 DATA READING IS FUN
810 DATA HE GOES FAST
820 DATA IN ALL THINGS
830 DATA GREEN GRASS
840 DATA TWO BIRDS FLY
850 DATA LATE LAST NIGHT
860 DATA THEY ARE HOME
870 DATA ON THE PHONE
880 DATA THROUGH A DOOR
890 DATA WE CAN TRY
900 DATA MY FOOT HURTS
910 DATA HAPPY NEW YEAR
9999 DATA XXX
```

EASY CHANGES

1. Change the phrases that are displayed by changing the DATA statements that start at line 720. Add more and/or replace those shown with your own phrases or words. Line 160 must specify a number that is at least as large as the number of DATA statements. So, to allow for up to 100 DATA statements, change line 160 to say

$$160 \ L = 100$$

Be sure to enter your DATA statements in the same form shown in the program listing. To begin with, you may want to start off with shorter phrases or single words. Later, try longer phrases. Do not alter line 9999, which has to be the last DATA statement. In a 16K cassette system or a 64K disk system, you have room for several hundred phrases of the approximate size shown in the program listing. Be sure to have at least 5.

2. To change the length of time the first phrase is displayed, change the value of T in line 150. Double it to double the length of time, etc. Don't make it less than 16.

3. To cause all phrases to be displayed for the same length of time, remove lines 560 and 650, and insert these lines:

    575 R$ = "AT THE SAME SPEED"
    655 R$ = "AT THE SAME SPEED":GOTO 580

4. If you want to change the waiting period before the phrase is flashed on the screen, change the 1500 in line 470. To make the delay five seconds, change it to 5500. To make it one second, change it to 1100.

5. To put the program into a sort of flashcard mode, in which the phrases are flashed, but no replies are necessary, insert these three lines:

    515 GOTO 640
    575 R$ = "AT THE SAME SPEED"
    645 GOTO 575

    This will cause each phrase to be flashed (all for the same length of time), and then displayed again so you can verify what it was. Use Easy Change 2 to alter the display time.

6. If you would prefer to display lowercase letters instead of all capitals, enter the DATA in lines 720-910 in lower case, and delete line 370.

MAIN ROUTINES

150- 180	Initializes variables.
190- 240	Reads DATA statements into T$ array.
250- 380	Displays introduction.
390- 430	Waits for operator to press a key.
440- 460	Picks random phrase from T$ array. Ensures no duplication from previous five phrases.
470	Clears screen and displays horizontal lines.
480- 500	Displays phrase for appropriate length of time.
510- 530	Asks what the phrase was.
540	Determines if typed phrase matches the phrase displayed.
550- 620	Shortens time for next phrase if reply was correct. Saves subscript to avoid repetition. Goes back to wait for key to be pressed.
630- 670	Shows what phrase was. Lengthens time for next phrase. Ensures that time period does not exceed maximum.
680- 710	Subroutine to display horizontal dash lines.
720-9999	DATA statements with phrases to be displayed.

MAIN VARIABLES

T	Time that phrase will be displayed.
J	Loop variable.
L	Limit of number of phrases.

T$	Array of phrases (read into from DATA statements).
C	Count of number of phrases actually read.
I	Constant one.
R$	Temporary string variable. Also, reply of operator.
R	Work variable. Also, subscript of phrase to be displayed.
P1,P2, P3,P4,P5	Subscripts of the five previous phrases.
K	Temporary work variable.

SUGGESTED PROJECTS

1. Instead of picking phrases at random, go through the list once sequentially.
2. Instead of only verifying that the current phrase does not duplicate any of the previous five phrases, modify the program to avoid duplication of the previous ten or more. Changes will be needed to lines 450, 460, and 580.
3. Keep score of the number of correct and incorrect replies, and display the percentage each time. Alternatively, come up with a rating based on the percentage correct and the speed attained, possibly in conjunction with a difficulty factor for the phrases used.
4. Add the capability to the program to also have a mode in which it can display a two to seven digit number, chosen at random. Have the operator try several of the numbers first (maybe five-digit ones) before trying the phrases. The phrases will seem easy after doing the numbers.

VOCAB

PURPOSE

Did you ever find yourself at a loss for words? Well, this vocabulary quiz can be used in a self-teaching environment or as reinforcement for classroom instruction to improve your ability to remember the jargon of any subject. It allows you to drill at your own pace, without the worry of ridicule from other students or judgment by an instructor. When you make mistakes, only the computer knows, and it's not telling anyone except you. Modifying the program to substitute a different vocabulary list is very simple, so you can accumulate many different versions of this program, each with a different set of words.

HOW TO USE IT

This program is pretty much self-explanatory from the sample run. After you enter RUN, it asks how many questions you want to try. Any number that is five or more is acceptable. Then the program asks you to press a key to start.

Next, you get a series of multiple choice questions. Each question is formatted in one of two ways—either you are given a word and asked to select from a list of definitions, or you are given a definition and asked to select from a list of words. The format is chosen at random. You respond with the number of the choice you think is correct. If you are right, you are told so. If not, you are shown the correct answer. From the second answer on, you are shown a status report of the number correct out of the number attempted so far.

Finally, after the last question, you are shown the percentage you got correct, along with a comment on your performance. Then you have the option of going back for another round of questions or stopping.

SAMPLE RUN

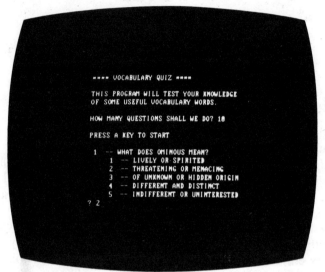

The operator decides to try 10 questions and selects the answer to the first question.

The program responds that the first answer was correct, and asks the next question.

At the end of ten questions, the program gives a final score and asks about trying again.

PROGRAM LISTING

```
100 REM: VOCAB
110 REM: A vocabulary drill/quiz.
120 REM: COPYRIGHT 1982 Tom Rugg and Phil Feldman.
130 REM: Any BASIC, 80 column CRT.
140 GOSUB 230
150 GOSUB 400
160 GOSUB 580
170 GOSUB 710
180 GOSUB 840
190 GOSUB 990
200 IF E=0 THEN 160
210 GOTO 140
220 REM
230 IF E<>0 THEN 290
240 KEY OFF:SCREEN 0,0:WIDTH 80:COLOR 7,0:CLS
250 PRINT"**** VOCABULARY QUIZ ****"
260 PRINT
270 PRINT"THIS PROGRAM WILL TEST YOUR KNOWLEDGE"
280 PRINT"OF SOME USEFUL VOCABULARY WORDS."
290 PRINT
300 DEF SEG:POKE 106,0
310 INPUT"HOW MANY QUESTIONS SHALL WE DO";L
320 IF L>4 THEN 340
330 PRINT"THAT'S NOT ENOUGH.   LET'S DO 5.":L=5
340 PRINT
350 PRINT"PRESS A KEY TO START"
360 R$=INKEY$:R=RND:IF LEN(R$)=0 THEN 360
370 IF ASC(R$)=27 THEN END
380 I=1:DEF SEG:POKE 106,0
390 RETURN
400 IF E<>0 THEN 540
410 C=5
420 D=26
430 DIM D$(D),E$(D)
440 DIM P(C)
450 J=1
460 READ D$(J)
470 IF D$(J)="XXX" OR D$(J)="xxx" THEN 530
480 READ E$(J)
490 J=J+1
500 IF J<=D THEN 460
510 PRINT"TOO MANY DATA STATEMENTS."
520 PRINT"ONLY THE FIRST";D;"ARE USED."
530 D=J-1
540 Q=1
550 E=0
560 Q1=0
570 RETURN
580 FOR J=1 TO C
590 P(J)=0
```

```
600 NEXT
610 FOR J=1 TO C
620 P=INT(D*RND)+1
630 IF P=P1 OR P=P2 OR P=P3 THEN 620
640 FOR K=1 TO J
650 IF P(K)=P THEN 620
660 NEXT K
670 P(J)=P
680 NEXT J
690 A=INT(C*RND)+1
700 RETURN
710 PRINT
720 M=RND
730 IF M>.5 THEN 790
740 PRINT Q;" -- WHAT WORD MEANS ";E$(P(A));"?"
750 FOR J=1 TO C
760 PRINT TAB(5);J;" -- ";D$(P(J))
770 NEXT
780 GOTO 830
790 PRINT Q;" -- WHAT DOES ";D$(P(A));" MEAN?"
800 FOR J=1 TO C
810 PRINT TAB(5);J;" -- ";E$(P(J))
820 NEXT
830 RETURN
840 INPUT R
850 IF R>=1 AND R<=C THEN 880
860 PRINT"I NEED A NUMBER FROM 1 TO";C
870 GOTO 840
880 IF R=A THEN 910
890 PRINT"NO, THE ANSWER IS NUMBER";A
900 GOTO 930
910 PRINT"RIGHT!"
920 Q1=Q1+1
930 IF Q=1 THEN 950
940 PRINT
    "YOU HAVE";Q1;"RIGHT OUT OF";Q;"QUESTIONS."
950 P3=P2
960 P2=P1
970 P1=P(A)
980 RETURN
990 Q=Q+1
1000 IF Q<=L THEN RETURN
1010 E=1
1020 Q=Q1*100/(Q-1)
1030 IF Q>0 THEN 1060
1040 PRINT"WELL, THAT'S A 'PERFECT' SCORE..."
1050 GOTO 1180
1060 PRINT"THAT'S";Q;"PERCENT."
1070 IF Q>25 THEN 1100
1080 PRINT"CONGRATULATIONS ON AVOIDING A SHUTOUT."
1090 GOTO 1180
1100 IF Q>50 THEN 1130
```

```
1110 PRINT"YOU CAN USE SOME MORE PRACTICE."
1120 GOTO 1180
1130 IF Q>75 THEN 1160
1140 PRINT"NOT BAD, BUT ROOM FOR IMPROVEMENT."
1150 GOTO 1180
1160 PRINT"VERY GOOD!"
1170 IF Q>95 THEN PRINT
     "YOU'RE ALMOST AS SMART AS I AM!"
1180 PRINT
1190 INPUT"WANT TO TRY AGAIN";R$
1200 R$=LEFT$(R$,1):
     IF R$<>"N" AND R$<>"n" THEN 1220
1210 PRINT:PRINT"CHECK YOU LATER.":PRINT:END
1220 IF R$<>"Y" AND R$<>"y" THEN 1180
1230 RETURN
1240 REM
     *************************************************
1250 REM:
         ON LINE 420, D MUST BE AT LEAST ONE GREATER
1260 REM: THAN THE NUMBER OF DIFFERENT WORDS.
1270 REM
     *************************************************
1280 DATA ANONYMOUS,"OF UNKNOWN OR HIDDEN ORIGIN"
1290 DATA OMINOUS,"THREATENING OR MENACING"
1300 DATA AFFLUENT,"WEALTHY"
1310 DATA APATHETIC,"INDIFFERENT OR UNINTERESTED"
1320 DATA LACONIC,"TERSE"
1330 DATA INTREPID,"FEARLESS OR COURAGEOUS"
1340 DATA GREGARIOUS,"SOCIAL OR COMPANY-LOVING"
1350 DATA ENERVATED,"WEAK OR EXHAUSTED"
1360 DATA VENERABLE,
     "WORTHY OF RESPECT OR REVERENCE"
1370 DATA DISPARATE,"DIFFERENT AND DISTINCT"
1380 DATA VIVACIOUS,"LIVELY OR SPIRITED"
1390 DATA ASTUTE,"KEEN IN JUDGMENT"
1400 DATA URSINE,"BEARLIKE"
1410 DATA PARSIMONIOUS,"STINGY OR FRUGAL"
1420 DATA OMNISCIENT,"ALL-KNOWING"
1999 DATA XXX
```

EASY CHANGES

1. Add more DATA statements between lines 1280 and 1999,
    or replace them all with your own. Be careful not to use two
    or more words with very similar definitions; the program
    might select more than one of them as possible answers to
    the same question. Note that each DATA statement first has
    the vocabulary word, then a comma, and then the definition
    or synonym. Be sure there are no commas or colons in the
    definition (unless you enclose the definition in quotation

marks). If you add more DATA statements, you have to increase the value of D in line 420 to be at least one greater than the number of words. The number of DATA statements you can have depends on how long each one is and how much user memory your computer has. Using DATA statements that average the same length as these, you can have several hundred in a 16K cassette system or a 64K disk system. Be sure to leave statement 1999 as it is—it signals that there are no more DATA statements.

2. To get something other than five choices for each question, change the value of C in line 410. You might want only three or four choices per question.

3. To cause the program to always ask a fixed number of questions, such as 20, make this change:

    310 PRINT "WE'LL DO 20 QUESTIONS.":L = 20

4. To make the program pause longer after a wrong answer, insert:

    895 FOR J = 1 TO 5000:NEXT

5. To change to a 40 column display, change the WIDTH 80 in line 240 to WIDTH 40.

MAIN ROUTINES

140- 210	Mainline routine. Calls major subroutines.
230- 390	Displays introduction. Initializes RND function. Determines number of questions to be asked.
400- 570	Reads vocabulary words and definitions into arrays. Performs housekeeping.
580- 700	Selects choices for answers and determines which will be the correct one.
710- 830	Determines in which format the question will be asked. Asks it.
840- 980	Accepts answer from operator. Determines if right or wrong. Keeps score. Saves subscripts of last three correct answers.
990-1230	Gives final score. Asks about doing it again.
1280-1999	DATA statements with vocabulary words and definitions.

MAIN VARIABLES

E	Set to 1 to avoid repeating introduction after the first round.

L	Limit of number of questions to ask.
I	Constant one.
R	Work variable. Also used for operator's reply to each question.
C	Number of choices of answers given for each question.
D	At least one greater than number of DATA statements. Used to DIM arrays.
D$	Array of vocabulary words.
E$	Array of definitions.
P	Array for numbers of possible answers to each question.
J	Work variable (subscript for FOR-NEXT loops).
Q	Number of questions asked so far (later used to calculate percent correct).
Q1	Number of questions correct so far.
P	Work variable.
P1,P2,P3	Last three correct answers.
A	Subscript of correct answer in P array.
M	Work variable to decide which way to ask question.
R$	Yes or no reply about doing another round.

SUGGESTED PROJECTS

1. Modify lines 1030 through 1180 to display the final evaluation messages based on a finer breakdown of the percent correct. For example, show one message if 100 percent, another if 95 to 99, another if 90 to 94, etc.
2. Ask the operator's name in the introduction routine, and personalize some of the messages with his/her name.
3. Instead of just checking about the last three questions, be sure that the next question has not been asked in the last eight or ten questions. (Check lines 630 and 950 to 970.)
4. Keep track of which questions the operator misses. Then, after going through the number of questions requested, repeat those that were missed.

Section 3

Game Programs

Almost everyone likes to play games. Computer games are a fun and entertaining use of your computer. Besides providing relaxation and recreation, they have some built-in practical bonuses. They often force you to think strategically, plan ahead, or at least be orderly in your thought processes. They are also a good way to help some friends over their possible "computer phobia." We present a collection of games to fit any game playing mood.

Maybe you desire a challenging all-skill game? Like chess or checkers, WARI involves no luck and considerable thinking. The computer will be your opponent, and a formidable one indeed.

Perhaps you're in the mood for a game with quick action and mounting excitement. GROAN is a fast-paced dice game involving mostly luck with a dash of skill (or intuition) thrown in. The computer is ready to take you on anytime.

Two word games are included. In JOT, you and the computer each pick secret words and then try to home in on each other's selection. In ARGO, you are challenged to make words by unscrambling letters in a race against time.

Do you like solving puzzles? If so, try DECODE. The computer will choose a secret code and then challenge you to find it.

Graphic electronic arcade games are a prevalent landmark of our times. We include two such games. ROADRACE puts you behind the wheel of a high speed race car. You must steer accurately to stay on course. OBSTACLE lets you and a friend compete in a game of cut and thrust. Each of you must avoid crossing the path laid by the other, and by yourself!

ARGO

PURPOSE

Argo is a word game that is both challenging and a lot of fun. The program displays 13 random letters, and your object is to try to score as many points as possible by creating words from them.

HOW TO USE IT

The program begins by displaying its name and asking you to press a key to start the game. After you press a key (other than ones like **SHIFT** or **Num Lock**, of course), the program displays 13 letters in alphabetical order and starts its "timer." When the timer in the upper left corner reaches 5000, the game is over.

Your object is to create words that are at least three, but no more than nine letters long. You can enter as many as ten words of each length, but only the first five will score points. This is to give you a chance to enter extra words of each length in case you mistyped a word or entered a word that is later disallowed.

Each word is entered by simply typing the letters of the word and pressing the **ENTER** key. As each letter of the word is typed, it is displayed at the top of the screen. When **ENTER** is pressed, the word is moved to the lower part of the screen, where a column of words is displayed for each length. The three letter words are at the left of the screen, and the nine letter words are at the right.

If you make a typing error before pressing **ENTER**, you can simply correct it as usual by using the "back arrow" key in the

top row. If you do not see the error until after you press
ENTER, there is no way to erase the erroneous word.

The program displays an error message to the right of your
word if you enter a duplicate word or if you try to enter a word
that is not made up of the letters shown. Of course, you can only
use a letter the number of times it is shown—to use a letter twice,
there must be two of them.

The program has no way of knowing whether or not you are
entering legitimate words. It only checks that you are using the
proper letters. It's up to you to determine if you want to allow
slang, proper names, foreign words, etc. If you are going to
compete with a friend, be sure you establish the ground rules
first.

After you enter each word, your current score is displayed at
the upper right portion of the screen.

At the end of your time limit, the program displays the score
again and ends. Scoring is based on how many words you
entered of each length. Each word counts the square of its word
length in points. So, each three letter word counts nine points.
Each four letter word is 16 points, a five letter word is 25 points,
a six letter word is 36 points, and so on. This means that the
maximum possible score is

$$5 \times (9 + 16 + 25 + 36 + 49 + 64 + 81) = 1400.$$

In our experience, however, any score over 200 is very good, and
anything over 300 is excellent. Needless to say, the scores vary
widely based on what letters you happen to get.

The program gives you a fair chance by making sure that you
have at least two vowels among your 13 letters. Other than that,
the letters are simply chosen at random.

SAMPLE RUN

The program waits for the operator to press a key to start the game.

The program selects 13 random letters and starts the timer.

The operator enters the first word, which will go in the column of five letter words when ENTER is pressed.

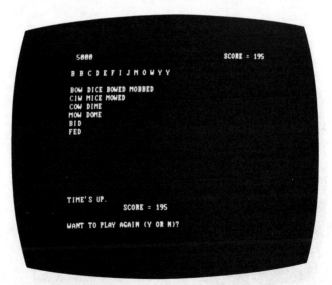

The timer reaches 5000 to end the game. Note that a typing error was made (CIW), so the operator entered an extra three letter word. This caused the scoring of five words of three letters to be correct.

PROGRAM LISTING

```
100 REM: ARGO
110 REM: A word unscrambling game.
120 REM: COPYRIGHT 1982 Tom Rugg and Phil Feldman.
130 REM: Any BASIC, 80 column CRT.
140 KEY OFF:SCREEN 0,0:WIDTH 80:COLOR 7,0
150 CLEAR:CLS:N=13:I=1
160 DIM W$(9,10),A(N),E(N),V(4)
170 V(0)=65:V(1)=69:V(2)=73:V(3)=79:V(4)=85
180 FOR J=3 TO 9:D(J)=5:NEXT
190 GOSUB 870
200 GOSUB 600:CLS:C=0:M=5000:GOTO 800
210 W$="":REM--no space between quotation marks
220 A$=INKEY$:C=C+1:IF C>M THEN 490
230 LOCATE 1,1:PRINT C;:IF LEN(A$)=0 THEN 220
240 IF ASC(A$)=13 THEN 300
250 IF ASC(A$)=8 THEN 650
260 IF A$<"A" OR A$>"Z" THEN 220:REM--upper case
270 W$=W$+A$:LOCATE 1,10:PRINT W$;
280 IF LEN(W$)>10 THEN 300
290 GOTO 220
300 L=LEN(W$)
310 IF L<3 OR L>9 THEN 420
320 GOSUB 690
330 IF F=1 THEN M$="DUPLICATE":GOTO 440
340 GOSUB 730:IF F=1 THEN 420
350 T(L)=T(L)+1:IF T(L)>10 THEN 430
360 W$(L,T(L))=W$
370 LOCATE D(L),(L*(L+1))/2-5:PRINT W$;
380 LOCATE 1,10:PRINT BL$
390 IF T(L)>5 THEN 410
400 SC=SC+L*L:LOCATE 1,40:PRINT"SCORE =";SC
410 D(L)=D(L)+1:GOTO 210
420 M$="ILLEGAL":GOTO 440
430 T(L)=T(L)-1:M$="TOO MANY":GOTO 440
440 LOCATE 1,20:PRINT M$;:SOUND 40,2
450 FOR J=1 TO 50:C=C+1:LOCATE 1,1
460 PRINT C;:NEXT
470 LOCATE 1,10:PRINT BL$
480 GOTO 210
490 LOCATE 18,1:PRINT"TIME'S UP."
500 SOUND 440,2
510 SC=0:FOR J=3 TO 9
520 K=T(J):IF K>5 THEN K=5
530 SC=SC+J*J*K:NEXT
540 PRINT TAB(15);"SCORE =";SC
550 PRINT:PRINT"WANT TO PLAY AGAIN (Y OR N)?"
560 A$=INKEY$:J=RND:IF LEN(A$)=0 THEN 560
570 IF A$="Y" OR A$="y" THEN 150
580 IF A$<>"N" AND A$<>"n" THEN 560
590 END
```

```
600 FOR J=1 TO N:R=INT(26*RND)+65
610 A(J)=R:NEXT
620 FOR J=1 TO 2
630 A(J)=V(INT(5*RND)):NEXT
640 RETURN
650 IF LEN(W$)<2 THEN 470
660 W$=LEFT$(W$,LEN(W$)-1)
670 LOCATE 1,10:PRINT BL$
680 LOCATE 1,10:PRINT W$;:GOTO 220
690 F=0:IF T(L)=0 THEN RETURN
700 FOR J=1 TO T(L)
710 IF W$(L,J)=W$ THEN F=1
720 NEXT:RETURN
730 F=0:FOR J=1 TO N:E(J)=A(J)
740 NEXT:FOR J=1 TO L
750 K=ASC(MID$(W$,J,1))
760 FOR X=1 TO N
770 IF E(X)=K THEN E(X)=0:GOTO 790
780 NEXT:F=1
790 NEXT J:RETURN
800 FOR J=N TO 2 STEP -1:X=A(1):F=1
810 FOR L=2 TO J:IF A(L)>X THEN X=A(L):F=L
820 NEXT:A(F)=A(J):A(J)=X:NEXT
830 LOCATE 3,1
840 FOR J=1 TO N:PRINT CHR$(A(J));CHR$(32);
850 NEXT
860 GOTO 470
870 PRINT TAB(15);"A R G O"
880 PRINT:PRINT"Be sure CAPS LOCK is in effect."
890 PRINT:PRINT"Press a key to start."
900 DEF SEG:POKE 106,0
910 A$=INKEY$:J=RND
920 IF LEN(A$)=0 THEN 910
930 POKE 106,0:BL$=STRING$(20,32)
940 RETURN
```

EASY CHANGES

1. You can easily change the program to give you more or less
    than 13 letters to choose from. Values from nine to 15 are
    best, although values from 3 to 40 could be used. As an ex-
    ample, make this change to use 15 letters:

    150 CLEAR:CLS:N = 15:I = 1

2. The program currently guarantees at least two vowels
    among the list of letters. Change the 2 at the end of line 620
    to alter this. For example, to guarantee at least three vowels,
    it should be:

    620 FOR J = 1 TO 3

3. Give the player more or less time to create words by chang-
    ing the value of M in line 200. For example, to make each
    game last about twice as long, change the 5000 to 10000.

MAIN ROUTINES

140-200	Initializes variables, displays title, chooses letters.
210-290	Gets word from player. Timer runs while waiting.
300-430	Examines word for legality. Saves it. Displays score.
440-480	Displays and erases error message.
490-590	Computes score and asks about playing again.
600-640	Subroutine to select N letters.
650-680	Backspaces during word entry.
690-720	Subroutine to check for duplicate word.
730-790	Subroutine to check that legal letters were used.
800-860	Alphabetizes and displays letters.
870-940	Subroutine to display title and initialize RND.

MAIN VARIABLES

N	Number of letters to choose from.
W$	Array that words are saved in.
A	Array holding ASCII values of letters.
E	Array for evaluating whether legal letters were used.
V	Array with ASCII values of the vowels.
D	Array of screen locations of each word length.
C	Counter for timer.
M	Maximum value for timer.
D	Screen location for word being entered.
W$	Word being entered.
A$	Key pressed during word entry.
L	Length of word entered. Also work variable.
F	Flag set to 1 if word is illegal. Also work variable.
M$	Error message.
BL$	String of 20 blanks.
T	Array to count the number of words entered of each length.
J,X	Loop and work variables.
R	Random number used in selecting letters.
SC	Number of points scored.

SUGGESTED PROJECTS

1. Allow the player to erase the last word entered, in case of typographical error.

DECODE

PURPOSE

Decode is really more of a puzzle than a game, although you can still compete with your friends to see who can solve the puzzles the fastest. Each time you play, you are presented with a new puzzle to solve.

The object is to figure out the computer's secret code in as few guesses as possible. The program gives you information about the accuracy of each of your guesses. By carefully selecting your guesses to make use of the information you have, you can determine what the secret code must be in a surprisingly small number of guesses. Five or six is usually enough.

The first few times you try, you will probably require quite a few more guesses than that, but with practice, you'll discover that you can learn a lot more from each guess than you originally thought.

HOW TO USE IT

The program starts off by displaying a brief introduction. Here are some more details.

The program selects a secret code for you to figure out. The code is a four digit number that uses only the digits 1 through 6. For example, your computer might pick 6153 or 2242 as a secret code.

Your object is to guess the code in the fewest possible guesses. After each of your guesses, the program tells you a "black" and a "white" number. The black number indicates the number of digits in your guess that were correct—the digit was correct *and* in the correct position. So, if the secret code is 6153 and your guess is 4143, you will told that black is 2 (because the 1 and the 3 will have been correct). Of course, you aren't told *which* digits are correct. That is for you to figure out by making use of the information you get from other guesses.

Each of the white numbers indicates a digit in your guess that was correct, but which is in the wrong position. For example, if the secret code is 6153 and your guess is 1434, you will be told that white is 2. The 1 and 3 are correct, but in wrong positions.

The white number is determined by ignoring any digits that accounted for a black number. Also, a single position in the secret code or guess can only account for one black or white number. These facts become significant when the secret code and/or your guess have duplicate digits. For example, if the code is 1234 and your guess is 4444, there is only one black, and no whites. If the code is 2244 and your guess is 4122, there are no blacks and three whites.

This may sound a little tricky, but you will quickly get the hang of it.

At any time during the game, you can ask for a summary by entering an **S** instead of a guess. This causes the program to clear the screen and display each guess (with the corresponding result) that has occurred so far.

Also, if you get tired of trying and want to give up, you can enter a **Q** (for quit) to end your misery and find out the answer. Otherwise, you continue guessing until you get the code right (four black, zero white), or until you have used up the maximum of twelve guesses.

SAMPLE RUN

```
          **** DECODE ****

     FIGURE OUT A 4 POSITION CODE
     USING THE DIGITS 1 THRU 6

     'BLACK' INDICATES A CORRECT DIGIT
     IN THE RIGHT POSITION.
     'WHITE' INDICATES SOME OTHER CORRECT
     DIGIT, BUT IN THE WRONG POSITION.
     PRESS A KEY TO START.
     I'VE CHOSEN MY SECRET CODE.
     GUESS NUMBER 1 ? 6413

     GUESS NO. 1 -- BLACK = 2    WHITE = 0

     GUESS NUMBER 2 ? _
```

The program displays an introduction, chooses its secret code, and asks for the operator's first guess. After the operator makes a guess, the program responds with a "black" and a "white" number, and asks for the second guess.

```
     NO.    GUESS    BLACK    WHITE
      1     6413       2        0
      2     6414       1        1
      3     6452       1        0
      4     6611       0        0
      5     4433       3        0

     GUESS NUMBER 6 ? 4443

     GUESS NO. 6 -- BLACK = 4    WHITE = 0

     YOU GOT IT IN 6 GUESSES.
     ...THAT'S PRETTY GOOD
     WANT TO TRY AGAIN?
```

Later in the same game, the operator asks for a summary, then makes the guess that turns out to be correct. The program acknowledges that the guess is correct and asks about trying another game.

PROGRAM LISTING

```
100 REM: DECODE
110 REM: Figure out the computer's secret code.
120 REM: COPYRIGHT 1982 Tom Rugg and Phil Feldman.
130 REM: Any BASIC, any CRT.
140 D=6:P=4:L=12
150 DIM G$(L),G(P),C(P),B(L),W(L)
160 GOSUB 790:I=1
170 GOSUB 290
180 PRINT"GUESS NUMBER";G;
190 INPUT A$:R$=LEFT$(A$,1)
200 IF R$="S" OR R$="s" THEN 370
210 IF R$="Q" OR R$="q" THEN 450
220 GOSUB 540:IF K=1 THEN 180
230 GOSUB 620
240 GOSUB 760
250 IF B(G)=P THEN 970
260 G$(G)=A$
270 G=G+1:IF G>L THEN 1120
280 GOTO 180
290 G=1:C$="":
    REM--no space between quotation marks.
300 FOR J=1 TO P
310 R=INT(D*RND)+1
320 C$=C$+MID$(STR$(R),2,1)
330 NEXT J
340 PRINT"I'VE CHOSEN MY SECRET CODE."
350 PRINT
360 RETURN
370 IF G=1 THEN PRINT"NO GUESSES YET.":GOTO 180
380 CLS:PRINT TAB(10);"SUMMARY":PRINT
390 PRINT"NO.    GUESS    BLACK    WHITE"
400 PRINT:FOR J=1 TO G-1
410 PRINT J;TAB(7);G$(J);TAB(16);B(J);TAB(24);W(J)
420 IF G<10 THEN PRINT
430 NEXT:PRINT
440 GOTO 180
450 PRINT
460 PRINT"CAN'T TAKE IT, HUH?"
470 PRINT:PRINT"WELL, MY CODE WAS ";
480 FOR J=1 TO 4
490 PRINT" .";
500 FOR K=1 TO 900:NEXT
510 NEXT J
520 PRINT C$:PRINT
530 GOTO 1060
540 K=0:IF LEN(A$)<>P THEN 600
550 FOR J=1 TO P
560 R=VAL(MID$(A$,J,1))
570 IF R<1 OR R>D THEN 600
580 NEXT
```

```
590 RETURN
600 BEEP:PRINT"ILLEGAL.   TRY AGAIN."
610 K=1:RETURN
620 B=0:W=0
630 FOR J=1 TO P
640 G(J)=VAL(MID$(A$,J,1))
650 C(J)=VAL(MID$(C$,J,1))
660 IF G(J)=C(J) THEN B=B+1:G(J)=0:C(J)=0
670 NEXT
680 FOR J=1 TO P:IF C(J)=0 THEN 740
690 H=0:FOR K=1 TO P
700 IF C(J)=0 THEN 730
710 IF C(J)<>G(K) THEN 730
720 H=1:G(K)=0:C(J)=0
730 NEXT K:W=W+H
740 NEXT J
750 RETURN
760 B(G)=B:W(G)=W:PRINT
770 PRINT
    "GUESS NO.";G;"-- BLACK =";B;"  WHITE =";W
780 PRINT:RETURN
790 KEY OFF:SCREEN 0,0:WIDTH 40:COLOR 7,0:CLS
800 PRINT TAB(5);"**** DECODE ****"
810 PRINT:PRINT
820 PRINT"FIGURE OUT A";P;"POSITION CODE"
830 PRINT
840 PRINT"USING THE DIGITS 1 THRU";D
850 PRINT:PRINT
860 PRINT"'BLACK' INDICATES A CORRECT DIGIT"
870 PRINT:PRINT"IN THE RIGHT POSITION."
880 PRINT
890 PRINT"'WHITE' INDICATES SOME OTHER CORRECT"
900 PRINT
910 PRINT"DIGIT, BUT IN THE WRONG POSITION."
920 PRINT
930 PRINT"PRESS A KEY TO START."
940 DEF SEG:POKE 106,0
950 R$=INKEY$:R=RND:IF LEN(R$)=0 THEN 950
960 POKE 106,0:RETURN
970 PRINT
980 PRINT"YOU GOT IT IN";G;"GUESSES."
990 IF G<5 THEN B$="OUTSTANDING!"
1000 IF G=5 OR G=6 THEN B$="PRETTY GOOD"
1010 IF G=7 THEN B$="NOT BAD"
1020 IF G=8 THEN B$="NOT TOO GREAT"
1030 IF G>8 THEN B$="PRETTY BAD"
1040 PRINT:PRINT"...THAT'S ";B$
1050 PRINT
1060 INPUT"WANT TO TRY AGAIN";A$
1070 A$=LEFT$(A$,1)
1080 IF A$="Y" OR A$="y" THEN 160
1090 IF A$<>"N" AND A$<>"n" THEN 1060
```

```
1100 PRINT:PRINT"COWARD.":PRINT
1110 END
1120 PRINT
1130 PRINT"THAT'S YOUR LIMIT OF";L;"GUESSES."
1140 PRINT
1150 PRINT"MY CODE WAS ";C$
1160 GOTO 1050
```

EASY CHANGES

1. Modify line 140 to change the complexity of the code and/or the number of guesses you are allowed. For example, the following line would allow fifteen guesses at a five position code using the digits 1 through 8:

    140 D = 8:P = 5:L = 15

    The introduction will automatically reflect the new values for D and P. Be sure that neither D nor P is set greater than 9.

2. To change the program so it will always display the summary information after each guess automatically, replace line 280 with this:

    280 GOTO 370

MAIN ROUTINES

140- 170	Initializes variables. Displays introduction. Chooses secret code.
180- 240	Gets a guess from operator. Analyzes reply. Displays result.
250	Determines if operator guessed correctly.
260- 280	Saves guess. Adds one to guess counter. Determines if limit on number of guesses was exceeded.
290- 360	Subroutine to initialize variables, choose secret code and inform operator.
370- 440	Subroutine to display summary of guesses so far.
450- 530	Subroutine to slowly display secret code when operator quits.
540- 610	Subroutine to determine if operator's guess was legal.
620- 750	Subroutine to determine number of black and white responses for the guess.
760- 780	Subroutine to display number of black and white responses for guess.

790- 960 Subroutine to display title and introduction.

970-1110 Subroutine to analyze operator's performance after correct answer is guessed and ask about playing again.

1120-1160 Subroutine to display secret code after operator exceeds limit of number of guesses.

MAIN VARIABLES

I	Constant one.
D	Number of possible digits in each position of the code (i.e., a digit from 1 to D).
P	Number of positions in the code.
L	Limit of number of guesses that can be made.
G$	Array in which guesses are saved.
G,C	Work arrays in which each guess is analyzed.
B,W	Arrays in which the number of black and white responses is saved for each guess.
R,H	Work variables.
G	Counter of the number of guesses made.
A$	Reply by the operator.
C$	Secret code chosen by the program.
J,K	Loop variables.
B,W	Number of black and white responses for this guess.
B$	String with message about operator's performance.
R$	Reply from operator; work string variable.

SUGGESTED PROJECTS

1. Change the analysis at the end of the game to take into account the difficulty of the code as well as the number of guesses it took to figure the code out. A four position code using the digits 1 through 6 has 1296 possibilities, but a five position code using 1 through 8 has 32768 possibilities. Change lines 990 through 1030 to determine the message to be displayed based on the number of possibilities in the code as well as G.

2. At the beginning of the game, give the operator the option of deciding the complexity of the code. Ask for the number of positions and the number of digits. Make sure only "reasonable" numbers are used — do not try to create a code with zero positions, for example. Another approach is to ask the operator if he/she wants to play the easy, intermediate, or

advanced version. Then set the values of D and P accordingly. Suggestions are:

        Easy: $D = 3$ and $P = 3$
        Intermediate: $D = 6$ and $P = 4$
        Advanced: $D = 8$ and $P = 5$

3. In addition to using the number of guesses to determine how
   well the operator did, keep track of the amount of time. You
   could do this by using the TIME$ feature of Disk BASIC, or
   else you could make use of the INKEY$ function instead of
   the INPUT function in line 190, and a bit of logic to build
   the A$ reply one character at a time. By counting the
   number of null strings encountered while waiting for keys to
   be pressed, you can "time" the operator.

Color Section

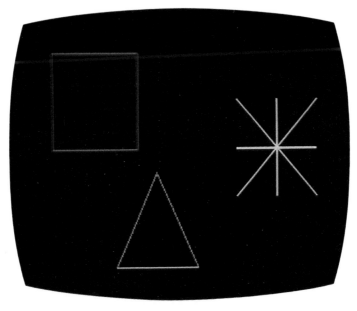

NUMBERS

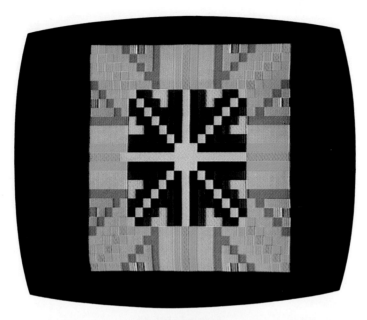

KALEIDO

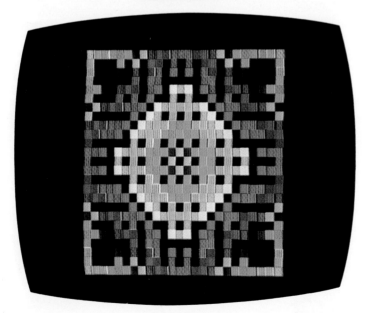

SPARKLE

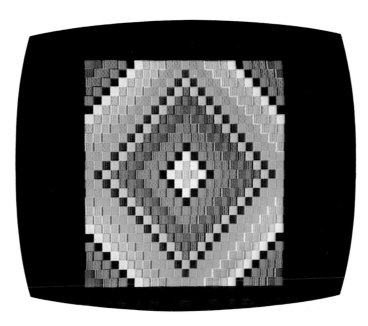

SPARKLE

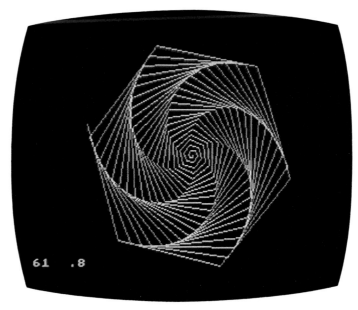

SPIRALS

SPIRALS

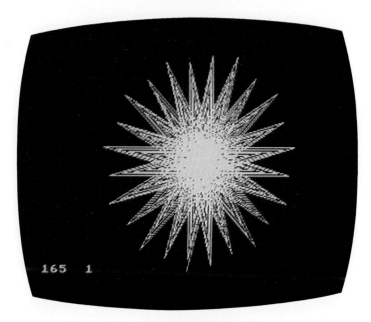

SPIRALS

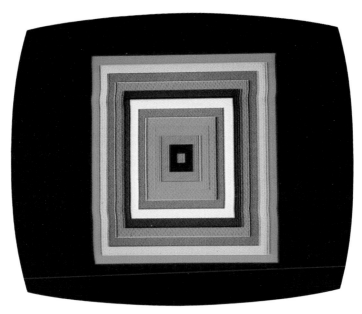

SQUARES

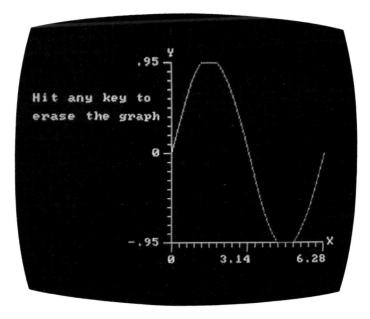

GRAPH

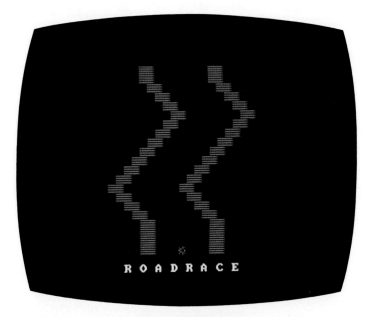

ROADRACE

ROADRACE

ROADRACE

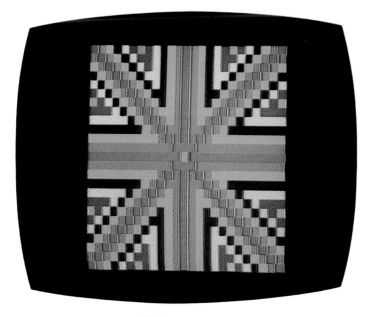

KALEIDO

GROAN

PURPOSE

Do you like the thrills of fast-paced dice games? If so, GROAN is right up your alley. It is a two-person game with the computer playing directly against you. There is a considerable amount of luck involved. However, the skill of deciding when to pass the dice to your opponent also figures prominently.

The computer will roll the dice for both players, but don't worry—it will not cheat. (We wouldn't think of stooping to such depths.)

Why is the game called GROAN? You will know soon after playing it.

HOW TO USE IT

NOTE: It is assumed that the program is being run on a system with the Color Graphics adapter card. If your system has only the Monochrome Display adapter, see Easy Change 4.

The game uses two dice. They are just like regular six-sided dice except for one thing. The die face where the 1 would normally be has a picture of a frowning face instead. The other five faces of each die contain the usual numbers (two through six).

The object is to be the first player to achieve a score agreed upon before the start of the game. Players alternate taking turns. A turn consists of a series of dice rolls (at least one roll, possibly several) subject to the following rules.

As long as no frown appears on either die, the roller builds a running score for this current series of rolls. After each roll with no frown, he has the choice of rolling again or passing the dice to his opponent. If he passes the dice, his score achieved on the current series is added to any previous total he may have had.

But if he rolls and a frown appears, he will be groaning. A frown on only one die cancels any score achieved for the current series of rolls. Any previous score is retained in this case. However, if he rolls a double frown, his entire previous total is wiped out as well as his current total. Thus, he reverts back to a total score of zero—true despair.

The program begins by asking what the winning score should be. Values between 50 and 100 tend to produce the best games, but any positive value less than 1000 is acceptable. Next, you are asked to hit any key to begin the simulated coin toss which randomly decides who will get the first roll.

Each dice roll is portrayed with a short graphics display. The dice are shown rolling and then the outcome is displayed pictorially. Before each roll, the computer indicates whose roll is coming up.

Each roll is followed by a display of the scoreboard. This scoreboard gives all relevant information: score needed to win, both players' scores before the current series of rolls, and the total score for the current series.

If a frown should appear on a die, the scoreboard will indicate the current running total as zero. In addition, the previous total will become zero in the case of the dreaded double frown. In either case, the dice will be passed automatically to the other player.

If a scoring roll results, the roller must decide whether to roll again or to pass the dice. The program has a built-in strategy to decide this for the computer. For you, the question will be asked after the scoreboard is displayed. The two legal replies are **P** and **R**. You may use either upper or lowercase letters. The **R** means that you wish to roll again. The **P** means that you choose to pass the dice to the computer. If you should score enough to win, you must still pass the dice to add the current series to your previous total.

The first player to pass the dice with a score greater than or equal to the winning score is the victor. This will surely cause his opponent to GROAN. The computer will acknowledge the winner and update the scoreboard before signing off.

SAMPLE RUN

G R O A N
How much needed to win
(between 50-100 is best)? 50

Hit any key to begin coin toss.

The operator has decided to challenge the computer to a fifty point game of GROAN. He must now hit any key to begin the simulated coin toss.

The coin is in the air and ...,
I get first roll.

The computer wins the coin toss and gets the first dice roll.

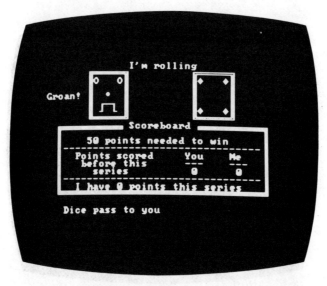

The computer's roll, however, results in a "groan" and a four. This
scores no points and the dice pass to the operator.

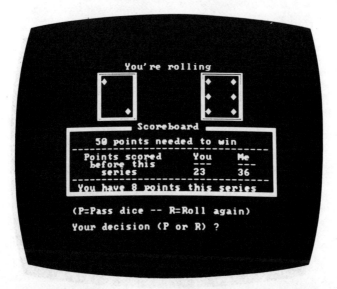

Much later in the same game, the operator rolls an 8 to start a series of
rolls. The score was operator-23, computer-36 before the roll. The
operator must now decide whether to pass the dice or risk rolling again.

PROGRAM LISTING

```
100 REM: GROAN
110 REM: A fast-paced dice game.
120 REM: COPYRIGHT 1982 Phil Feldman and Tom Rugg.
130 REM: Any BASIC, graphics interface card.
140 KEY OFF:SCREEN 0,0,0,0:WIDTH 40:COLOR 7,0,0
150 CLEAR:CLS:DEF SEG:POKE 106,0
160 B$=CHR$(32):P=0:H=0:T=0:
    PRINT TAB(15);"G R O A N":PRINT
170 PRINT"How much needed to win"
180 INPUT"(between 50-100 is best)";W
190 W=INT(W):IF W<=0 OR W>999 THEN BEEP:GOTO 150
200 PRINT:PRINT"Hit any key to begin coin toss."
210 Q$=INKEY$:Q=RND:IF Q$="" THEN 210
220 GOSUB 460:IF Q=2 THEN 350
230 Q$="You're rolling":GOSUB 550:T=T+R1+R2:
    IF F>0 THEN T=0
240 P$="You":IF F=2 THEN H=0
250 GOSUB 890:IF F=0 THEN 270
260 LOCATE 20,5:GOSUB 340:GOTO 350
270 LOCATE 20,5:
    PRINT"(P=Pass dice -- R=Roll again)"
280 LOCATE 22,5:PRINT"Your decision (P or R) ?"
290 R$=INKEY$:IF R$="" THEN 290
300 IF R$="r" OR R$="R" THEN 230
310 IF R$<>"p" AND R$<>"P" THEN 290
320 H=H+T:IF H>=W THEN 850
330 T=0:LOCATE 24,5:GOSUB 340:GOTO 350
340 COLOR 23:PRINT"Dice pass to me";:COLOR 7:
    GOSUB 1020:RETURN
350 T=0:Q$=B$+B$+"I'm rolling":P$=B$+"I"
360 GOSUB 550:T=T+R1+R2:IF F>0 THEN T=0
370 IF F=2 THEN P=0
380 GOSUB 890:IF F=0 THEN 400
390 LOCATE 20,5:GOSUB 450:T=0:GOTO 230
400 GOSUB 1030:LOCATE 20,5:IF X=0 THEN 420
410 COLOR 23:PRINT"I'll roll again":COLOR 7:
    GOSUB 1020:GOTO 360
420 PRINT"I'll stop with this":P=P+T
430 IF P>=W THEN GOSUB 1020:GOTO 850
440 LOCATE 22,5:GOSUB 450:T=0:GOTO 230
450 COLOR 23:PRINT"Dice pass to you";:COLOR 7:
    GOSUB 1020:RETURN
460 FOR J=1 TO 6:GOSUB 500:Q=19-J*3:GOSUB 540:
    NEXT:FOR J=6 TO 1 STEP -1
470 GOSUB 500:Q=22-J*3:GOSUB 540:NEXT:
    SCREEN 0,0,0,0
480 LOCATE 24,7:Q=1:Q$="You":IF RND<.5 THEN Q=2:
    Q$="I"
```

```
490 PRINT Q$;B$;"get first roll.";:GOSUB 1020:
    RETURN
500 SCREEN 0,0,1,0:CLS:K=19-J*3:FOR Q=K TO K+3:
    LOCATE Q,20
510 PRINT CHR$(221):NEXT:GOSUB 520:
    SCREEN 0,0,0,1:CLS:RETURN
520 FOR Q=1 TO 100:NEXT:LOCATE 22,1
530 PRINT"The coin is in the air and ...":RETURN
540 LOCATE Q,18:PRINT STRING$(5,220):GOSUB 520:
    RETURN
550 R1=INT(RND*6+1):R2=INT(RND*6+1):F=0:
    IF R1=1 THEN F=1
560 SCREEN 0,0,3,0:CLS:SCREEN 0,0,0,3:
    IF R2=1 THEN F=F+1
570 SCREEN 0,0,1,3:CLS:YC=2:XC=9:GOSUB 690:
    SCREEN 0,0,0,3:CLS:GOSUB 690
580 XC=26:GOSUB 690:LOCATE 1,14:PRINT Q$:
    SCREEN 0,0,1,3:GOSUB 690
590 LOCATE 1,14:PRINT Q$:SCREEN 0,0,2,3:CLS:
    YC=4:XC=11:GOSUB 690
600 XC=28:GOSUB 690:LOCATE 1,14:PRINT Q$:
    SCREEN 0,0,0,3
610 YC=2:XC=9:ON R1 GOSUB 790,720,730,740,760,77C
620 XC=26:ON R2 GOSUB 790,720,730,740,760,770
630 FOR J=1 TO 15:SCREEN 0,0,0,1:FOR K=1 TO 100:
    NEXT
640 SCREEN 0,0,0,2:FOR K=1 TO 100:NEXT:NEXT
650 SCREEN 0,0,0,0:YC=5:IF R1=1 THEN XC=2:
    GOSUB 830
660 IF R2=1 THEN XC=34:GOSUB 830
670 IF F=2 THEN LOCATE YC,17:PRINT"DESPAIR!";:
    SOUND 40,30
680 RETURN
690 LOCATE YC,XC:
    PRINT CHR$(201);STRING$(5,205);CHR$(187)
700 FOR K=YC+1 TO YC+5:LOCATE K,XC:
    PRINT CHR$(186);SPACE$(5);CHR$(186):NEXT
710 LOCATE YC+6,XC:PRINT CHR$(200);STRING$(5,
    205);CHR$(188):RETURN
720 LOCATE YC+1,XC+1:PRINT CHR$(4);:
    LOCATE YC+5,XC+5:PRINT CHR$(4);:RETURN
730 LOCATE YC+3,XC+3:PRINT CHR$(4);:GOSUB 720:
    RETURN
740 LOCATE YC+1,XC+5:PRINT CHR$(4);:
    LOCATE YC+5,XC+1
750 PRINT CHR$(4);:GOSUB 720:RETURN
760 GOSUB 730:GOSUB 740:RETURN
770 LOCATE YC+3,XC+1:PRINT CHR$(4);:
    LOCATE YC+3,XC+5
780 PRINT CHR$(4);:GOSUB 740:RETURN
790 LOCATE YC+1,XC+1:
    PRINT CHR$(79);STRING$(3,32);CHR$(79);
```

```
800 LOCATE YC+3,XC+3:PRINT CHR$(248):
    LOCATE YC+4,XC+2
810 PRINT CHR$(218);CHR$(196);CHR$(191);:
    LOCATE YC+5,XC+2
820 PRINT CHR$(217);B$;CHR$(192);:RETURN
830 LOCATE YC,XC:PRINT"Groan!";:SOUND 75,20
840 FOR J=1 TO 2500:NEXT:RETURN
850 GOSUB 890:LOCATE 24,5:IF P>=W THEN 870
860 PRINT "You win -- it was sheer luck!":
    SOUND 75,20:GOSUB 1020:END
870 PRINT "I win -- skill triumphs again!":
    FOR J=1 TO 4:SOUND 1000,2
880 FOR Q=1 TO 350:NEXT:NEXT:GOSUB 1020:END
890 LOCATE 9,4:PRINT STRING$(34,220):
    FOR J=1 TO 8:LOCATE,4
900 PRINT CHR$(221);:LOCATE,37:PRINT CHR$(222):
    NEXT
910 LOCATE,4:PRINT STRING$(34,223):LOCATE 9,15
920 PRINT B$;"Scoreboard";B$;:LOCATE 11,8
930 PRINT W;"points needed to win";:LOCATE 12,5
940 PRINT STRING$(32,45);:LOCATE 13,7:
    PRINT"Points scored";
950 LOCATE 14,8:PRINT"before this";:
    LOCATE 15,10:PRINT"series";
960 LOCATE 13,25:PRINT"You";SPACE$(4);"Me";
970 LOCATE 14,25:
    PRINT STRING$(3,45);SPACE$(4);STRING$(3,45);
980 Q=24:IF H<10 THEN Q=25
990 LOCATE 15,Q:PRINT H;:Q=31:IF P<10 THEN Q=32
1000 LOCATE 15,Q:PRINT P;:LOCATE 16,5:
     PRINT STRING$(32,45);
1010 LOCATE 17,6:PRINT P$;B$;
     "have";T;"points this series";:RETURN
1020 FOR K=1 TO 5000:NEXT:RETURN
1030 V=P+T:IF V>=W THEN 1090
1040 IF (W-H)<10 THEN 1100
1050 IF P>=H THEN L=T/25:GOTO 1080
1060 IF V<H THEN L=T/35:GOTO 1080
1070 L=T/30
1080 IF RND>L THEN 1100
1090 X=0:RETURN
1100 X=1:RETURN
```

EASY CHANGES

1. If you wish to set the program for a fixed value of the winning score, it can be done by changing line 170 and deleting lines 180 and 190. Simply set W to the winning score desired. For example:

$$170 \ W = 100$$

would make the winning score 100. Don't forget to delete lines 180 and 190.

2. The rolling dice graphics display before each roll can be eliminated by adding line 625 as follows:

625 GOTO 650

This has the effect of speeding up the game by showing each dice roll immediately.

3. After you play the game a few times, you may wish to change the delay constant in line 1020. It controls the "pacing" of the game (i.e., the time delay between various messages, etc.). To speed up the game try

1020 FOR K = 1 TO 2000:NEXT:RETURN

Of course, if desired, the constant can be set to a larger value to slow down the pacing.

4. The animated graphics displays work only with the Color Graphics adapter. If your system has only the Monochrome Display adapter, make these changes:

```
460 GOSUB 520:GOTO 480
560 IF R2 = 1 THEN F = F + 1
570 CLS:YC = 2:XC = 9:GOSUB 690
580 XC = 26:GOSUB 690:LOCATE 1,14:PRINT Q$
```

In addition, delete lines 590, 600, 630, and 640. These changes will remove the animated dice rolling but still display each dice roll pictorially.

MAIN ROUTINES

150- 160	Initializes constants.
170- 220	Initial display. Gets winning score.
230- 340	Human rolls.
350- 450	Computer rolls.
460- 540	Coin toss for first roll.
550- 680	Determines dice roll, drives its display.
690- 710	Draws die outline at YC, XC.
720- 820	Draws die face.
830- 840	Displays groan messages and sounds.
850- 880	Ending messages.
890-1010	Displays scoreboard.
1020	Delay loop.
1030-1100	Computer's strategy. Sets X = 0 to stop rolling or X = 1 to continue rolling.

MAIN VARIABLES

W	Amount needed to win.
H	Previous score of human.
P	Previous score of computer.
T	Score of current series of rolls.
X	Computer strategy flag (0 = stop rolling; 1 = roll again).
L	Cutoff threshold used in computer's built-in strategy.
V	Score computer would have if it passed the dice.
Q,Q$	Work variable, work string variable.
J,K	Loop indices.
P$	String of name of current roller.
R1,R2	Outcome of roll for die 1, die 2.
F	Result of roll (0 = no frown; 1 = one frown; 2 = double frown).
XC,YC	Column, row of die printing positions.
B$	String of one blank character.
R$	User reply string.

SUGGESTED PROJECTS

1. The computer's built-in strategy is contained from line 1030 on. Remember, after a no frown roll, the computer must decide whether or not to continue rolling. See if you can improve on the current strategy. You may use, but not modify, the variables P, T, H, W. The variable X must be set before returning. Set X = 0 to mean the computer passes the dice or X = 1 to mean the computer will roll again.

2. Ask the operator for his/her name. Then personalize the messages and scoreboard.

3. Dig into the workings of the graphics routines connected with the dice rolling. Then modify them to produce new, perhaps more realistic, effects.

JOT

PURPOSE

JOT is a two player word game involving considerable mental deduction. The IBM PC will play against you. But be careful! You will find your computer quite a formidable opponent.

The rules of JOT are fairly simple. The game is played entirely with three-letter words. All letters of each word must be distinct — no repeats. (See the "Easy Changes" section for further criteria used in defining legal words.)

To begin the game, each player chooses a secret word. The remainder of the game involves trying to be the first player to deduce the other's secret word.

The players take turns making guesses at their opponent's word. After each guess, you are told how many letters (or hits) your guess had in common with your opponent's secret word. The position of the letters in the word does not matter. For example, if the secret word was OWN, a guess of WHO would have 2 hits. The winner is the first one to correctly guess his opponent's secret word.

HOW TO USE IT

The program starts by requesting that you hit any key to begin. It displays some introductory messages while asking you to think of your secret word. You are requested to press the **CAPS LOCK** key to insure the use of capital letters in all your subsequent responses. It then asks whether or not you wish to make the first guess. This is followed by you and the computer alternating guesses at each other's secret word.

After the computer guesses, it will immediately ask you how it did. Possible replies are **0, 1, 2, 3,** or **R**. The response of **R** (for right) means the computer has just guessed your word correctly—a truly humbling experience. The numerical replies indicate that the word guessed by the computer had that number of hits in your secret word. A response of **3** means that all the letters were correct, but they need to be rearranged to form the actual secret word (e.g., a guess of EAT with the secret word being TEA).

After learning how it did, the computer will take some time to process its new information. If this time is not minimal, the PC will display the message: "I'M THINKING" so you do not suspect it of idle daydreaming. If it finds an inconsistency in its information, it will ask you for your secret word and then analyze what went wrong.

When it is your turn to guess, there are two special replies you can make. These are the single letters **S** or **Q**. The **S**, for summary, will display a table of all previous guesses and corresponding hits. This is useful as a concise look at all available information. It will then prompt you again for your next guess. The **Q**, for quit, will simply terminate the game.

When not making one of these special replies, you will input a guess at the computer's secret word. This will be, of course, a three letter word. If the word used is not legal, the computer will so inform you. After a legal guess, you will be told how many hits your guess had. If you correctly guess the computer's word, you will be duly congratulated. The computer will then ask you for your secret word and verify that all is on the "up and up."

SAMPLE RUN

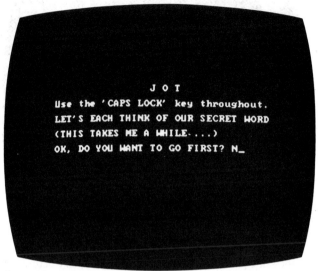

The player hits a key to begin. Then he and the computer each select their secret words. The computer is given the first guess.

The computer and player exchange the first few guesses and their results with each other.

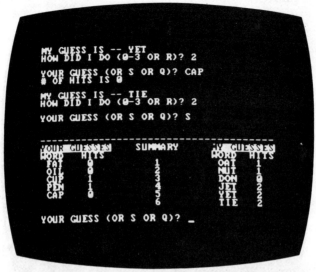

Later in the same game, the player requests a summary before making
his guess.

The computer, however, guesses correctly to win the game. After reveal-
ing its secret word, the computer offers another game but the player has
had enough.

PROGRAM LISTING

```
100 REM: JOT
110 REM: A word and logic game.
120 REM: COPYRIGHT 1982 Phil Feldman and Tom Rugg.
130 REM: Any BASIC, any CRT.
140 KEY OFF:SCREEN 0,0,0,0:WIDTH 40:COLOR 7,0,0:
    CLEAR
150 M=25
160 N=406
170 DIM G1$(M),G2$(M),H1(M),H2(M),A$(N)
180 DEF SEG:POKE 106,0:CLS:PRINT:
    PRINT"Hit any key to begin."
190 Q$=INKEY$:Q=RND:IF LEN(Q$)=0 THEN 190
200 CLS:PRINT TAB(17);"J O T":PRINT
210 PRINT"Use the 'CAPS LOCK' key throughout.":
    PRINT
220 G1=0:G2=0:L=N:GOSUB 910:Q=RND*N+1
230 PRINT"LET'S EACH THINK OF OUR SECRET WORD"
240 PRINT:PRINT"(THIS TAKES ME A WHILE ...)"
250 GOSUB 860:M$=A$(Q):PRINT:PRINT"OK, ";
260 INPUT"DO YOU WANT TO GO FIRST";Q$
270 Q$=LEFT$(Q$,1):IF Q$="N" THEN 380
280 IF Q$="Y" THEN 300
290 BEEP:PRINT:PRINT"YES OR NO PLEASE":PRINT:
    GOTO 260
300 PRINT:INPUT"YOUR GUESS (OR S OR Q)";P$:
    IF P$="S" THEN GOSUB 610:GOTO 300
310 IF P$="Q" THEN 730
320 IF P$=M$ THEN G1=G1+1:G1$(G1)=P$:H1(G1)=9:
    GOTO 950
330 GOSUB 820:IF F=0 THEN BEEP:PRINT"THAT'S NOT
    A LEGAL WORD -- TRY AGAIN":GOTO 300
340 Q$=M$:GOSUB 890:Q$=P$:GOSUB 770
350 PRINT"# OF HITS IS";Q
360 G1=G1+1:G1$(G1)=Q$:H1(G1)=Q
370 IF G1=M THEN 1020
380 Q$=A$(L):G2=G2+1:G2$(G2)=Q$
390 PRINT:PRINT"MY GUESS IS -- ";Q$
400 INPUT "HOW DID I DO (0-3 OR R)";P$
410 P$=LEFT$(P$,1)
420 IF P$="R" THEN H2(G2)=9:GOTO 920
430 P=VAL(P$):IF P>3 OR (P=0 AND P$<>
    "0") THEN PRINT"BAD ANSWER":BEEP:GOTO 390
440 IF L>100 THEN PRINT:PRINT"I'M THINKING ..."
450 H2(G2)=P:GOSUB 470
460 GOTO 300
470 Q$=G2$(G2):H=H2(G2):J=0:GOSUB 890:L=L-1:
    IF L<1 THEN 550
480 J=J+1:IF J>L THEN 540
490 Q$=A$(J):GOSUB 770
500 IF Q=H THEN 480
```

```
510 A=J:B=L:GOSUB 880:L=L-1
520 IF L<1 THEN 550
530 IF L >=J THEN 490
540 RETURN
550 PRINT:BEEP:PRINT"SOMETHING'S WRONG !!"
560 PRINT:INPUT"WHAT'S YOUR SECRET WORD";P$:
      GOSUB 820
570 IF F=0 THEN PRINT:PRINT"ILLEGAL WORD -- I
      NEVER HAD A CHANCE":GOTO 730
580 PRINT:
      PRINT"YOU GAVE A BAD ANSWER SOMEWHERE --"
590 PRINT"CHECK THE SUMMARY": GOSUB 610
600 GOTO 730
610 PRINT:Q=G1:IF G2>G1 THEN Q=G2
620 IF Q=0 THEN PRINT"NO GUESSES YET":RETURN
630 PRINT:PRINT STRING$(38,45)
640 COLOR 0,7:PRINT"YOUR GUESSES";:COLOR 7,0
650 PRINT SPC(4);"SUMMARY";SPC(5);:COLOR 0,7
660 PRINT"MY GUESSES":COLOR 7,0
670 PRINT"WORD";SPC(3);"HITS";TAB(29);"WORD";
      SPC(2);"HITS";SPC(2)
680 FOR J=1 TO Q:K=1:IF J>9 THEN K=0
690 IF J>G1 THEN PRINT TAB(18+K);J;TAB(30);
      G2$(J);TAB(35);H2(J):GOTO 720
700 IF J>G2 THEN PRINT TAB(2);G1$(J);TAB(8);
      H1(J);TAB(18+K);J:GOTO 720
710 PRINT TAB(2);G1$(J);TAB(8);H1(J);TAB(18+K);
      J;TAB(30);G2$(J);TAB(35);H2(J)
720 NEXT:RETURN
730 PRINT:INPUT"HOW ABOUT ANOTHER GAME";Q$
740 Q$=LEFT$(Q$,1):IF Q$="Y" THEN 200
750 IF Q$="N" THEN PRINT:END
760 PRINT:BEEP:PRINT"YES OR NO PLEASE":GOTO 730
770 P$=LEFT$(Q$,1):Q=0:GOSUB 800
780 P$=MID$(Q$,2,1):GOSUB 800
790 P$=RIGHT$(Q$,1):GOSUB 800:RETURN
800 IF P$=M1$ OR P$=M2$ OR P$=M3$ THEN Q=Q+1
810 RETURN
820 F=0
830 FOR J=1 TO N
840 IF A$(J)=P$ THEN F=1
850 NEXT:RETURN
860 FOR A=N TO 2 STEP -1:B=INT(RND*A)+1
870 GOSUB 880:NEXT:RETURN
880 SWAP A$(B),A$(A):RETURN
890 M1$=LEFT$(Q$,1):M2$=MID$(Q$,2,1)
900 M3$=RIGHT$(Q$,1):RETURN
910 RESTORE:FOR P=1 TO N:READ A$(P):NEXT:RETURN
920 PRINT:PRINT"IT SURE FEELS GOOD"
930 PRINT:PRINT"MY WORD WAS -- ";M$
940 GOTO 730
```

```
950 PRINT:PRINT"CONGRATULATIONS - THAT WAS IT":
    PRINT
960 INPUT "WHAT WAS YOUR WORD";P$:GOSUB 820:J=1
970 IF F=0 THEN PRINT:BEEP:PRINT
    "ILLEGAL WORD - I HAD NO CHANCE": GOTO 730
980 IF A$(J)=P$ THEN PRINT:PRINT"NICE WORD":
    GOTO 730
990 J=J+1:IF J<=L THEN 980
1000 PRINT:BEEP:PRINT"YOU MADE AN ERROR
     SOMEWHERE":PRINT"-- CHECK THE SUMMARY"
1010 GOSUB 610:GOTO 730
1020 PRINT:PRINT"SORRY, I'M OUT OF MEMORY":PRINT
1030 PRINT"MY WORD WAS - ";M$:GOTO 730
1040 DATA ACE,ACT,ADE,ADO,ADS,AFT,AGE
1050 DATA AGO,AID,AIL,AIM,AIR,ALE,ALP
1060 DATA AND,ANT,ANY,APE,APT,ARC,ARE
1070 DATA ARK,ARM,ART,ASH,ASK,ASP,ATE
1080 DATA AWE,AWL,AXE,AYE,BAD,BAG,BAN
1090 DATA BAR,BAT,BAY,BED,BEG,BET,BID
1100 DATA BIG,BIN,BIT,BOA,BOG,BOW,BOX
1110 DATA BOY,BUD,BUG,BUM,BUN,BUS,BUT
1120 DATA BUY,BYE,CAB,CAD,CAM,CAN,CAP
1130 DATA CAR,CAT,COB,COD,COG,CON,COP
1140 DATA COT,COW,COY,CRY,CUB,CUD,CUE
1150 DATA CUP,CUR,CUT,DAB,DAM,DAY,DEN
1160 DATA DEW,DIE,DIG,DIM,DIN,DIP,DOE
1170 DATA DOG,DON,DOT,DRY,DUB,DUE,DUG
1180 DATA DYE,DUO,EAR,EAT,EGO,ELK,ELM
1190 DATA END,ELF,ERA,FAD,FAG,FAN,FAR
1200 DATA FAT,FED,FEW,FIG,FIN,FIR,FIT
1210 DATA FIX,FLY,FOE,FOG,FOR,FOX,FRY
1220 DATA FUN,FUR,GAP,GAS,GAY,GEM,GET
1230 DATA GIN,GNU,GOB,GOD,GOT,GUM,GUN
1240 DATA GUT,GUY,GYP,HAD,HAG,HAM,HAS
1250 DATA HAT,HAY,HEN,HEX,HID,HIM,HIP
1260 DATA HIS,HIT,HER,HEM,HOE,HOG,HOP
1270 DATA HOT,HOW,HUB,HUE,HUG,HUM,HUT
1280 DATA ICE,ICY,ILK,INK,IMP,ION,IRE
1290 DATA IRK,ITS,IVY,JAB,JAR,JAW,JAY
1300 DATA JOB,JOG,JOT,JOY,JUG,JAG,JAM
1310 DATA JET,JIB,JIG,JUT,KEG,KEY,KID
1320 DATA KIN,KIT,LAB,LAD,LAG,LAP,LAW
1330 DATA LAY,LAX,LED,LEG,LET,LID,LIE
1340 DATA LIP,LIT,LOB,LOG,LOP,LOT,LOW
1350 DATA LYE,MAD,MAN,MAP,MAR,MAT,MAY
1360 DATA MEN,MET,MID,MOB,MOP,MOW,MUD
1370 DATA MIX,MUG,NAB,NAG,NAP,NAY,NET
1380 DATA NEW,NIL,NIP,NOD,NOT,NOR,NOW
1390 DATA NUT,OAF,OAK,OAR,OAT,ODE,OIL
1400 DATA OLD,ONE,OPT,ORE,OUR,OUT,OVA
1410 DATA OWE,OWL,OWN,PAD,PAL,PAN,PAR
```

```
1420 DATA PAT,PAW,PAY,PEA,PEG,PEN,PET
1430 DATA PEW,PIE,PIG,PIT,PLY,POD,POT
1440 DATA POX,PER,PIN,PRO,PRY,PUB,PUN
1450 DATA PUS,PUT,RAG,RAM,RAN,RAP,RAT
1460 DATA RAW,RAY,RED,RIB,RID,REV,RIG
1470 DATA RIM,RIP,ROB,ROD,ROE,ROT,ROW
1480 DATA RUB,RUE,RUG,RUM,RUN,RUT,RYE
1490 DATA SAD,SAG,SAP,SAT,SAW,SAY,SET
1500 DATA SEW,SEX,SHY,SEA,SIN,SHE,SIP
1510 DATA SIR,SIT,SIX,SKI,SKY,SLY,SOB
1520 DATA SOD,SON,SOW,SOY,SPA,SPY,STY
1530 DATA SUE,SUM,SUN,TAB,TAD,TAG,TAN
1540 DATA TAP,TAX,TAR,TEA,TEN,THE,THY
1550 DATA TIC,TIE,TIN,TIP,TOE,TON,TOP
1560 DATA TOW,TOY,TRY,TUB,TUG,TWO,URN
1570 DATA USE,UPS,VAN,VAT,VEX,VIA,VIE
1580 DATA VIM,VOW,YAK,YAM,YEN,YES,YET
1590 DATA YOU,WAD,WAG,WAN,WAR,WAS,WAX
1600 DATA WAY,WEB,WED,WET,WHO,WHY,WIG
1610 DATA WIN,WIT,WOE,WON,WRY,ZIP,FIB
```

EASY CHANGES

1. It is fairly common for players to request a summary before most guesses that they make. If you want the program to automatically provide a summary before each guess, change lines 300 to read

    300   GOSUB 610:PRINT:
          INPUT "YOUR GUESS (OR Q)";P$

2. The maximum number of guesses allowed, M, can be changed in line 150. You may wish to increase it in conjunction with Suggested Project 2. You might decrease it to free some memory needed for other program additions. The current value of twenty-five is really somewhat larger than necessary. An actual game almost never goes beyond fifteen guesses. To set M to 15 change line 150 to read

    150 M = 15

3. Modifying the data list of legal words is fairly easy. Our criteria for legal words were as follows: they must have three distinct letters and *not* be

    —capitalized
    —abbreviations
    —interjections (like "ugh," "hey" etc.)
    —specialized words (like "ohm," "sac," "yaw" etc.)

In line 160, N is set to be the total number of words in the data list. The data list itself is from line 1040 on.

To add word(s), do the following. Enter them in data statements after the current data (use line numbers larger than 1610). Then redefine the value of N to be 406 plus the number of new words added. For example, to add the words "ohm" and "yaw" onto the list, change line 160 to read

160 N = 408

and add a new line

1620 DATA OHM,YAW

To delete word(s), the opposite must be done. Remove the words from the appropriate data statement(s) and decrease the value of N accordingly.

MAIN ROUTINES

150- 170	Dimensions arrays.
180- 290	Initializes new game.
300- 370	Human guesses at the computer's word.
380- 460	Computer guesses.
470- 540	Evaluates human's possible secret words. Moves them to the front of A$ array.
550- 600	Processes inconsistency in given information.
610- 720	Displays the current summary table.
730- 760	Inquires about another game.
770- 810	Compares a guess with key word.
820- 850	Checks if input word is legal.
860- 870	Shuffles A$ array randomly.
880	Swaps elements A and B in the A$ array.
890- 900	Breaks word Q$ into separate letters.
910	Fills A$ array from data.
920- 940	Post-mortem after computer wins.
950-1010	Post-mortem after human wins.
1020-1030	Error routine—too many guesses.
1040-1610	Data.

MAIN VARIABLES

N	Total number of data words.
M	Maximum number of guesses allowed.
A$	String array holding data words.
G1$,G2$	String arrays of human's, computer's guesses.

H1,H2	Arrays of human's, computer's hits corresponding to G1$,G2$.
G1,G2	Current number of human's, computer's guesses.
M$	Computer's secret word.
M1$,M2$, M3$	First, second, and third letters of a word.
P$,Q$	String temporaries and work variables.
L	Current number of human's possible secret words.
F	Flag for input word legality.
H	Number of hits in last guess.
A,B	A$ array locations to be swapped.
J,P,Q	Temporaries; array and loop indices.
K	Formatting variable for the summary display.

SUGGESTED PROJECTS

1. Additional messages during the course of the game can personify the program even more. After the computer finds out how its last guess did, you might try an occasional message like one of these:

    > JUST AS I THOUGHT...
    > HMM, I DIDN'T EXPECT THAT...
    > JUST WHAT I WAS HOPING TO HEAR...

    The value of L is the number of words to which the computer has narrowed down the human's secret word. You might check its value regularly and when it gets low, come out with something like

    > BE CAREFUL, I'M CLOSING IN ON YOU.

2. Incorporate a feature to allow the loser to continue guessing at the other's word. The summary display routine will already work fine even if G1 and G2 are very different from each other. It will display a value of 9 for the number of hits corresponding to the correct guess of a secret word.

3. Make words with repeat letters legal as both possible secret words and possible guesses. This involves compiling such a word list, adding it to the data, and modifying the program to allow the new kind of words.

OBSTACLE

PURPOSE

This program allows you and a friend (or enemy) to play the game of OBSTACLE, an arcade-like game that's one of our favorites. A combination of physical skills (reflex speed, hand to eye coordination, etc.) and strategic skills are needed to beat your opponent. Each game generally takes only a minute or two, so you'll want to play a match of several games to determine the better player.

HOW TO USE IT

The object of the game is to keep moving longer than your opponent without bumping into an obstacle. When the program starts, it asks in turn for the name of the player on the left and on the right. Then it displays the playing field, shows the starting point for each player, and tells you to press a key to start.

After a key is pressed, each player begins moving independently in one of four random directions—up, down, left, or right. As each player moves, he or she builds a "wall" inside the playing field. The computer determines the speed of the move; the player can only control his own direction. The player on the left can change direction to up, down, left, or right by pressing the key **W, Z, A,** or **D,** respectively. The player on the right does the same by using the four cursor movement keys. Find these keys on the keyboard and you will see the logic behind these choices.

The first time either player bumps into the wall surrounding the playing field or the obstacle wall built by either player, he or she loses. When this happens, the program indicates the point of impact for a few seconds and displays the name of the winner. Then the game starts over.

The strategic considerations for this game are interesting. Should you attack your opponent, trying to build a wall around him that he must crash into? Or should you stay away from him and try to make efficient moves in an area until your opponent runs out of room on his own? Try both approaches and see which yields the most success.

When pressing a key to change direction, be sure to press it quickly and release it. *Do not* hold a key down—you might inhibit the computer from recognizing a move your opponent is trying to make.

SAMPLE RUN

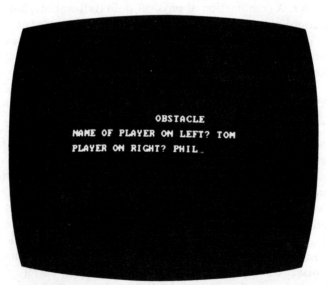

The program starts off by asking for the names of the two players.

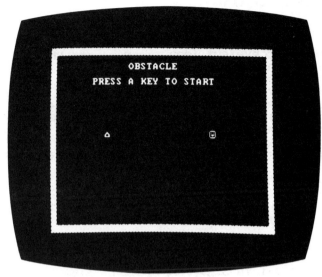

The program draws the playing field and waits for a key to be pressed.

The program redraws the playing field and starts both players moving in a random direction (in this case, both start moving upward). Phil (on the right) doesn't change directions soon enough and crashes into the wall, making Tom the winner.

PROGRAM LISTING

```
100 REM: OBSTACLE
110 REM: A two player video game.
120 REM: COPYRIGHT 1982 Tom Rugg and Phil Feldman.
130 REM: Any BASIC, any CRT.
140 GOSUB 590:I=1
150 KEY OFF:SCREEN 0,0:COLOR 7,0:WIDTH WD:CLS
160 A$=CHR$(127):B$=CHR$(1):T=WD-4:H=24
170 AX=INT(T/4)+1:AY=INT(H/2):BX=3*AX-3:BY=AY
180 E$=CHR$(178)
190 LOCATE 3,T/2-4,0:PRINT"OBSTACLE"
200 LOCATE 5,T/2-10:PRINT"PRESS A KEY TO START"
210 GOSUB 750:GOSUB 720
220 DEF SEG:POKE 106,0
230 FOR J=1 TO 10:R$=INKEY$:NEXT
240 R$=INKEY$:J=RND:IF LEN(R$)=0 THEN 240
250 AD=INT(4*RND)+1:BD=INT(4*RND)+1
260 CLS
270 IF R$=CHR$(27) THEN END
280 GOSUB 750:GOSUB 720
290 FOR J=1 TO 5:R$=INKEY$:NEXT
300 X=AX:Y=AY:D=AD:GOSUB 800
310 AR=R:AX=X:AY=Y
320 X=BX:Y=BY:D=BD:GOSUB 800
330 BR=R:BX=X:BY=Y
340 IF AR=1 OR BR=1 THEN 490
350 GOSUB 720
360 FOR J=1 TO 8:R$=INKEY$
370 IF LEN(R$)=0 THEN R=0:GOTO 400
380 R=ASC(R$):
    IF LEN(R$)=2 THEN R=ASC(RIGHT$(R$,1))
390 IF R>96 THEN R=R-32
400 IF R=87 THEN AD=1:REM W=UP
410 IF R=90 THEN AD=2:REM Z=DOWN
420 IF R=65 THEN AD=3:REM A=LEFT
430 IF R=68 THEN AD=4:REM D=RIGHT
440 IF R=56 OR R=72 THEN BD=1:REM UP
450 IF R=50 OR R=80 THEN BD=2:REM DOWN
460 IF R=52 OR R=75 THEN BD=3:REM LEFT
470 IF R=54 OR R=77 THEN BD=4:REM RIGHT
480 NEXT J:GOTO 300
490 GOSUB 650:IF AR=1 THEN R$=CHR$(32)
500 IF BR=1 THEN Z$=CHR$(32)
510 FOR J=1 TO 15:LOCATE AY,AX:PRINT A$;
520 LOCATE BY,BX:PRINT B$;
530 FOR K=1 TO 200:NEXT K
540 LOCATE AY,AX:PRINT R$;
550 LOCATE BY,BX:PRINT Z$;
560 FOR K=1 TO 200:NEXT K
570 NEXT J
```

```
580 GOTO 150
590 CLS:PRINT TAB(15);"OBSTACLE":PRINT
600 INPUT"NAME OF PLAYER ON LEFT";AN$
610 PRINT
620 INPUT"PLAYER ON RIGHT";BN$
630 WD=40
640 RETURN
650 PRINT
660 BEEP:LOCATE H+1,1
670 IF AR=0 OR BR=0 THEN 690
680 PRINT"YOU BOTH LOSE!";:GOTO 710
690 R$=AN$:IF AR=1 THEN R$=BN$
700 PRINT R$;" WINS!";
710 R$=A$:Z$=B$:RETURN
720 LOCATE AY,AX:PRINT A$;
730 LOCATE BY,BX:PRINT B$;
740 RETURN
750 FOR X=1 TO T:LOCATE 1,X:PRINT E$;
760 LOCATE H,X:PRINT E$;:NEXT X
770 FOR Y=1 TO H:LOCATE Y,1:PRINT E$;
780 LOCATE Y,T:PRINT E$;:NEXT Y
790 RETURN
800 IF D=1 THEN Y=Y-1
810 IF D=2 THEN Y=Y+1
820 IF D=3 THEN X=X-1
830 IF D=4 THEN X=X+1
840 R=0:IF SCREEN (Y,X)<>32 THEN R=1
850 RETURN
```

EASY CHANGES

1. To speed the game up, change the 8 in line 360 to a 5 or so. To slow it down, make it 12 or 15.
2. To make both players always start moving upward at the beginning of each game (instead of in a random direction), insert the following statement:

$$255 \; AD = 1:BD = 1$$

To make the players always start off moving toward each other, use this statement instead:

$$255 \; AD = 4:BD = 3$$

3. To change the length of time that the final messages are displayed after each game, modify line 510. Change the 15 to 8 (or so) to shorten it, or to 25 to lengthen it.
4. Change the markers of the players and/or the boundary of the playing field by changing lines 160 and 180. For exam-

ple, to make the player on the left an asterisk and the player on the right a solid square, do this:

160 A$ = CHR$(42):B$ = CHR$(219):T = WD − 4:H = 24

The character of the playing field boundary can be changed similarly by changing the value of E$ in line 180. Refer to the appendix on ASCII character codes in the BASIC manual.

5. Change the keys that are used to determine each player's direction by altering the appropriate values in lines 400 through 470. For example, to make the X key cause the player on the left to go down, make this change:

410 IF R = 88 THEN AD = 2

6. If you have an 80 column CRT, you can play on a larger playing field by making this change:

630 WD = 80

MAIN ROUTINES

140-210	Initializes variables. Gets players' names. Displays titles, playing field.
220-290	Waits for key to be pressed to start game. Redisplays playing field. Picks starting directions.
300-350	Makes move for player A (on left side) and B (on right). Saves results.
360-480	Accepts moves from keyboard and translates direction.
490-580	Displays winner's name at bottom of screen. Flashes a square where collision occurred. Goes back to start next game.
590-640	Subroutine that gets each player's name.
650-710	Subroutine that displays winner's name.
720-740	Subroutine that displays each marker of each player's obstacle on the screen.
750-790	Subroutine that displays playing field.
800-850	Subroutine that moves marker and determines if space moved to is empty.

MAIN VARIABLES

I	Constant one.
AX,AY	Player A's current coordinates.

BX,BY	Player B's current coordinates.
A$	A's marker.
B$	B's marker.
AD,BD	Current direction that A and B are going (1 = up, 2 = down, 3 = left, 4 = right).
E$	Graphics character for edge of playing field.
R$	Character being read from keyboard; also work variable.
R	ASCII value of key pressed.
H	Height of playing field.
T	Width of playing field.
X,Y	Coordinates of temporary position on screen.
D	Temporary direction.
AR,BR	Result of A's and B's moves (0 = okay, 1 = loser).
AN$,BN$	Names of players A and B.
Z$	Work variable.
J,K	Loop and work variables.
WD	Width of screen (40 or 80).

SUGGESTED PROJECTS

1. Keep score over a seven game (or so) match. Display the current score after each game. Don't forget to allow for ties.
2. Modify the program to let each player press only two keys — one to turn left from the current direction of travel, and one to turn right.
3. Instead of a game between two people, make it a game of a person against the computer. Develop a computer strategy to keep finding open areas to move to and/or to cut off open areas from the human opponent.

ROADRACE

PURPOSE

Imagine yourself at the wheel of a high-speed race car winding your way along a treacherous course. The road curves unpredictably. To stay on course, you must steer accurately or risk collision. How far can you go in one day? How many days will it take you to race cross-country? Thrills galore without leaving your living room!

The difficulty of the game is completely under your control. By adjusting the road width and visibility conditions, ROADRACE can be made as easy or as challenging as you wish.

HOW TO USE IT

The program begins with a short graphics display. It then asks you to hit any key to begin. Next you are requested to provide two inputs: road width and visibility. The road width (in characters) can be set anywhere between 3 and 15. The degree of difficulty changes appreciably with different widths. A very narrow setting will be quite difficult and a wide one relatively easy. Visibility can be set to any of four settings, ranging from "terrible" to "good." When visibility is good, the car appears high on the screen. This allows a good view of the twisting road ahead. When visibility is poor, the car appears low on the screen allowing only a brief look at the upcoming road.

Having set road width and visibility, the race is ready to start. The car appears on the road at the starting line. A five-step starting light counts down the start. When the bottom light goes on,

the race begins. The road moves continually up the screen. Its
twists and turns are controlled randomly. You must steer the car
accurately to keep it on track.

The car is controlled with the use of two keys on the
keyboard. Pressing the comma (,) will cause the car to move to
the left while pressing the period (.) will cause a move to the
right. On these keys are the helpful symbols, < and >, respectively. Doing neither will cause the car to continue straight
down.

The race proceeds until the car goes "off the road." Each such
collision is considered to terminate one day of the race. After
each day, you are shown the number of miles achieved that day
along with the cumulative miles achieved for consecutive days of
the race.

After each collision, you can proceed by pressing either **C, R,**
or **Q.** Selecting **C** will continue the race for another day with the
same road conditions. Cumulative totals will be retained. **R** will
restart the race. This allows changing the road conditions and in-
itializing back to day one. **Q** simply quits the race and returns
the computer back to direct BASIC. Either of the last two options will produce a display of the average miles travelled per
day for the race.

There are several different ways to challenge yourself with the
program. You can try to see how far you get in a given number
of days. You might see how many days it takes you to go a given
number of miles—say 3000 miles for a cross-country trip. As
you become proficient at one set of road conditions, make the
road narrower and/or the visibility poorer. This will increase the
challenge. Different road conditions can also be used as a han-
dicapping aid for two unequally matched opponents.

SAMPLE RUN

The program displays its logo.

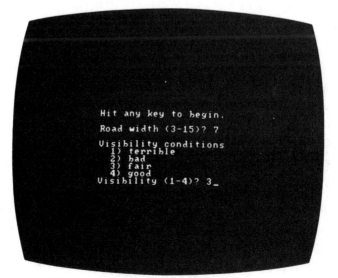

After requesting a key be hit to begin, the short input phase begins. The operator selects a course with a 7 character road width and fair visibility.

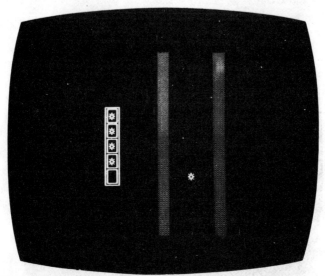

The car is on the starting line. The starting light counts down the beginning of the race. When the last light goes on, the race will be off and running.

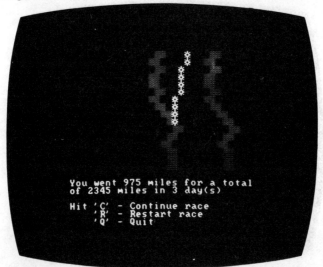

The operator, steering the car from the keyboard, finally crashes. A distance of 975 miles is obtained on this leg for a total of 2345 miles in 3 days (legs). The options for continuing are displayed while the program waits for the operator's choice.

PROGRAM LISTING

```
100 REM: ROADRACE
110 REM: A car-driving video game.
120 REM: COPYRIGHT 1982 Phil Feldman and Tom Rugg.
130 REM: Any BASIC, graphics interface optional.
140 KEY OFF:SCREEN 0,1,0,0:COLOR 7,0,0:WIDTH 40
150 CLEAR:CLS
160 FC=7:BC=0:CC=4:CR=1
170 C$=CHR$(15)
180 LC=.4
190 RC=1-LC
200 TC=177
210 L$=CHR$(44):R$=CHR$(46)
220 GOSUB 740:CLS
230 DEF SEG:POKE 106,0
240 PRINT"Hit any key to begin."
250 Q$=INKEY$:Q=RND: IF LEN(Q$)=0 THEN 250
260 T=0:N=0:GOSUB 820
270 H=0:N=N+1:GOSUB 290
280 END
290 COLOR FC,BC:CLS
300 L=18-W/2:
    T$=STRING$(2,TC)+SPACE$(W)+STRING$(2,TC)
310 EL=1:ER=35-W
320 RA=26-V*3
330 CA=20
340 COLOR CR,BC
350 FOR Q=1 TO 24
360 LOCATE Q,L:PRINT T$;:NEXT:Q=24
370 COLOR CC,BC:LOCATE RA,CA:PRINT C$;
380 COLOR FC,BC:LOCATE RA-9,6:
    PRINT CHR$(201);CHR$(205);CHR$(187);
390 FOR J=0 TO 4:R=RA-8+J*2:LOCATE R,6:
    PRINT CHR$(186);
400 LOCATE R,8:PRINT CHR$(186);:NEXT
410 FOR J=0 TO 3:R=RA-7+J*2:LOCATE R,6
420 PRINT CHR$(204);CHR$(205);CHR$(185);:NEXT
430 R=RA+1:LOCATE R,6:
    PRINT CHR$(200);CHR$(205);CHR$(188);
440 FOR K=1 TO 2500:NEXT
450 COLOR CC,BC:FOR J=0 TO 4:R=RA-8+J*2:LOCATE R,7
460 FOR K=1 TO 900:NEXT:PRINT CHR$(15);:NEXT:BEEP
470 H=H+1:K=RND: IF K>RC AND L<ER THEN L=L+1:
    GOTO 490
480 IF K<LC AND L>EL THEN L=L-1
490 LOCATE Q,L:COLOR CR,BC:PRINT T$
500 Q$=INKEY$:IF Q$=L$ THEN CA=CA-1:GOTO 520
510 IF Q$=R$ THEN CA=CA+1
520 LOCATE RA,CA:COLOR CC,BC
530 IF SCREEN(RA,CA)=32 THEN PRINT C$;:GOTO 470
```

```
540 BEEP:FOR J=1 TO 8
550 GOSUB 730:COLOR CR,BC:
    PRINT CHR$(177);CHR$(29);
560 GOSUB 730:COLOR CC,BC:PRINT C$;CHR$(29);:NEXT
570 DEF SEG:POKE 106,0:LOCATE 24,1
580 COLOR FC,BC:M=H*5:T=T+M:PRINT
590 PRINT"You went";M;"miles for a total"
600 PRINT"of";T;"miles in";N;"day(s)":PRINT
610 PRINT"Hit 'C' - Continue race"
620 PRINT SPC(4);"'R' - Restart race"
630 PRINT SPC(4);"'Q' - Quit"
640 Q$=INKEY$
650 IF Q$="C" OR Q$="c" THEN 270
660 IF Q$="R" OR Q$="r" THEN 680
670 IF Q$<>"Q" AND Q$<>"q" THEN 640
680 PRINT
690 PRINT"Your average was";T/N
700 PRINT"miles per day."
710 IF Q$="R" OR Q$="r" THEN 260
720 RETURN
730 FOR K=1 TO 200:NEXT:RETURN
740 T$=STRING$(2,TC)+SPACE$(7)+STRING$(2,177):
    RESTORE:COLOR CR,BC
750 FOR J=1 TO 21:READ Q:R=11+Q:LOCATE J,R:
    PRINT T$:NEXT:FOR K=1 TO 500:NEXT
760 RESTORE:FOR J=1 TO 20:READ Q:R=16+Q:
    LOCATE J,R:COLOR CC,BC
770 PRINT C$;:FOR K=1 TO 200:NEXT:LOCATE J,R:
    COLOR BC,BC:PRINT C$;:NEXT
780 LOCATE 21,20:COLOR CC,BC:PRINT C$;
790 DATA 4,4,5,6,7,8,7,6,5,4,3,2,1,0,1,2,3,4,4,4,4
800 COLOR 31,BC:BEEP:LOCATE 23,13:
    PRINT"R O A D R A C E"
810 FOR K=1 TO 5000:NEXT:COLOR FC,BC:RETURN
820 COLOR 7,0:PRINT:INPUT"Road width (3-15)";W
830 W=INT(W):IF W<3 OR W>15 THEN BEEP:GOTO 820
840 PRINT:PRINT"Visibility conditions"
850 PRINT SPC(2);"1) terrible":
    PRINT SPC(2);"2) bad"
860 PRINT SPC(2);"3) fair":PRINT SPC(2);"4) good"
870 INPUT"Visibility (1-4)";V
880 V=INT(V):IF V<1 OR V>4 THEN BEEP:GOTO 870
890 RETURN
```

EASY CHANGES

1. The keys which cause the car to move left and right can be
    easily changed. You may wish to do this if you are left-
    handed or find that two widely separated keys would be
    more convenient. The changes are to be made in line 210.

Left and right movements are controlled by the two string variables L$ and R$. If, for example, you wanted **1** to cause a left move and **9** to cause a right move, change line 210 to read

210 L$ = "1":R$ = "9"

2. The amount of twists in the road can be adjusted by changing the value of LC in line 180. Maximum curves are achieved with a value of 0.5 for LC. To get a straighter road, make LC smaller. A value of 0. will produce a completely straight road. LC should lie between 0. and 0.5 or else the road will drift to one side and linger there. To get a somewhat more winding road, you might change line 180 to read

180 LC = 0.45

3. The colors used for the road and for the car are assigned to the variables CR and CC respectively. These are set in line 160. Currently blue is used for the road and red for the car. You may wish to use different colors for variety. (Don't use black, however, for that is the color of the background.) Consult your reference manual for the numerical values corresponding to the different colors. For example, to get a brown road and cyan car, change line 160 to read

160 FC = 7:BC = 0:CC = 3:CR = 6

4. If you do not have a color monitor (or TV) or do not have the graphics card, you can get a black and white version of the game by setting the color of both the car and the road to white. To do this, change line 160 to:

160 FC = 7:BC = 0:CC = 7:CR = 7

MAIN ROUTINES

150-250	Initializes variables and displays graphics.
260-280	Processes next race day.
290-370	Initializes the road and car.
380-460	Graphics to begin race.
470-490	Determines the next road condition.
500-530	Updates the car position.
540-720	Processes end of race day.
730	Time wasting subroutine.
740-810	Initial graphics display.
820-890	Gets road condition from user.

MAIN VARIABLES

W	Road width.
V	Visibility.
M	Miles driven on current day.
N	Number of days of the race.
T	Total miles driven for whole race.
H	Elapsed time during race.
L$,R$	String characters to move car left, right.
L	Position of left side of road.
LC,RC	Random value cutoff to move road left, right.
EL,ER	Leftmost, rightmost allowable road position.
Q$	User replies.
CR	Color of road.
CC	Color of car.
C$	Character string for car.
J,K,Q,R	Loop indices and work variables.
FC,BC	Colors of foreground, background.
TC	ASCII value of road piece.
T$	Character string for road segment.
RA	Screen row of car location.
CA	Screen column of car location.

SUGGESTED PROJECTS

1. Write a routine to evaluate a player's performance after each collision. Display a message rating him anywhere from "expert" to "back seat driver." This should involve comparing his actual miles achieved against an expected (or average) number of miles for the given road width and visibility. For starters, you might use

$$\text{Expected miles} = W^3 + (10*V) - 35$$

This formula is crude, at best. The coding can be done between lines 600 and 610.

2. Incorporate provisions for two players racing one at a time. Keep cumulative totals separately. After each collision, display the current leader and how far he is ahead.

3. Add physical obstacles or other hazards onto the road in order to increase the challenge. This can be done with appropriate PRINT statements after line 490. The program will recognize a collision if the car moves into any non-blank square.

WARI

PURPOSE

The origins of this game go back thousands of years to a variety of other similar games, all classified as members of the Mancala family. Other variations on Wari are Awari, Oware, Pallanguli, Kalah, and countless other offshots.

The program matches you against the computer. You are probably going to lose a few games before you win one—the computer plays a pretty good game. This may hurt your ego a little bit, since Wari is purely a skill game (like chess or checkers). There is no element of luck involved, as would be the case with backgammon, for example. When you lose, it's because you were outplayed.

HOW TO USE IT

When you start the program, the first thing it does is display the Wari board and ask you if you want to go first. The board is made up of twelve squares in two rows of six. Your side is the bottom side, numbered one through six from left to right. The computer's side is on the top, numbered seven through twelve from right to left.

At the start of the game, each square has four "stones" in it. There is no way to differentiate between your stones and the computer's. They all look alike and will move from one side to the other during the course of play.

The first player "picks up" all the stones in one of the squares on his side of the board and drops them, one to a square, starting with the next highest numbered square. The stones continue

to be dropped consecutively in each square, continuing over onto the opponent's side if necessary (after square number 12
comes square number 1 again).

If the last stone is dropped onto the opponent's side *and* leaves
a total of either two or three stones in that square, these stones
are captured by the player who moved, and removed from the
board. Also, if the next-to-last square in which a stone was dropped meets the same conditions (on the opponent's side and now
with two or three stones), its stones are also captured. This continues backwards until the string of consecutive squares of two
or three on the opponent's side is broken.

Regardless of whether any captures are made, play alternates
back and forth between the two players.

The object of the game is to be the first player to capture
twenty-four or more stones. That's half of the forty-eight stones
that are on the board at the beginning of the game.

There are a few special rules to cover some situations that can
come up in the game. It is not legal to capture all the stones on
the opponent's side of the board, since this would leave the opponent with no moves on his next turn. By the same token, when
your opponent has no stones on his side (because he had to move
his last one to your side on his turn), you have to make a move
that gives him at least one stone to move on his next turn, if
possible. If you cannot make such a move, the game is over and
counted as a draw.

During the course of the game, it's possible for a square to accumulate twelve or more stones in it. Moving from such a square
causes stones to be distributed all the way around the board.
When this happens, the square from which the move was made
is skipped over. So, the square moved from is always left empty.

It takes the computer anywhere from five seconds to about
twenty seconds to make a move, depending on the complexity of
the board position. The word THINKING is displayed during
this time, and a period is added to it as each possible move is
evaluated in sequence (seven through twelve).

SAMPLE RUN

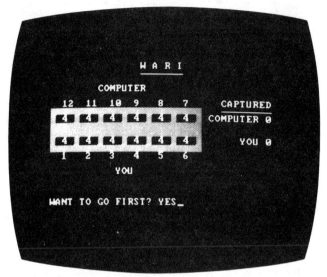

The program starts off by drawing the playing "board" and asking who should move first. The operator decides to go first.

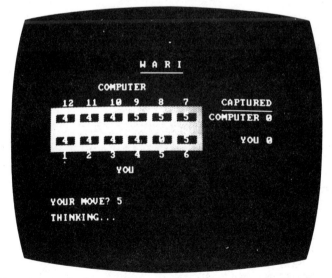

The program asks for the operator's move. He or she decides to move square number 5. The program alters the board accordingly, and begins "thinking" about what move to make.

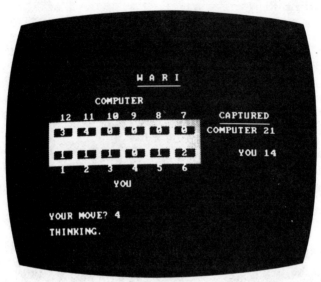

Later in the same game, the computer is about to move either square
number 11 or 12, which will capture six more stones and win the game.

PROGRAM LISTING

```
100 REM: WARI
110 REM: A game of skill against the computer.
120 REM: COPYRIGHT 1982 Tom Rugg and Phil Feldman.
130 REM: Any BASIC, any CRT.
140 DEFINT A-D,J-T,W-Y:J=1:K=1:Q=14:P=13:F=50:
    D=12:I=1
150 DIM T(Q),Y(Q),W(Q),V(6),E(6),B(Q)
160 ZB=RND:ZB=ZB/Q:ZA=.25+ZB:ZB=.25-ZB:GOSUB 730
170 FOR J=1 TO D:B(J)=4:NEXT:B(P)=0:B(Q)=0:MN=0:
    GOSUB 940:GOSUB 830
180 GOSUB 910:INPUT"WANT TO GO FIRST";R$
190 GOSUB 910:PRINT D$:R$=LEFT$(R$,1):
    IF R$="Y" OR R$="y" THEN 280
200 IF R$<>"N" AND R$<>"n" THEN 180
210 GOSUB 920:PRINT D$;D$;D$;:GOSUB 920:
    PRINT"THINKING";:GOSUB 530
220 IF M<1 THEN 1030
230 GOSUB 920:PRINT D$;:GOSUB 920:
    PRINT"MY MOVE IS";M
240 FOR J=1 TO Q:T(J)=B(J):NEXT:GOSUB 370
250 FOR J=1 TO Q:B(J)=T(J):NEXT:GOSUB 830
260 IF B(Q)<24 THEN 280
270 GOSUB 920:PRINT"I WIN!";D$: GOTO 770
```

```
280 GOSUB 910:PRINT D$;D$:GOSUB 910:
    INPUT "YOUR MOVE";R$
290 M=INT(VAL(R$)):IF M>6 OR M<1 THEN 360
300 FOR J=1 TO Q:T(J)=B(J):NEXT
310 GOSUB 370:IF M<0 THEN 360
320 FOR J=1 TO Q:B(J)=T(J):NEXT
330 MN=MN+1:GOSUB 830
340 IF B(P)<24 THEN 210
350 GOSUB 920:PRINT"YOU WIN!";D$:GOTO 770
360 GOSUB 910:PRINT TAB(15);" ILLEGAL ";:BEEP:
    FOR J=1 TO 3000:NEXT:GOTO 280
370 IF T(M)=0 THEN M=-1:RETURN
380 R$="H":IF M>6 THEN R$="C":GOTO 400:
    REM--H and C are upper case
390 FOR J=1 TO Q:Y(J)=T(J):NEXT:GOTO 420
400 FOR J=1 TO 6:Y(J)=T(J+6):Y(J+6)=T(J):NEXT
410 Y(P)=T(Q):Y(Q)=T(P):M=M-6
420 C=M:N=Y(C):FOR J=1 TO N:C=C+1
430 IF C=P THEN C=1
440 IF C=M THEN C=C+1:GOTO 430
450 Y(C)=Y(C)+1:NEXT:Y(M)=0:L=C
460 IF L<7 OR Y(L)>3 OR Y(L)<2 THEN 480
470 Y(P)=Y(P)+Y(L):Y(L)=0:L=L-1:GOTO 460
480 S=0:FOR J=7 TO D:S=S+Y(J):NEXT
490 IF S=0 THEN M=-2:RETURN
500 IF R$="H" THEN FOR J=1 TO Q:T(J)=Y(J):NEXT:
    RETURN:REM--upper case H
510 FOR J=1 TO 6:T(J)=Y(J+6):T(J+6)=Y(J):NEXT
520 T(Q)=Y(P):T(P)=Y(Q):RETURN
530 FOR A=1 TO 6:M=A+6:IF B(M)=0 THEN E(A)=-F:
    GOTO 700
540 FOR J=1 TO Q:T(J)=B(J):NEXT:GOSUB 370
550 IF M<0 THEN E(A)=-F:GOTO 700
560 IF T(Q)>23 THEN M=A+6:RETURN
570 FOR J=1 TO Q:W(J)=T(J):NEXT:FOR K=1 TO 6
580 IF T(K)=0 THEN V(K)=F:GOTO 680
590 FOR J=1 TO Q:T(J)=W(J):NEXT:M=K:GOSUB 370
600 IF M<0 THEN V(K)=F:GOTO 680
610 FA=0:FB=.05:FC=0:FD=0:FOR J=7 TO D
620 FB=FB+T(J):IF T(J)>0 THEN FA=FA+1
630 IF T(J)<3 THEN FC=FC+1
640 IF T(J)>FD THEN FD=T(J)
650 NEXT:FE=FB:FOR J=1 TO 6:FE=FE+T(J):NEXT
660 FA=FA/6:FD=1-FD/FB:FC=1-FC/6:FB=FB/FE
670 V(K)=ZA*(FA+FB)+ZB*(FC+FD)+T(Q)+B(P)-B(Q)-T(P)
680 NEXT:E(A)=F:FOR J=1 TO 6:
    IF V(J)<E(A) THEN E(A)=V(J)
690 NEXT
700 PRINT".";:NEXT:M=0:FA=-F:FOR J=1 TO 6
710 IF(E(J)>FA) THEN FA=E(J):M=J+6
720 NEXT:RETURN
```

```
730 A$=CHR$(177)
740 B$=A$:FOR J=1 TO 24:B$=B$+A$:NEXT
750 D$=CHR$(32):FOR J=1 TO 5:D$=D$+D$:NEXT
760 RETURN
770 PRINT"GOOD GAME!"
780 INPUT "WANT TO PLAY AGAIN";R$
790 R$=LEFT$(R$,1):IF R$="Y" OR R$="y" THEN 160
800 IF R$<>"N" AND R$<>"n" THEN 780
810 PRINT"SEE YOU LATER"
820 PRINT:END
830 LOCATE 8
840 FOR J=0 TO 5:PRINT TAB(4*J+2);B(12-J);:
    IF B(12-J)=0 THEN GOSUB 930
850 NEXT:PRINT TAB(27);"COMPUTER";B(Q)
860 LOCATE 11:FOR J=0 TO 5
870 PRINT TAB(4*J+2);B(J+1);:
    IF B(J+1)=0 THEN GOSUB 930
880 NEXT:PRINT TAB(32);"YOU";B(P)
890 FOR J=1 TO 25 STEP 4:LOCATE 8,J:PRINT A$;
900 LOCATE 11,J:PRINT A$;:NEXT:RETURN
910 LOCATE 19,1:RETURN
920 LOCATE 21,1:RETURN
930 PRINT CHR$(32);:RETURN
940 KEY OFF:SCREEN 0,0:WIDTH 40:COLOR 7,0:CLS
950 PRINT TAB(16);"W A R I":
    PRINT TAB(16);STRING$(7,196)
960 PRINT:PRINT TAB(9);"COMPUTER": PRINT
970 FOR J=0 TO 5:PRINT TAB(4*J+2);12-J;:NEXT
980 PRINT TAB(29);"CAPTURED":
    PRINT B$;TAB(29);STRING$(8,196)
990 PRINT:PRINT B$:PRINT B$:PRINT:PRINT B$
1000 FOR J=0 TO 5:PRINT TAB(4*J+2);J+1;:NEXT
1010 PRINT:PRINT:PRINT TAB(12);"YOU"
1020 PRINT:RETURN
1030 PRINT"NO LEGAL MOVES."
1040 PRINT"GAME IS A DRAW."
1050 GOTO 780
```

EASY CHANGES

1. Want a faster moving game against an opponent who isn't
    quite such a good player? Insert the following two lines:

    565 GOTO 610
    675 E(A) = V(K):GOTO 700

    In the standard version of the game, the computer looks at
    each of its possible moves and each of your possible replies
    when evaluating which move to make. This change causes
    the computer to look only at each of its moves, without

bothering to look at any of your possible replies. As a result, the computer does not play as well, but it takes only a few seconds to make each move.

2. If you are curious about what the computer thinks are the relative merits of each of its possible moves, you can make this change to find out. Change line 700 so it looks like this:

700 PRINT E(A);:NEXT:M = 0:FA = − F:FOR J = 1 TO 6

This will cause the program to display its evaluation number for each of its moves in turn (starting with square seven). It will select the largest number of the six. A negative value means that it will lose stones if that move is made, assuming that you make the best reply you can. A value of negative 50 indicates an illegal move. A positive value greater than one means that a capture can be made by the computer, which will come out ahead after your best reply. You may want to press **CTRL** and **NumLock** to make the program pause before writing over some of the evaluation numbers. Pressing a key will make the program continue.

MAIN ROUTINES

140- 170	Initializes variables. Displays board.
180- 200	Asks who goes first. Evaluates answer.
210- 250	Determines computer's move. Displays new board position.
260- 270	Determines if computer's move resulted in a win. Displays a message if so.
280- 330	Gets operator's move. Checks for legality. Displays new board position.
340- 350	Determines if operator's move resulted in a win.
360	Displays message if illegal move attempted.
370- 520	Subroutine to make move M in T array.
380- 410	Copies T array into Y array (inverts if computer is making the move).
420- 450	Makes move in Y array.
460- 470	Checks for captures. Removes stones. Checks previous square.
480- 490	Sees if opponent is left with a legal move.
500- 520	Copies Y array back into T array.
530- 720	Subroutine to determine computer's move.

730- 760	Subroutine to create graphics strings for board display.
770- 820	Displays ending message. Asks about playing again.
830- 900	Subroutine to display stones on board and captured, and "cross-bars" of board squares.
910	Subroutine to move cursor to YOUR MOVE position on screen.
920	Subroutine to move cursor to MY MOVE position on screen.
930	Subroutine to display one blank character.
940-1020	Subroutine to display Wari board (without stones), titles, and square numbers.
1030-1050	Displays message when computer has no legal move.

MAIN VARIABLES

J,K	Subscript variables.
Q,P,F,D	Constant values of 14, 13, 50 and 12, respectively.
I	Constant one.
T,Y,W	Arrays with temporary copies of the Wari board.
V	Array with evaluation values of operator's six possible replies to computer's move being considered.
E	Array with evaluation values of computer's six possible moves.
B	Array containing Wari board. Thirteenth element has stones captured by operator. Fourteenth has computer's.
ZA,ZB	Weighting values for the evaluation function.
MN	Move number.
R$	Operator's reply. Also used as switch to indicate whose move it is (C for computer, H for human).
M	Move being made (1-6 for operator, 7-12 for computer). Set negative if illegal.
C	Subscript used in dropping stones around board.
L	Last square in which a stone was dropped.
S	Stones on opponent's side of the board after a move.
A	Subscript used to indicate which of the six possible computer moves is currently being evaluated.

FA	First evaluation factor used in determining favorability of board position after a move (indicates computer's number of occupied squares).
FB	Second evaluation factor (total stones on computer's side of the board).
FC	Third evaluation factor (number of squares with two or less stones).
FD	Fourth evaluation factor (number of stones in most populous square on computer's side).
FE	Total stones on board.
A$,B$	Strings of graphics characters used to display the Wari board.
D$	String of 32 blanks.

SUGGESTED PROJECTS

1. Modify the program to declare the game a draw if neither player has made a capture in the past thirty moves. Line 330 adds one to a counter of the number of moves made. To make the change, keep track of the move number of the last capture, and compare the difference between it and the current move number with 30.

2. Modify the evaluation function used by the computer strategy to see if you can improve the quality of its play. Lines 610 through 670 examine the position of the board after the move that is being considered. Experiment with the factors and/or the weighting values, or add a new factor of your own.

3. Change the program so it can allow two people to play against each other, instead of just a person against the computer.

Section 4

Graphics Display
Programs

The IBM Personal Computer is an amazing machine. With the graphics interface, it has very useful color graphics capabilities in addition to its other capacities. Programs in the other sections of this book take advantage of these graphics to facilitate and "spice up" their various output. Here we explore their use for sheer fun, amusement, and diversion.

Ever look through a kaleidoscope and enjoy the symmetric changing patterns produced? KALEIDO will create such effects to keep you hypnotized.

Three other programs produce ever changing patterns but with much different effects. SPARKLE will fascinate you with a changing shimmering collage. SQUARES uses geometric shapes to obtain its pleasing displays. SPIRALS displays beautiful patterns by rotating ever-increasing lines at various angles.

WALLOONS demonstrates a totally different aspect of the computer. This program will keep you entertained with an example of computer animation.

KALEIDO

PURPOSE

If you have ever played with a kaleidoscope, you were probably fascinated by the endless symmetrical patterns you saw displayed. This program creates a series of kaleidoscope-like designs, with each one overlaying the previous one.

HOW TO USE IT

There is not much to say about how to use this one. Just type RUN, press a key to start, then sit back and watch. Turning down the lights and playing a little music is a good way to add to the effect.

Have a few friends bring their IBM Personal Computers over (all your friends *do* have PCs, don't they?), and get them all going with KALEIDO at once. Let us know if you think you have set a new world's record. Please note that we will not be responsible for any hypnotic trances induced this way.

To fully appreciate this program, you need to have the color/graphics interface and a color video display. However, even if you have only a black and white display (with either the color/graphics or the monochrome interface), you should find these designs interesting. If you use the monochrome interface, only the left side of the screen will be used.

To stop the program after the current design is finished, press a key.

SAMPLE RUN

One of the patterns generated by the KALEIDO program.

PROGRAM LISTING

```
100 REM: KALEIDO
110 REM: A kaleidoscope-like display.
120 REM: COPYRIGHT 1982 Tom Rugg and Phil Feldman.
130 REM: Any BASIC, any CRT.
140 I=1
150 KEY OFF:SCREEN 0,1:COLOR 7,0,0:WIDTH 40:CLS
160 GOSUB 590
170 P=12
180 A=20:B=13:D=-1:R$=CHR$(219)
190 M=16
200 DIM R(7)
210 FOR J=0 TO 7
220 R(J)=INT(M*RND)
230 NEXT J
240 COLOR 0,INT(8*RND)
250 D=-D:K=1:L=P:IF D>0 THEN 270
260 K=P:L=1
270 IF D>0 THEN LOCATE B,A:COLOR R(7):PRINT R$;
280 FOR J=K TO L STEP D
290 X=A+J:Y=B:GOSUB 430
300 X=A-J:GOSUB 430
310 X=A:Y=B+J:GOSUB 430
320 Y=B-J:GOSUB 430
330 X=A+J:Y=B+J:GOSUB 430
340 X=A-J:Y=B-J:GOSUB 430
```

```
350 Y=B+J:GOSUB 430
360 X=A+J:Y=B-J:GOSUB 430
370 NEXT J
380 IF D<0 THEN LOCATE B,A:COLOR R(7):PRINT R$;
390 FOR J=1 TO 2000:NEXT J
400 A$=INKEY$:IF LEN(A$)=0 THEN 210
410 SCREEN 0,0,0
420 END
430 LOCATE Y,X:COLOR R(0):PRINT R$;
440 IF J=1 THEN RETURN
450 W=INT(J/2):T=J-W-1
460 FOR N=1 TO W
470 IF X<>(A) THEN 490
480 Y2=Y:X2=X+N:GOSUB 580:X2=X-N:GOSUB 580:
    GOTO 570
490 IF Y<>B THEN 510
500 X2=X:Y2=Y+N:GOSUB 580:Y2=Y-N:GOSUB 580:
    GOTO 570
510 Y2=Y:IF X>=(A) THEN 530
520 X2=X+N:GOSUB 580:GOTO 540
530 X2=X-N:GOSUB 580
540 X2=X:IF Y>=B THEN 560
550 Y2=Y+N:GOSUB 580:GOTO 570
560 Y2=Y-N:GOSUB 580
570 NEXT N:RETURN
580 LOCATE Y2,X2:COLOR R(N):PRINT R$;:RETURN
590 LOCATE 1,17,0:PRINT"KALEIDO"
600 LOCATE 4,10
610 PRINT"PRESS A KEY TO START"
620 DEF SEG:POKE 106,0
630 R$=INKEY$:J=RND:IF LEN(R$)=0 THEN 630
640 CLS:RETURN
```

EASY CHANGES

1. To clear the screen before the next pattern about 20% of the time (chosen at random), insert this:

    242 IF RND<.2 THEN CLS

    For 50%, use .5 instead of .2, etc.

2. To use different characters at each point of the design, try replacing the 219 in line 180 with 223, 221, 254, 176, 1, 2, 4, or 15.

3. To randomly change the size of the patterns, insert:

    244 P = INT(9*RND)+4

4. To cause only the outward patterns to be displayed, insert this line:

    246 D = -1

To cause only inward patterns, change it to say

$$246 \ D = 1$$

5. To alter the number of graphics colors used in the pattern, insert:

$$395 \ M = INT(14*RND) + 2$$

6. To lengthen the delay after each pattern is drawn, change the 2000 in line 390 to 5000 or 10000. To eliminate the delay, delete line 390.

Note: These changes add a lot to the appeal of the designs. Experiment! Each change can be done by itself or in combination with other changes.

MAIN ROUTINES

140-200	Housekeeping. Initializes variables, RND.
210-230	Picks 8 random graphics colors.
240	Picks random background color.
250-380	Displays a full screen of the pattern.
390	Waits about two seconds.
400	Goes back to create next pattern if no key was pressed.
410-420	Resets screen to black and white text and ends.
430-570	Displays points on and between axes of symmetry.
580	Subroutine to display points between axes.
590-640	Subroutine to display title and initialize RND.

MAIN VARIABLES

I	Constant one.
A,B	Pointer to center of design (B down, A across).
D	Direction in which design is drawn (1 = outward, -1 = inward).
M	Multiplier used to determine the range of random graphics colors.
J,K,L	Subscript variables.
A$	Temporary string variable.
P	Distance from center to edge of design.
R	Array of 8 random colors.
R$	Graphics character to be displayed.
X,Y	Coordinates of a point to be displayed on axes.

X2,Y2   Coordinates of a point to be displayed between axes.

N,W   Work variables.

SPARKLE

PURPOSE

This graphics display program provides a continuous series of hypnotic patterns, some of which seem to sparkle at you while they are created. Two types of patterns are used. The first is a set of concentric diamond shapes in the center of the screen. Although the pattern is regular, the sequence in which it is created is random, which results in the "sparkle" effect.

The second type of pattern starts about two seconds after the first has finished. It is a series of "sweeps" across the screen— left to right and top to bottom. Each sweep uses a random graphics color that is spaced equally across the screen. The spacing distance is chosen at random for each sweep. Also, the number of sweeps to be made is chosen at random each time in the range from 11 to 30.

After the second type of pattern is complete, the program goes back to the first type, which begins to overlay the second type.

HOW TO USE IT

Confused by what you just read? Never mind. You have to see it to appreciate it. Just enter the program into your computer, then sit back and watch the results of your labor.

SPARKLE looks best in color (see the comments in the last two paragraphs of "How To Use It" in KALEIDO).   To stop the program, simply press any key.

SAMPLE RUN

One of the patterns generated by the SPARKLE program.

PROGRAM LISTING

```
100 REM: SPARKLE
110 REM: A sparkling graphics display.
120 REM: COPYRIGHT 1982 Tom Rugg and Phil Feldman.
130 REM: Any BASIC, any CRT.
140 I=1
150 KEY OFF:SCREEN 0,1:COLOR 7,0,0:WIDTH 40:CLS
160 S=12
170 DIM A(S),B(S):X=20:Y=13
180 GOSUB 540
190 R$=CHR$(219)
200 T=INT(16*RND)
210 COLOR 0,INT(8*RND)
220 FOR J=0 TO S:A(J)=J:B(J)=J:NEXT J
230 FOR J=0 TO S:R=INT((S+1)*RND)
240 W=A(J):A(J)=A(R):A(R)=W:NEXT J
250 FOR J=0 TO S:R=INT((S+1)*RND)
260 W=B(J):B(J)=B(R):B(R)=W:NEXT J
270 FOR J=0 TO S:FOR K=0 TO S
280 R=A(J):W=B(K):C=R+W+T
290 IF C>15 THEN C=C-16:GOTO 290
300 COLOR C
```

```
310 LOCATE Y+W,X+R:PRINT R$;
320 LOCATE Y-W,X+R:PRINT R$;
330 LOCATE Y-W,X-R:PRINT R$;
340 LOCATE Y+W,X-R:PRINT R$;
350 LOCATE Y+R,X+W:PRINT R$;
360 LOCATE Y-R,X+W:PRINT R$;
370 LOCATE Y-R,X-W:PRINT R$;
380 LOCATE Y+R,X-W:PRINT R$;
390 NEXT K:NEXT J
400 FOR J=1 TO 2000:NEXT J
410 A$=INKEY$:IF LEN(A$)=0 THEN 430
420 SCREEN 0,0,0:END
430 M=15
440 N=INT(20*RND)+11
450 FOR J=1 TO N
460 R=INT(22*RND)+1:W=INT(M*RND)
470 COLOR W
480 FOR L=Y-S TO Y+S STEP INT(R/4)+1
490 FOR K=X-S TO X+S STEP R
500 LOCATE L,K:PRINT R$;
510 NEXT K:NEXT L:NEXT J
520 A$=INKEY$:IF LEN(A$)=0 THEN 200
530 SCREEN 0,0,0:END
540 LOCATE 1,17,0:PRINT"SPARKLE"
550 LOCATE 4,10
560 PRINT"PRESS A KEY TO START"
570 DEF SEG:POKE 106,0
580 R$=INKEY$:J=RND:IF LEN(R$)=0 THEN 580
590 CLS:RETURN
```

EASY CHANGES

1. Make the second type of pattern appear first by inserting this line:

    195 GOTO 430

    Or, eliminate the first type of pattern by inserting:

    205 GOTO 430

    Or, eliminate the second type of pattern by inserting:

    435 GOTO 200

2. Increase the delay after the first type of pattern by increasing the 2000 in line 400 to, say, 5000. Remove line 400 to eliminate the delay.

3. Increase the number of sweeps across the screen of the second type of pattern by changing the 11 at the right end of

line 440 into a 30 or a 50, for example. Decrease the number of sweeps by changing the 11 to a 1, and also changing the 20 in line 440 to 5 or 10.

4. Watch the effect on the second type of pattern if you change the 22 in line 460 into various integer values between 2 and 40.

5. Change the value of M in line 430 to alter the graphics colors used in the second type of pattern. For example, try

$$430 \ M = 4$$

Be sure M in an integer from 2 to 15.

MAIN ROUTINES

140-190	Initializes variables.
200-390	Displays first type of pattern.
220-260	Shuffles the numbers 0 through 12 in the A and B arrays.
270-390	Displays graphics colors on the screen.
400	Delays for about 2 seconds.
410-420	Ends program if a key is pressed.
430-510	Overlays the entire screen with a random graphics color spaced at a fixed interval chosen at random.
520-530	Ends program if a key is pressed.
540-590	Displays title, initializes RND, clears screen.

MAIN VARIABLES

I	Constant one.
S	Size of patterns (center to edge).
R	Random integer. Also, work variable.
A,B	Arrays in which shuffled integers from 0 to S are stored for use in making first type of pattern.
X,Y	Coordinates of center of screen (20 across, 13 down).
T	Integer from 0 to 15, used in creating random graphics colors.
J,K,L	Work and loop variables.
W	Work variable.
C	Graphics color to be displayed on screen.
N	Number of repetitions of second type of pattern.
M	Multiplier used in getting a random color for the second type of pattern.

| A\$ | Input key to end the display. |
| R\$ | Graphics character to be displayed. |

SUGGESTED PROJECTS

Make the second type of pattern alternate between "falling from the top" (as it does now) and rising from the bottom of the screen.

SPIRALS

PURPOSE

This graphics display program draws spiraling geometric designs. You can either let the program draw them at random for you, or you can specify just what kind of design you want to be displayed.

HOW TO USE IT

The program starts by displaying its title and a menu of four options. Enter a digit from one through four to select the one you want. There's no need to press the **ENTER** key.

Option 1 draws spirals at random. After each spiral is drawn, it will remain on the screen for about five seconds, and then the next one will begin. To go back to the menu after the current spiral finishes, press a key on the keyboard.

Option 2 allows you to specify the parameters that cause the spiral to be drawn. First you are asked for the angle, and then for the increment. Here's a brief explanation of how these numbers are used to create the spirals.

Each spiral is drawn as a series of lines. Each line is slightly longer than the last line, and drawn at a specified angle from the last line. The angle is the amount in degrees by which the next line will deflect from the last line. 180 degrees causes the next line to continue in a straight line from the last one. 90 degrees deflects by a right angle and draws a spiraling square. 120 degrees leaves an interior angle of 60 degrees (180 minus 120), and draws a spiraling equilateral triangle. Angles which are close, but not equal, to those which produce equilateral polygons produce some of the most interesting designs. Try angles like 59, 73, 88, 89, 91, 119, 122, 162, and 178.

The increment is both the starting length of the line, and the amount by which each subsequent line lengthens from the previous one. So, if you give 2 as the increment, the first line is 2 units long, the second is 4, the third is 6, and so on. The screen is 200 units high and 320 units wide. When you give a small increment (such as .5 or 1), you get an intricate, tightly-woven design. A larger increment (3 or 4) leaves much more space in the resulting spiral. Each spiral is drawn until the program determines that the next line is so long that it would extend beyond the edge of the screen if drawn.

Experiment with various combinations of angles and increments, or simply use Option 1 to let the program randomly pick them for you while you watch the results. The angle and increment are shown in the lower left corner of the screen.

Option 3 simply repeats the last spiral drawn.

Option 4 ends the program.

This program requires the color/graphics interface. Either a black and white or a color screen can be used.

SAMPLE RUN

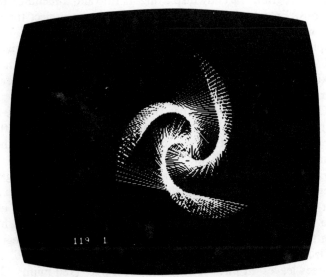

One of the patterns generated by the SPIRALS program.

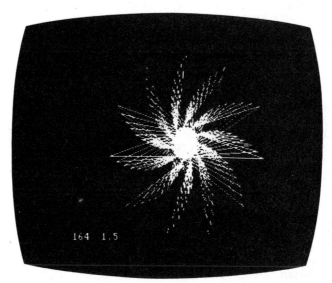

Another of the patterns from the SPIRALS program.

PROGRAM LISTING

```
100 REM: SPIRALS
110 REM: Draw "spirals" using straight lines.
120 REM: COPYRIGHT 1982 Tom Rugg and Phil Feldman.
130 REM: Any BASIC, graphics interface card.
140 KEY OFF:SCREEN 1,0,0,0:COLOR 0,1:CLS
150 GOTO 310
160 CLS:IF INCR=0 THEN 330
170 LOCATE 25:PRINT ANGLE;INCR;
180 PX=INT(XL/2):PY=INT(YL/2):A=ANGLE:L=INCR
190 C=3
200 X=L*COS(M*A)+PX:Y=L*SIN(M*A)+PY
210 IF X>XL OR X<0 OR Y>YL OR Y<0 THEN 260
220 LINE (PX,PY)-(X,Y),C
230 L=L+INCR:A=A+ANGLE
240 PX=X:PY=Y
250 GOTO 200
260 FOR J=1 TO 6000:NEXT
270 A$=INKEY$:IF LEN(A$)=0 THEN 290
280 GOTO 330
290 IF SPEC$="Y" OR SPEC$="y" THEN 330
300 GOTO 480
310 M=3.141593/180:I=1:INCR=0
320 XL=319:YL=199
330 CLS:PRINT"**** SPIRALS ****"
```

```
340 PRINT:PRINT
350 PRINT"OPTIONS:"
360 PRINT"1 - DRAW RANDOM SPIRALS"
370 PRINT"2 - DRAW SPECIFIC SPIRAL"
380 PRINT"3 - REPEAT LAST SPIRAL"
390 PRINT"4 - END PROGRAM"
400 PRINT
410 DEF SEG:POKE 106,0
420 R$=INKEY$:X=RND:IF LEN(R$)=0 THEN 420
430 IF R$<"1" OR R$>"4" THEN 420
440 PRINT R$:PRINT
450 ON VAL(R$) GOTO 470,510,160,600
460 PRINT"ERROR":BEEP:STOP
470 SPEC$="N"
480 ANGLE=INT(121*RND)+59
490 INCR=(INT(4*RND)+1)/2
500 GOTO 160
510 PRINT"ENTER ANGLE"
520 PRINT"    (59 - 179 RECOMMENDED)"
530 INPUT ANGLE
540 PRINT
550 PRINT"ENTER INCREMENT"
560 PRINT"    (.5 - 2 RECOMMENDED)"
570 INPUT INCR
580 SPEC$="Y"
590 GOTO 160
600 SCREEN 0,0,0,0
610 END
```

EASY CHANGES

1. Change the delay after each spiral is drawn by changing the 6000 in line 260. Double it to double the delay, etc.
2. Instead of using medium resolution graphics (320 points wide by 200 high), you can use high resolution (640 wide by 200 high). This has the effect of squashing the design together so it looks tall and thin. To try it, make these changes:

    140 KEY OFF:SCREEN 2,0,0,0:CLS
    320 XL = 639:YL = 199

3. Delete line 170 to eliminate the display of the angle and increment.

MAIN ROUTINES

140-150   Initializes screen and goes to menu routine.
160-250   Clears screen, displays angle and increment, and draws spiral on screen.
260   Delays about 5 seconds.

270-300	Goes to display menu if a key is pressed or if Option 2 is in effect. If neither, picks next random spiral.
310-400	Initializes variables and displays menu.
410-460	Gets response for menu display; cycles RND; goes to appropriate routine.
470-500	Picks random angle and increment for Option 1.
510-590	Gets angle and increment from operator (Option 2).
600-610	Resets screen to text mode and ends program.

MAIN VARIABLES

ANGLE	Angle used in drawing spiral.
INCR	Increment used in drawing spiral.
PX,PY	Previous X,Y coordinates of line end.
XL,YL	Upper limits of X and Y that fit on screen.
A	Current angle on screen.
L	Current line length.
C	Color of design.
X,Y	Coordinates of end point of new line.
M	Constant to convert angles from degrees to radians.
J	Loop variable.
A$	Key pressed during display of spiral.
SPEC$	Set to Y if specific spiral (Option 2), or N otherwise.
I	Constant one.
R$	Reply of operator to menu options.

SUGGESTED PROJECTS

1. Modify the random angle and increment selection so that it will only select the designs that you find most interesting. For example, if you only like angles from 88 to 160 degrees, and increments of .5, 1, and 1.5, you might make these changes:

    480 ANGLE = INT(73*RND) + 88
    490 INCR = (INT(3*RND) + 1)/2

2. Modify the program to redraw the current design on a high resolution plotter after it has been displayed on the screen.

3. If you are using a color screen, make changes to use different colors effectively. A simple start would be:

    190 COLOR 0,0:C = INT(3*RND) + 1

    or

    215 C = INT(3*RND) + 1

SQUARES

PURPOSE

This is another graphics-display program. It draws a series of concentric squares with the graphics color used for each one chosen at random. After a full set of concentric squares is drawn, the next set starts again at the center and overlays the previous one. They are actually rectangles, not squares, but let's not be nit-pickers.

HOW TO USE IT

As with most of the other graphics display programs, you just sit back and enjoy watching this one once you get it started.

You get the maximum effect from SQUARES in color (see the comments in the last two paragraphs of "How To Use It" in KALEIDO).

The program can be stopped by simply pressing any key.

SAMPLE RUN

One of the patterns generated by the SQUARES program.

PROGRAM LISTING

```
100 REM: SQUARES
110 REM: A graphics display program.
120 REM: COPYRIGHT 1982 Tom Rugg and Phil Feldman.
130 REM: Any BASIC, any CRT.
140 I=1
150 R$=CHR$(219)
160 KEY OFF:SCREEN 0,1:COLOR 7,0,0:WIDTH 40:CLS
170 GOSUB 320
180 X=20:Y=13:N=1
190 COLOR INT(16*RND):LOCATE Y-1,X:PRINT R$;
200 C=INT(16*RND):COLOR C
210 FOR J=0 TO N:LOCATE Y,X+J:PRINT R$;:NEXT
220 X=X+N:N=N+1
230 FOR J=0 TO N:LOCATE Y-J,X:PRINT R$;:NEXT
240 Y=Y-N:FOR J=0 TO N:LOCATE Y,X-J:PRINT R$;:NEXT
250 X=X-N
260 FOR J=0 TO N:LOCATE Y+J,X:PRINT R$;:NEXT
270 N=N+1:Y=Y+N
280 IF N<23 THEN 200
290 FOR J=1 TO 1000:NEXT J
300 A$=INKEY$:IF LEN(A$)=0 THEN 180
310 SCREEN 0,0,0:END
320 LOCATE 1,17,0:PRINT"SQUARES"
```

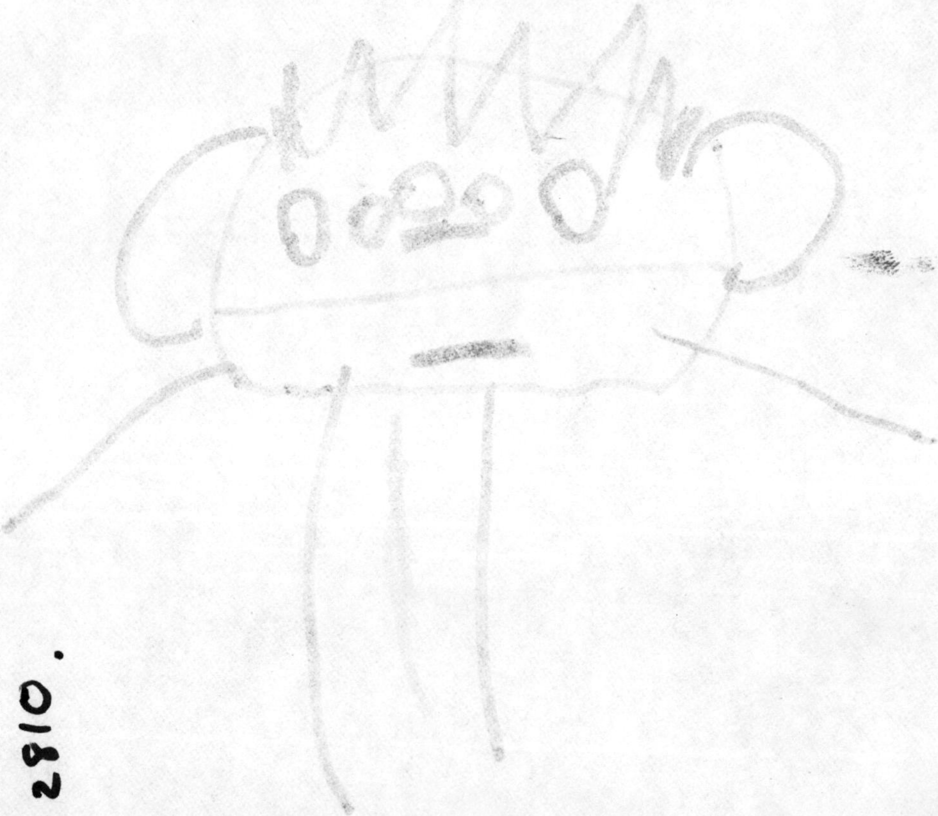

946-2810.

```
330 LOCATE 4,10
340 PRINT"PRESS A KEY TO START"
350 DEF SEG:POKE 106,0
360 A$=INKEY$:J=RND:IF LEN(A$)=0 THEN 360
370 CLS:RETURN
```

EASY CHANGES

1. Change the delay after each set of patterns by changing the
   1000 in line 290. A bigger number causes a longer delay.
2. To occasionally blank out the screen (about 20% of the
   time), insert this:

$$295 \text{ IF RND} < = .2 \text{ THEN CLS}$$

MAIN ROUTINES

140-170	Displays title and initializes RND function.
180	Initializes counters for the pattern. Points to the center of the screen.
190	Draws random color in center.
200	Picks a graphics color.
210-220	Draws the bottom side of the square.
230	Draws the right side.
240-250	Draws the top side.
260-270	Draws the left side.
280	Tests if the outermost square has been drawn.
290	Delays about one second.
300	Goes back to start again at the center if no key has been pressed.
320-370	Subroutine to display title and set RND.

MAIN VARIABLES

I	Constant one.
N	Length of the side currently being drawn.
X,Y	Location of center of screen.
C	Numeric equivalent of the random graphics color chosen.
J	Loop variable.
R$	Graphics character to be displayed.
A$	Key pressed to start or end display.

WALLOONS

PURPOSE

The IBM Personal Computer is quite a versatile machine. This program takes advantage of its powerful graphics capability to produce computer animation. That's right, animation! WALLOONS will entertain you with a presentation from the PC Playhouse.

The PC Playhouse searches the world over to bring you the best in circus acts and other performing artists. Today, direct from their performance before the uncrowned heads of Europe, the Playhouse brings you the Flying Walloons.

HOW TO USE IT

Just sit back, relax, and get ready to enjoy the show. Type RUN and the Flying Walloons will be ready to perform. You have a front row center seat and the show is about to begin.

Applause might be appropriate if you enjoy their performance. Please note that the Walloons have been working on a big new finish to their act which they haven't yet quite perfected.

A note for those typing the program into their computer: It will be helpful to use the **CAPS LOCK** key. The string literal arguments (i.e., the text between the quote marks) of the DRAW statements in lines 440, 1640, 1650, and 1680 contain 0 (zeros), not O (the letter "oh"). The DATA statements in lines 2020 and 2040 contain O ("ohs") and not 0 (zeros). On the other hand, the DATA statement in line 2010 contains a zero.

SAMPLE RUN

The billboard announces a new presentation of the (in)famous PC Playhouse.

"The Flying Walloons" are to perform!

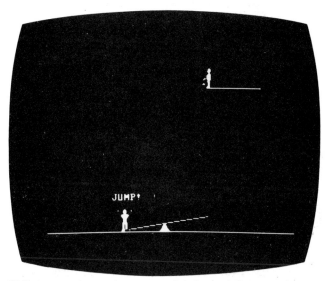

The Walloons attempt a dangerous trick from their repertoire.

PROGRAM LISTING

```
100 REM: WALLOONS
110 REM: An animated graphics show.
120 REM: COPYRIGHT 1982 Phil Feldman and Tom Rugg.
130 REM: Advanced BASIC, graphics interface card.
140 KEY OFF:SCREEN 1,0:COLOR 0,1
150 CLEAR:CLS:DEFINT A-Z
160 DIM A(270),B(270),C(8),VR(220),VL(220)
170 DIM WN(60),WA(60),WL(60),WP(30),WK(40),WM(60)
180 DIM WB(60),WE(60),WF(60),WG(60),WQ(30)
190 DIM WR(30),WT(20),WJ(30)
200 GOSUB 1210:CLS:D=3000:GOSUB 230:GOSUB 1570
210 D=3000:GOSUB 230:CLS:D=1000:GOSUB 230
220 GOSUB 540:CLS:END
230 FOR K=1 TO D:NEXT:RETURN
240 PUT(X,Y),WN:FOR K=1 TO D:NEXT
250 PUT(X,Y),WN:RETURN
260 PUT(X,Y),WG:FOR K=1 TO D:NEXT
270 PUT(X,Y),WG:RETURN
280 PUT(X,Y),WP:FOR K=1 TO D:NEXT
290 PUT(X,Y),WP:RETURN
300 PUT(X,Y),WF:FOR K=1 TO D:NEXT
310 PUT(X,Y),WF:RETURN
320 PUT(X,Y),WE:FOR K=1 TO D:NEXT
330 PUT(X,Y),WE:RETURN
```

```
340 PUT(X,Y),WK:FOR K=1 TO D:NEXT
350 PUT(X,Y),WK:RETURN
360 PUT(X,Y),WQ:FOR K=1 TO D:NEXT
370 PUT(X,Y),WQ:RETURN
380 PUT(X,Y),WM:FOR K=1 TO D:NEXT
390 PUT(X,Y),WM:RETURN
400 PUT(X,Y),WA:FOR K=1 TO D:NEXT
410 PUT(X,Y),WA:RETURN
420 PUT(X,Y),WL:FOR K=1 TO D:NEXT
430 PUT(X,Y),WL:RETURN
440 Q=Q+2:PSET(150,100):CLS:DRAW"S=Q;AOXWN$;"
450 PSET(50,50):DRAW"S4XW$;":PAINT(X,Y):RETURN
460 CLS:LINE(149,Y)-(V,182):LINE(V,182)-(161,Y)
470 LINE(149,Y)-(161,Y):PAINT(V,186):RETURN
480 X=95:Y=168:PUT(X,Y),WN:PUT(X,Y),WA
490 LOCATE 20,12:PRINT"JUMP!";:BEEP
500 D=4000:GOSUB 230:PUT(X,Y),WA:PUT(X,Y),WN
510 LOCATE 20,12:PRINT SPACE$(5);:RETURN
520 FOR J=1 TO 7:SOUND 1000,1:D=150
530 GOSUB 230:NEXT:RETURN
540 LINE(0,190)-(319,190):LINE(280,0)-(280,190)
550 LINE (212,40)-(280,40):PUT(100,175),VL
560 PUT(284,169),WN:X=5:Y=169:D=5000:GOSUB 240
570 D=3000:GOSUB 420:X=26:Y=171:D=400:GOSUB 260
580 X=52:Y=169:GOSUB 300:X=73:Y=171:GOSUB 320
590 X=95:Y=168:D=2500:GOSUB 240:D=1500:GOSUB 400
600 PUT(X,Y),WN:GOSUB 520:D=3000:GOSUB 230
610 Y=169:PUT(284,Y),WN:X=282:D=2000:GOSUB 280
620 D=200:FOR Y=164 TO 19 STEP-5:X=277:GOSUB 340
630 X=282:GOSUB 280:NEXT:Y=19
640 FOR X=277 TO 212 STEP-5:GOSUB 340:GOSUB 280
650 NEXT:PUT(207,Y),WK:D=4000:GOSUB 230
660 GOSUB 480:D=2000:GOSUB 230:Y=19:D=150
670 PUT(207,Y),WK:FOR X=212 TO 227 STEP 5
680 GOSUB 280:GOSUB 340:NEXT:X=232:D=1000
690 GOSUB 280:PUT(203,35),WT:D=3500:GOSUB 230
700 GOSUB 480:D=2000:GOSUB 230:PUT(203,35),WT
710 D=300:PUT(204,26),WR:GOSUB 230
720 PUT(204,26),WR:X=188:Y=46:GOSUB 360:X=203
730 D=150:FOR Y=58 TO 153 STEP 5:GOSUB 280:NEXT
740 PUT(95,168),WN:D=100
750 FOR J=1 TO 3
760 X=95:PUT(100,175),VR,PSET:PUT(197,168),WA
770 FOR Y=154 TO 54 STEP -5:GOSUB 240:NEXT
780 FOR Y=54 TO 154 STEP 5:GOSUB 400:NEXT
790 X=197:PUT(X,168),WA:PUT(100,175),VL,PSET
800 PUT(95,168),WA:FOR Y=154 TO 54 STEP -5
810 GOSUB 240:NEXT:FOR Y=54 TO 154 STEP 5
820 GOSUB 400:NEXT:PUT(95,168),WA:NEXT
830 PUT(100,175),VR,PSET:PUT(X,168),WA
840 D=150:FOR J=154 TO 54 STEP -20:X=95:Y=J
850 GOSUB 420:X=93:Y=J-5:GOSUB 320:X=95:Y=J-9
```

```
860 GOSUB 300:X=93:Y=J-14:GOSUB 260:NEXT
870 FOR J=34 TO 134 STEP 20:X=95:Y=J:GOSUB 420
880 X=93:Y=J+6:GOSUB 260:X=95:Y=J+11:GOSUB 300
890 X=93:Y=J+15:GOSUB 320:NEXT:PUT(197,168),WA
900 PUT(100,175),VL,PSET:PUT(95,168),WA
910 FOR J=154 TO 54 STEP -20:X=197:Y=J:GOSUB 420
920 X=195:Y=J-5:GOSUB 320:X=197:Y=J-9:GOSUB 300
930 X=195:Y=J-14:GOSUB 260:NEXT:BEEP
940 X=197:D=200:FOR J=45 TO 145 STEP 10:Y=J
950 GOSUB 380:Y=J+5:GOSUB 300:NEXT:PUT(95,168),WA
960 PUT(100,175),VR,PSET:PUT(197,168),WB:BEEP
970 X=91:Y=160:FOR J=1 TO 25:X=X+4:Y=Y-6
980 GOSUB 240:NEXT:X=197:Y=9:GOSUB 400:X=202:Y=14
990 GOSUB 400:X=207:Y=19:D=1500:GOSUB 400
1000 X=202:Y=14:D=200:GOSUB 240:X=197:Y=9
1010 GOSUB 240:X=195:Y=4:FOR J=1 TO 12:X=X-4:Y=Y+6
1020 GOSUB 400:PUT(197,168),WB:PUT(197,168),WF
1030 X=X-4:Y=Y+6:GOSUB 400:PUT(197,168),WF
1040 PUT(197,168),WB:NEXT:PUT(197,168),WB
1050 PUT(100,175),VL,PSET:PUT(95,168),WA:X=203
1060 D=250:Y=159:FOR J=1 TO 13:X=X-6:Y=Y-5
1070 PUT(X,Y),WB:GOSUB 230:PUT(X,Y),WB
1080 X=X-6:Y=Y-5:GOSUB 300:NEXT:D=100
1090 FOR Y=29 TO 169 STEP 5:GOSUB 380:NEXT
1100 FOR Y=164 TO 134 STEP -5:GOSUB 380:NEXT
1110 FOR Y=139 TO 164 STEP 5:GOSUB 380:NEXT:BEEP
1120 Y=169:D=800:GOSUB 380:PUT(36,182),WQ
1130 D=2500:GOSUB 230:PUT(95,168),WA
1140 PUT(100,168),WP:D=2500:GOSUB 230
1150 X=36:Y=182:D=3000:PUT(X,Y),WQ:PUT(X,Y),WJ
1160 GOSUB 230:PUT(X,Y),WJ:PUT(X,Y),WQ
1170 GOSUB 230:X=95:Y=168:PUT(100,Y),WP
1180 GOSUB 240:PUT(X,Y),WA:GOSUB 520:D=4000
1190 GOSUB 230:CLS:LOCATE 12,16:PRINT"F I N I S"
1200 D=5000:GOSUB 230:RETURN
1210 AB$="R3U1H1U2E1R2F1D2G1D1R3":CD$="G2D3F1"
1220 GH$="E1U3H2":RAD$="F5D1H1L1H3"
1230 LAD$="G3L1G1U1E5":LD$="D6F1L3U6H1G1D6L3E1U6"
1240 RAU$="E5D2G5":LAU$="H5U2F5"
1250 LU$="F6D1L2H7G7L2U1E6"
1260 WN$="BL4XLAD$;XAB$;XRAD$;XCD$;XLD$;XGH$;"
1270 WA$="BL4XLAU$;XAB$;XRAU$;XCD$;XLD$;XGH$;"
1280 WL$="BL4XLAU$;XAB$;XRAU$;XCD$;XLU$;XGH$;"
1290 M$=
     "E2U1L1U1L1E1U1E1R1F1D2G1D1F1D6G1D7L4E1R1U6"
1300 K$=M$+"G5L3E1R1E5U3G2L1G1L1E5":L$=M$+"H1U5"
1310 H$=M$+"G4L3E1R1E4U3G2L1G1L1E5"
1320 X=50:Y=52:T=41:U=43:V=59:W=63:Q=2
1330 W$=WN$:GOSUB 440:GOSUB 2000
1340 W$=WN$:GOSUB 440:GET(T,U)-(V,W),WN
1350 W$=WA$:GOSUB 440:GET(T,U)-(V,W),WA
1360 W$=WL$:GOSUB 440:GET(T,U)-(V,W),WL
```

```
1370 W$="BL2XL$;":GOSUB 440:PAINT(X,45)
1380 GET(47,U)-(52,W),WP
1390 W$="BL2XH$;":GOSUB 440:PAINT(X,45)
1400 GET(42,U)-(52,W),WK:U=37:W=57:Y=49
1410 W$="A2XWA$;":GOSUB 440:GET(T,U)-(V,W),WB
1420 W$="A2XWN$;":GOSUB 440:GET(T,U)-(V,W),WM
1430 Y=51:W$="A2XWL$;":GOSUB 440:GET(T,U)-(V,W),WF
1440 W$="A1XWL$;":GOSUB 440:GET(42,T)-(65,V),WE
1450 W$="A3XWL$;":GOSUB 440:GET(35,T)-(58,V),WG
1460 W$="A1BL2XL$;":X=52:Y=50:GOSUB 440:
     PAINT(45,50)
1470 GET(43,48)-(65,52),WT
1480 X=50:Y=48:W$="A2BL2XL$;":GOSUB 440:
     PAINT(X,55)
1490 GET(48,37)-(53,57),WR
1500 X=48:Y=50:W$="A3BL2XL$;":GOSUB 440:
     PAINT(55,Y)
1510 GET(35,45)-(57,52),WQ
1520 X=55:W$="A3BL2XH$;":GOSUB 440:PAINT(48,51)
1530 GET(35,45)-(57,52),WJ
1540 X=210:Y=189:T=175:V=155:W=100:GOSUB 460
1550 LINE(W,Y)-(X,T):GET(W,T)-(X,Y),VL:GOSUB 460
1560 LINE(W,T)-(X,Y):GET(W,T)-(X,Y),VR:RETURN
1570 LOCATE 9,9:PRINT"P C   P L A Y H O U S E"
1580 LOCATE 12,14:PRINT"P R O U D L Y"
1590 LOCATE 15,13:PRINT"P R E S E N T S"
1600 D=9000:GOSUB 230:C(0)=14:C(1)=7
1610 C(2)=-16369:C(3)=-4036:C(4)=15600:C(5)=C(4)
1620 C(6)=C(4):C(7)=C(3):C(8)=C(2)
1630 P$="U3E3R5F3D3L1":FOR X=2 TO 100 STEP 2
1640 LINE (1,86)-(X,86):DRAW"AOXP$;":D=100:
     GOSUB 230
1650 LINE (1,86)-(X,86),0:DRAW"COXP$;":NEXT
1660 FOR Y=87 TO 90:LINE(1,Y)-(102,Y):DRAW P$
1670 GOSUB 230:LINE(1,Y)-(102,Y),0
1680 DRAW "COXP$;":NEXT:LINE(1,91)-(102,91)
1690 DRAW P$:LOCATE 12,14:PRINT"P":FOR J=1 TO 70
1700 GET(1,85)-(210,94),A:GET(4,85)-(210,94),B
1710 PUT (1,85),A:PUT(1,85),B:NEXT
1720 D=9000:GOSUB 230:CLS:FOR X=33 TO 5 STEP-1
1730 D=100:GOSUB 230:LOCATE 8,X:B$=CHR$(32)
1740 PRINT"T H E";B$;B$:NEXT:FOR X=27 TO 9 STEP-1
1750 GOSUB 230:LOCATE 12,X
1760 PRINT"F L Y I N G";B$;B$:NEXT
1770 FOR X=22 TO 13 STEP -1:GOSUB 230
1780 LOCATE 16,X:
     PRINT"W A L L";SPACE$(5);"N S";B$;B$
1790 NEXT:D=2000:GOSUB 230:X=16:Y=32:DY=1:D=20
1800 GOSUB 1990:X=X+1:Y=Y+DY
1810 IF Y=48 THEN DY=-1:BEEP
1820 IF Y=32 THEN DY=1
1830 IF X=81 THEN 1840 ELSE 1800
```

```
1840 D=99:Y=32:FOR X=81 TO 96:Y=Y+3:GOSUB 1990:
     NEXT
1850 D=50:BEEP:Y=80:FOR X=97 TO 112:Y=Y-1:
     GOSUB 1990
1860 NEXT:FOR X=113 TO 128:Y=Y+1:GOSUB 1990:NEXT
1870 BEEP:FOR X=129 TO 144:Y=Y-1:GOSUB 1990:NEXT
1880 FOR X=145 TO 176:Y=Y+2:GOSUB 1990:NEXT:BEEP
1890 FOR Y=124 TO 122 STEP -2:GOSUB 1990:NEXT
1900 PUT (176,120),C:D=2000:GOSUB 230:X=176:D=30
1910 FOR Y=2 TO 112 STEP 2:GOSUB 1990:NEXT:BEEP
1920 FOR Y=110 TO 80 STEP -2:GOSUB 1990:NEXT
1930 FOR Y=82 TO 110 STEP 2:GOSUB 1990:NEXT:BEEP
1940 PUT (X,112),C:D=1000:GOSUB 230:D=70
1950 Y=120:PUT(176,Y),C:FOR X=175 TO 162 STEP -1
1960 GOSUB 1990:NEXT:PUT(160,Y),C:X=176
1970 PUT(X,112),C:FOR Y=113 TO 119:GOSUB 1990
1980 NEXT:PUT (X,120),C:RETURN
1990 PUT(X,Y),C:GOSUB 230:PUT(X,Y),C:RETURN
2000 FOR J=1 TO 4:READ T$:PLAY T$:NEXT:RETURN
2010 DATA T190MB
2020 DATA MSO3L4DDGAL2BL8BBL404C03EE
2030 DATA L2AL4DDF#GABAAGEL2DL4DDGABBB
2040 DATA O4C03EEL2AL8DDL4DF#GABAL16.
```

EASY CHANGES

1. If you wish to have the Walloons perform more (or less)
    jumps during their performance, change the loop bound
    value of 3 in line 750 accordingly. To get six jumps, use

    750 FOR J = 1 TO 6

2. The speed of the Walloon's movement is controlled by the
    value of D when the subroutine at line 230 is called. To
    make the Walloons move faster, try changing line 230 to

    230 FOR K = 1 TO D/2:NEXT:RETURN

    To have them move slower, try

    230 FOR K = 1 TO D*2:NEXT:RETURN

3. You might want to personalize the title placard and make
    yourself the presenter of the Walloons. This can be done by
    altering the string literal, "PC PLAYHOUSE" in line 1570
    to something else. To say, for example, that Simon Fenster
    presents the Walloons, change line 1570 to:

    1570 LOCATE 9,9:PRINT "SIMON FENSTER"

MAIN ROUTINES

140- 190	Initializes, dimensions arrays.
200- 220	Main routine, drives Walloon's performance.
230	Time delay subroutine.
240- 450	Subroutines to draw Walloons.
460- 470	Subroutine to draw fulcrum.
480- 510	Subroutine for Walloon to request the other Walloon to jump.
520- 530	Subroutine to sound rapid beeps.
540-1200	Subroutine for Walloon's performance.
1210-1560	Subroutine to set graphics strings and arrays.
1570-1980	Subroutine to announce the performers.
1990	Utility subroutine.
2000-2040	Subroutine to play circus tune.

MAIN VARIABLES

AB$-WN$	Various graphics strings.
J,K	Loop indices.
D	Time delay length.
X,Y	Horizontal, vertical screen location.
DY	Increment in Y (vertical) direction.
T$	Tune string.
T,U,V,W	Work variables.
A,B,C	Put,get arrays for text.
VR,V1	Put,get arrays for lever.
WA-WT	Put,get arrays for Walloons.

SUGGESTED PROJECTS

1. There are many possibilities for "spicing up" the Walloons'
    act with extra tricks or improved ones. Perhaps you would
    like to change their finish to something less crude. To get
    you started, here are the changes to produce one alternate
    ending:

    ```
    1060 D=250:Y=159:FOR J=1 TO 9:X-6:Y=Y-5
    1082 FOR Y=72 TO 142 STEP 5:PUT (X,Y),WB
    1084 GOSUB 230:PUT(X,Y),WB:NEXT:Y=147
    1086 PUT(X,Y),WB:D=4000:GOTO 1190
    ```

2. If you add some alternate tricks or endings as suggested in
    the previous project, try randomizing if and when they will

be done. Thus, the Walloon's performance will be different each time the program is run. At least their ending may be variable.

3. Scour the world yourself for other acts to include in the PC Playhouse. Maybe someday we will have a complete software library of performing artists.

Section 5

Mathematics Programs

Since their invention, computers have been used to solve mathematical problems. Their great speed and reliability render solvable many otherwise difficult (or impossible) calculations. Several different numerical techniques lend themselves naturally to computer solution. The following programs explore some of them. They will be of interest mainly to engineers, students, mathematicians, statisticians, and others who encounter such problems in their work.

GRAPH takes advantage of the computer's graphic powers to draw the graph of a function $Y = f(X)$. You supply the function. INTEGRATE calculates the integral, or "area under the curve," for any such function.

Experimental scientific work frequently results in data at discrete values of X and Y. CURVE finds a polynomial algebraic expression to express this data with a formula.

Theoretical scientists (and algebra students) often must find the solution to a set of simultaneous linear algebraic equations. SIMEQN does the trick.

Much modern engineering work requires the solution of differential equations. DIFFEQN will solve any first-order ordinary differential equation that you provide.

STATS will take a list of data and derive standard statistical information describing it. In addition, it will sort the data list into ranking numerical order.

CURVE

PURPOSE AND DISCUSSION

CURVE fits a polynomial function to a set of data. The data must be in the form of pairs of X-Y points. This type of data occurs frequently as the result of some experiment, or perhaps from sampling tabular data in a reference book.

There are many reasons why you might want an analytic formula to express the functional relationship inherent in the data. Often you will have experimental errors in the Y values. A good formula expression tends to smooth out these fluctuations. Perhaps you want to know the value of Y at some X not obtained exactly in the experiment. This may be a point between known X values (interpolation) or one outside the experimental range (extrapolation). If you wish to use the data in a computer program, a good formula is a convenient and efficient way to do it.

This program fits a curve of the form

$$Y = C_0 + C_1 X^1 + C_2 X^2 + \ldots + C_D X^D$$

to your data. You may select D, the degree (or power) of the highest term, to be as large as 7. The constant coefficients, C_0-C_D, are the main output of the program. Also calculated is the goodness of fit, a guide to the accuracy of the fit. You may fit different degree polynomials to the same data and also ask to have Y calculated for specific values of X.

The numerical technique involved in the computation is known as least squares curve fitting. It minimizes the sum of the squares of the errors. The least squares method reduces the problem to a set of simultaneous algebraic equations. Thus these equations could be solved by the algorithm used in SIMEQN. In fact, once the proper equations are set up, CURVE uses the identical subroutine found in SIMEQN to solve the equations. For more information, the bibliography contains references to descriptions of the numerical technique.

HOW TO USE IT

The first thing you must do, of course, is enter the data into the program. This consists of typing in the pairs of numbers. Each pair represents an X value and its corresponding Y value. The two numbers (of each pair) are separated by a comma. A question mark will prompt you for each data pair. After you have entered them all, type

999,999

to signal the end of the data. When you do this, the program will respond by indicating how many data pairs have been entered. A maximum of 100 data pairs is allowed.

Next, you must input the degree of the polynomial to be fitted. This can be any non-negative integer subject to certain constraints. The maximum allowed is 7. Also, D must be less than the number of data pairs.

A few notes regarding the selection of D may be of interest. If $D = 0$, the program will output the mean value of Y as the coefficient C_0. If $D = 1$, the program will be calculating the best straight line through the data. This special case is known as "linear regression." If D is one less than the number of data pairs, the program will find an exact fit to the data (barring round-off and other numerical errors). This is a solution which passes exactly through each data point.

Once you have entered the desired degree, the program will begin calculating the results. There may be a slight pause while this calculation is performed. The time involved depends on the number of data pairs and the degree selected.

The results are displayed in a table. It gives the values of the coefficients for each power of X from 0 to D. That is, the values of C_0-C_D are output. Also shown is the percent goodness of fit, a number between 0 and 100. This is a measure of how accurately the program was able to fit the given case. A value of 100 means perfect fit, lesser values indicate correspondingly poorer fits. It is hard to say what value denotes *satisfactory* fit since much depends on the accuracy of data and the purpose at hand. But as a rule of thumb, anything in the high nineties is quite good. For those interested, the formula to calculate the percent goodness of fit is

$$P.G.F. = 100* \sqrt{1 - \frac{\sum_i (Y_i - \hat{Y}_i)^2}{\sum_i (Y_i - \bar{Y})^2}}$$

where Y_i are the actual Y data values, $\hat{Y}_i$ are the calculated Y values (through the polynomial expression), and $\bar{Y}$ is the mean value of Y.

Next, you are presented with three options for continuing the run. These are 1) determining specific points, 2) fitting another degree, 3) ending the program. Simply type **1**, **2**, or **3** to make your selection. A description of each choice now follows.

Option 1 allows you to see the value of Y that the current fit will produce for a given value of X. In this mode you are continually prompted to supply any value of X. The program then shows what the polynomial expression produces as the value for Y. Input 999 for an X value to leave this mode.

Option 2 allows you to fit another degree polynomial to the same data. Frequently, you will want to try successively higher values of D to improve the goodness of fit. Unless round-off errors occur, this will cause the percent goodness of fit to increase.

Option 3 simply terminates the program and with that we will terminate this explanation of how to use CURVE.

SAMPLE PROBLEM AND RUN

Problem: An art investor is considering the purchase of Primo's masterpiece, "Frosted Fantasy." Since 1940, the painting has been for sale at auction seven times. Here is the painting's sales record from these auctions.

Year	Price
1940	$ 8000.
1948	$13000.
1951	$16000.
1956	$20000.
1962	$28000.
1968	$39000.
1975	$53000.

The painting is going to be sold at auction in 1983. What price should the investor expect to have to pay to purchase the painting? If he resold it in 1987, how much profit should he expect to make?

Solution: The investor will try to get a polynomial function that expresses the value of the painting as a function of the year. This is suitable for CURVE. The year will be represented by the variable X, and the price is shown by the variable Y. To keep the magnitude of the numbers small, the years will be expressed as elapsed years since 1900, and the price will be in units of $1000. (Thus a year of 40 represents 1940, a price of 8 represents $8000.)

SAMPLE RUN

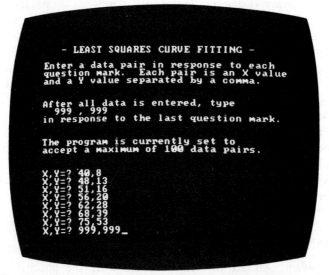

The operator enters the painting's previous auction sales records.

```
X,Y=? 75,53
X,Y=? 999,999

  7 data pairs entered.

Degree of polynomial to be fitted? 1

  X POWER          COEFFICIENT
  -------          -----------
     0              -48.27012
     1               1.287227

Percent Goodness of Fit = 97.53021

-- Continuation Options --

  1 - Determine specific points
  2 - Fit another degree to same data
  3 - End program

What next? 2_
```

He then selects a first degree fit to the data.

```
  2 - Fit another degree to same data
  3 - End program

What next? 2

Degree of polynomial to be fitted? 2

  X POWER          COEFFICIENT
  -------          -----------
     0               38.48421
     1              -1.835239
     2               2.703742E-02

Percent Goodness of Fit = 99.94857

-- Continuation Options --

  1 - Determine specific points
  2 - Fit another degree to same data
  3 - End program

What next? _
```

A second degree fit is attempted for the same data.

```
      1 - Determine specific points
      2 - Fit another degree to same data
      3 - End program
  What next? 1

  Enter 999 to leave this mode

  X=? 83
  Y=  72.42015

  X=? 87
  Y=  83.46465

  X=? 999
  -- Continuation Options --

      1 - Determine specific points
      2 - Fit another degree to same data
      3 - End program
  What next? 3_
```

The operator asks to see the predicted sales figures for 1983 and 1987.
He then exits from the program.

Initially, a first degree fit was tried and a percent goodness of
about 97 was obtained. The investor wanted to do better, so he
tried a second degree fit next. This had a very high goodness of
fit. He then asked for the extrapolation of his data to the years
1983 and 1987. He found that he should expect to pay about
$72400 to buy the painting in 1983. Around an $11000 profit
could be expected upon resale in 1987.

Of course, the investor did not make his decision solely on the
basis of this program. He used it only as one guide to his decision. There is never any guarantee that financial data will perform in the future as it has done in the past. Though CURVE is
probably as good a way as any, extrapolation of data can never
be a totally reliable process.

PROGRAM LISTING

```
100 REM: CURVE
110 REM: Least squares curve fitting.
120 REM: COPYRIGHT 1982 Phil Feldman and Tom Rugg.
130 REM: Any BASIC. any CRT.
```

```
140 KEY OFF:SCREEN 0,0,0,0:WIDTH 40:COLOR 7,0,0
150 CLEAR:CLS
160 MX=100
170 EF=999
180 MD=7
190 DIM X(MX),Y(MX)
200 Q=MD+1:DIM A(Q,Q),R(Q),V(Q)
210 Q=MD*2:DIM P(Q)
220 PRINT"   - LEAST SQUARES CURVE FITTING -":
    PRINT
230 PRINT"Enter a data pair in response to each"
240 PRINT"question mark.  Each pair is an X value"
250 PRINT"and a Y value separated by a comma.":
    PRINT
260 PRINT:PRINT"After all data is entered, type"
270 PRINT SPC(1);EF;",";EF
280 PRINT
    "in response to the last question mark.":PRINT
290 PRINT:PRINT"The program is currently set to"
300 PRINT"accept a maximum of";MX;"data pairs."
310 PRINT:PRINT:J=0
320 J=J+1:INPUT"X,Y=";X(J),Y(J)
330 IF X(J)=EF AND Y(J)=EF THEN J=J-1:GOTO 360
340 IF J=MX THEN PRINT:BEEP:
    PRINT"No More Data Allowed":GOTO 360
350 GOTO 320
360 NP=J:PRINT
370 IF NP=0 THEN GOSUB 760:
    PRINT"No data entered":STOP
380 PRINT NP;"data pairs entered.":PRINT
390 PRINT:INPUT
    "Degree of polynomial to be fitted";D:PRINT
400 IF D<0 THEN GOSUB 740:
    PRINT"Degree must be >= 0":GOTO 390
410 D=INT(D):IF D<NP THEN 430
420 GOSUB 740:PRINT"Not enough data":GOTO 390
430 D2=2*D:IF D>MD THEN GOSUB 740:
    PRINT"Degree too high":GOTO 390
440 N=D+1
450 FOR J=1 TO D2:P(J)=0:FOR K=1 TO NP
460 P(J)=P(J)+X(K)^J:NEXT:NEXT:P(0)=NP
470 R(1)=0:FOR J=1 TO NP:R(1)=R(1)+Y(J)
480 NEXT:IF N=1 THEN 510
490 FOR J=2 TO N:R(J)=0:FOR K=1 TO NP
500 R(J)=R(J)+Y(K)*X(K)^(J-1):NEXT:NEXT
510 FOR J=1 TO N:FOR K=1 TO N:A(J,K)=P(J+K-2):
    NEXT:NEXT
520 GOSUB 780
530 PRINT:
    PRINT SPC(1);"X POWER";SPC(6);"COEFFICIENT"
540 PRINT SPC(1);:FOR J=1 TO 7:PRINT"-";:NEXT:
    PRINT SPC(6);
```

```
550 FOR J=1 TO 11:PRINT"-";:NEXT:PRINT
560 FOR J=1 TO N:PRINT SPC(3);J-1,V(J):NEXT:
    PRINT:PRINT
570 Q=0:FOR J=1 TO NP:Q=Q+Y(J):NEXT:M=Q/NP:T=0:
    G=0:FOR J=1 TO NP
580 Q=0:FOR K=1 TO N:Q=Q+V(K)*X(J)^(K-1):NEXT:
    T=T+(Y(J)-Q)^2
590 G=G+(Y(J)-M)^2:NEXT:IF G=0 THEN T=100:GOTO 610
600 T=100*SQR(1-T/G)
610 PRINT"Percent Goodness of Fit =";T
620 PRINT:PRINT"-- Continuation Options --":PRINT
630 PRINT"  1 - Determine specific points"
640 PRINT"  2 - Fit another degree to same data"
650 PRINT"  3 - End program":PRINT
660 INPUT"What next";Q:Q=INT(Q):IF Q=3 THEN END
670 IF Q=2 THEN 390
680 IF Q<>1 THEN 620
690 PRINT:PRINT:
    PRINT"Enter";EF;"to leave this mode"
700 PRINT:INPUT"X=";XV:IF XV=EF THEN 620
710 YV=0:FOR K=1 TO N
720 YV=YV+V(K)*XV^(K-1):NEXT:PRINT"Y= ";YV
730 GOTO 700
740 PRINT"** ";:COLOR 23,0,0:PRINT"ERROR!";:
    COLOR 7,0,0
750 PRINT" ** -- ";:BEEP:RETURN
760 PRINT"** ";:COLOR 23,0,0:
    PRINT"FATAL ERROR!";:COLOR 7,0,0
770 PRINT" ** -- ";:BEEP:RETURN
780 IF N>1 THEN 800
790 V(1)=R(1)/A(1,1):RETURN
800 FOR K=1 TO N-1:M=K+1
810 L=K
820 Q=ABS(A(M,K))-ABS(A(L,K))
830 IF Q>0 THEN L=M
840 IF M<N THEN M=M+1:GOTO 820
850 IF L=K THEN 880
860 FOR J=K TO N:SWAP A(K,J),A(L,J):NEXT
870 SWAP R(K),R(L)
880 M=K+1
890 Q=A(M,K)/A(K,K):A(M,K)=0
900 FOR J=K+1 TO N
910 A(M,J)=A(M,J)-Q*A(K,J):NEXT
920 R(M)=R(M)-Q*R(K)
930 IF M<N THEN M=M+1:GOTO 890
940 NEXT
950 V(N)=R(N)/A(N,N)
960 FOR M=N-1 TO 1 STEP -1
970 Q=0:FOR J=M+1 TO N:Q=Q+A(M,J)*V(J)
980 V(M)=(R(M)-Q)/A(M,M):NEXT:NEXT:RETURN
```

EASY CHANGES

1. The program uses 999 as the flag number to terminate various input modes. This may cause a problem if your data include 999. You can easily change the flag number by modifying the value of EF in line 170 to any value not needed in your data. To use 10101, for example, make this change:

170 EF = 10101

2. To allow fits of higher degrees than seven, set MD in line 180 to the maximum degree desired. To achieve up to tenth degree fits, set the value of MD appropriately:

180 MD = 10

However, it must be stressed that it can be unreliable to attempt high degree fits. Unless your data is well behaved (X and Y values close to 1), the program will often not produce accurate results if D is greater than 5 or so. This is because sums of powers of X and Y are calculated up to powers of 2*D. These various sums are several orders of magnitude different from each other. Errors result because of the numerous truncation and round-off operations involved in doing arithmetic with them. A practical limit for MD is 7.

3. Currently a maximum value of 100 data pairs is allowed. If you need more, change the value of MX in line 160 to the number required. For example, to allow up to 300 data pairs, use

160 MX = 300

4. The demand on available RAM memory is increased if you raise the values of MD or MX as described in the above two easy Changes. As written, the program should run on a PC with 5K bytes free (see the Appendix). If your system has less you may need to decrease MD and/or MX to enable the program to run. Should MD or MX be set too large for your available memory an out of memory error will result after execution begins.

5. For some applications, significantly improved accuracy can be obtained by using "double-precision" computation. This can be achieved by simply inserting the following line:

155 DEFDBL A-H,P-Z

MAIN ROUTINES

150-180	Initializes constants.
190-210	Dimensions arrays.
220-300	Displays introductory messages.
310-380	Gets X-Y input data from the user.
390-440	Gets degree of polynomial from the user, determines if it is acceptable.
450-520	Sets up equations for the simultaneous equation solver and calls it.
530-610	Calculates goodness of fit, displays all results.
620-680	Gets user's continuation option and branches to it.
690-730	Determines Y value corresponding to any X value.
740-770	Subroutine to print flashing error messages.
780-980	Subroutine to solve simultaneous linear algebraic equations.

MAIN VARIABLES

MX	Maximum number of data pairs allowed.
MD	Maximum degree allowed to fit.
EF	Ending flag value for data input and X point mode.
X,Y	Arrays of X and Y data points.
NP	Number of data pairs entered.
D	Degree of polynomial to fit.
D2	2*D, the maximum power sum to compute.
N	D+1, number of simultaneous equations to solve.
A,R,V	Arrays for simultaneous linear equation solver.
P	Array for holding sums of various powers of X.
J,K,L,M	Loop indices.
Q,G	Work variables.
M	Mean value of Y.
T	Percent goodness of fit.
XV	Specific X point for which to calculate Y.
YV	Y value corresponding to XV.

SUGGESTED PROJECTS

1. No provision for modifying the data is incorporated into the program. Often it would be nice to add, subtract, or modify parts of the data after some results are seen. Build in a capability to do this.

2. You may desire other forms of output. A useful table for many applications might include the actual X values, calculated Y values, and/or percentage errors in Y.

3. Sometimes certain points (or certain regions of points) are known to be more accurate than others. It would be nice to weight these points as being more important than others. The least squares method can be modified to include such a weighting parameter with each data pair. Research this technique and incorporate it into the program. (Note: you can achieve some weighting with the current program by entering important points two or more times. There is a certain danger in this, however. You must only ask for a solution with D less than the number of *unique* data points. A division by zero error may result otherwise.)

4. Often you wish to try successively higher degree polynomials until a certain minimum goodness of fit is obtained. Modify the program to accept a minimally satisfactory goodness of fit from the user. Then have the program automatically try various polynomial fits until it finds the lowest degree fit, if any, with a satisfactory goodness of fit.

DIFFEQN

PURPOSE

Differential equations express functions by giving the rate of change of one variable with respect to another. This type of relation occurs regularly in almost all the physical sciences. The solution of these equations is necessary in many practical engineering problems.

For many such equations, a closed form (or exact analytical expression) solution can be obtained. However, for just as many, no such "simple" solution exists. The equation must then be solved numerically, usually by a computer program such as this.

There are many types and classes of differential equations. This program solves those of a simple type; namely, first order, ordinary differential equations. This means the equation to be solved can be written in the form

$$\frac{dY}{dX} = (\text{any function of } X, Y)$$

Here, X is the independent variable and Y is the dependent variable. The equation expresses the derivative (or rate of change) of Y with respect to X. The right-hand side is an expression which may involve X and/or Y.

To use the program, you must supply it with the differential equation to be solved. The procedure to do this is explained in the "How To Use It" section.

A technique known as the "fourth-order, Runge-Kutta" method is used to solve the equation. Space limitations prevent any detailed explanation of it here. However, it is discussed well in the numerical analysis books referenced in the bibliography.

The program allows two forms of output. The answers can be tabulated in columns or plotted graphically.

HOW TO USE IT

The first thing you must do is enter the differential equation into the program. This must be done at line 900. Currently this line contains a GOTO statement. This GOTO will cause an error message to be displayed if the program is run before you have changed line 900. The form of line 900 should be:

900 D = (your function of X,Y)

D represents dY/dX. GOSUBs are made to line 900 with X and Y set to their current values. Thus, when each RETURN is made, D will be set to the appropriate value of dY/dX for that given X and Y. If necessary, you may use the lines between 900 and 999 to complete the definition of D. Line 999 already contains a RETURN statement so you do not need to add another one.

The program begins by warning you that you should have already entered the equation at line 900. You acknowledge that this has been done by hitting the C or c key to continue.

Now the various initial conditions are input. You are prompted for them one at a time. They consist of: the initial values of X and Y, the stepsize interval in X at which to display the output, and the final value of X.

You now have a choice between two types of output. Enter a T (or t) for tabular output or a G (or g) for graphical output. The tabular form is simply a two-column display of the corresponding values of X and Y.

The graphical output plots the values of Y along a horizonal axis as each corresponding X value is displayed on successive lines of the screen. This graphical display requires you to input the minimum and maximum values of Y that will be used on the Y axis. You will be prompted for them if this output form is chosen. An asterisk (*) is used to plot the value of Y. If, however, the value of Y is "off-scale," an open circle is plotted at the appropriate edge of the graph.

With the input phase completed, the program initializes things to begin the output. A question mark will be displayed in the lower left of the screen, telling you the program is waiting for you to hit any key to begin the output.

The output is displayed at each interval of the stepsize until the final value of X is reached. Output may temporarily be halted at any time by simply hitting any key. This will stop the display until you hit any key to resume the output. The output may be started and stopped as often as desired, thus enabling you to leisurely view intermediate results before they scroll off the screen. It is applicable to both the tabular and graphical forms of output.

SAMPLE PROBLEM AND RUN

Problem: A body, originally at rest, is subjected to a force of 2000 dynes. Its initial mass is 200 grams. However, while it moves, it loses mass at the rate of 1 gram/sec. There is also an air resistance equal to twice its velocity retarding its movement. The differential equation expressing this motion is:

$$\frac{dY}{dX} = \frac{(2000 - 2Y)}{(200 - X)} \quad \text{where } Y = \text{velocity (cm./sec.)}$$
$$X = \text{time (sec.)}$$

Find the velocity of the body every 10 seconds up through two minutes. Also, plot this velocity as a function of time.

Solution and Sample Run: The solution and sample run are illustrated in the accompanying photographs.

```
************************************************
*                                              *
* The differential equation must be            *
* defined at line 900.  The form is            *
*                                              *
*    900 D = (Your function of X,Y)            *
*                                              *
* where D = DY/DX.                             *
*                                              *
************************************************
*                                              *
* If this has already been done, hit           *
* the 'C' key to continue.                     *
*                                              *
* If not, hit any other key.  Then             *
* enter line 900 and re-run the                *
* program.                                     *
*                                              *
************************************************

Ok
900 D=(2000-2*Y)/(200-X)
RUN
```

The operator hits a key to exit from the program. Then he enters the differential equation into line 900. He types RUN to restart the program.

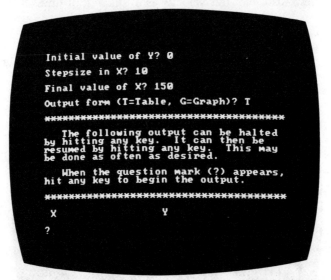

The operator has hit the "C" key. The program responds by beginning the input phase. The operator has responded to the first request.

The operator has completed the input. The program signals with a question mark that it is waiting for him to hit any key. It will not continue the run until he does so.

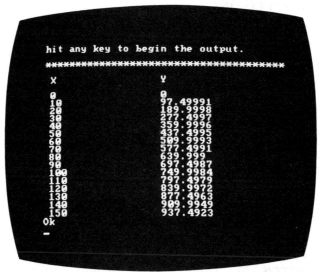

The operator hits a key and the program responds with the tabulated output. X is time in seconds and Y is velocity in cm./sec.

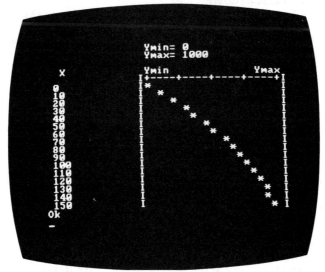

The graph is displayed as requested. The program waits for the operator to hit any key to end the program.

PROGRAM LISTING

```
100 REM: DIFFEQN
110 REM: Solve a differential equation.
120 REM: COPYRIGHT 1982 Phil Feldman and Tom Rugg.
130 REM: Any BASIC, any CRT.
140 KEY OFF:SCREEN 0,0,0,0:WIDTH 40:COLOR 7,0,0
150 CLEAR:CLS:DEF SEG:POKE 106,0:GOTO 280
160 IF F$="T" THEN PRINT XX;TAB(19);YY:
    GOSUB 250:RETURN
170 F=(YY-YL)/(YH-YL):V=INT(17+20*F+.5)
180 C=42:IF YY<YL THEN V=17:C=79
190 IF YY>YH THEN V=37:C=79
200 PRINT XX;TAB(16);CHR$(73);TAB(V);CHR$(C);
    TAB(38);CHR$(73)
210 GOSUB 250:RETURN
220 PRINT TAB(1);STRING$(38,42):RETURN
230 PRINT TAB(1);"*"; TAB( 38);"*": RETURN
240 PRINT TAB(38);"*": RETURN
250 R$=INKEY$:IF LEN(R$)=0 THEN RETURN
260 R$=INKEY$:IF LEN(R$)=0 THEN 260
270 RETURN
280 PRINT
    "First Order Differential Equation Solver"
290 GOSUB 220:GOSUB 230
300 PRINT TAB(1);"* The differential equation
    must be";: GOSUB 240
310 PRINT TAB(1);"* defined at line 900.  The
    form is";: GOSUB 240
320 GOSUB 230:PRINT TAB(1);"*    900 D = (Your
    function of X,Y)";: GOSUB 240
330 GOSUB 230:
    PRINT TAB(1);"* where D = DY/DX.";: GOSUB 240
340 GOSUB 230:GOSUB 220:GOSUB 230
350 PRINT TAB(1);"* If this has already been
    done, hit";: GOSUB 240
360 PRINT TAB(1);"* the 'C' key to continue.";:
    GOSUB 240
370 GOSUB 230:PRINT TAB(1);"* If not, hit any
    other key.  Then";: GOSUB 240
380 PRINT TAB(1);
    "* enter line 900 and re-run the";: GOSUB 240
390 PRINT TAB(1);"* program.";: GOSUB 240
400 GOSUB 230:GOSUB 220
410 R$=INKEY$:IF LEN(R$)=0 THEN 410
420 PRINT:IF R$<>"C" AND R$<>"c" THEN END
430 INPUT"Initial value of X";XX
440 PRINT:INPUT"Initial value of Y";YY:Y=YY:
    X=XX:GOSUB 900
450 PRINT:INPUT"Stepsize in X";DX
460 PRINT:INPUT"Final value of X";XF
470 PRINT:INPUT"Output form (T=Table, G=Graph)";F$
```

```
480 F$=LEFT$(F$,1):IF F$="t" THEN F$="T"
490 IF F$="g" THEN F$="G"
500 IF F$<>"T" AND F$<>"G" THEN 470
510 IF F$="T" THEN 580
520 PRINT:INPUT"Minimum Y for the graph axis";YL
530 PRINT:INPUT"Maximum Y for the graph axis";YH
540 IF YH>YL THEN 580
550 PRINT:BEEP
560 PRINT"*** Error! -- max Y must be > min Y ***"
570 GOTO 520
580 PRINT:GOSUB 220:PRINT
590 PRINT"   The following output can be halted"
600 PRINT"by hitting any key.  It can then be"
610 PRINT"resumed by hitting any key.  This may"
620 PRINT"be done as often as desired.": PRINT
630 PRINT"   When the question mark (?) appears,"
640 PRINT"hit any key to begin the output."
650 PRINT:GOSUB 220:PRINT
660 IF F$="T" THEN PRINT" X";TAB(20);"Y":GOTO 710
670 PRINT TAB(17);"Ymin=";YL:
    PRINT TAB( 17);"Ymax=";YH
680 PRINT:PRINT" X";TAB(17);"Ymin";TAB(34);"Ymax"
690 PRINT TAB(16);
700 PRINT"I+----+----+----+----+I";
710 PRINT:PRINT"?";
720 R$=INKEY$:IF LEN(R$)=0 THEN 720
730 PRINT CHR$(29);CHR$(32);CHR$(29);
740 DEF SEG:POKE 106,0: GOSUB 160
750 Q=XX+DX:IF Q>XF+9.999999E-06 THEN END
760 X=XX:Y=YY:GOSUB 900:K0=D:X=XX+DX/2:
    Y=YY+K0*DX/2
770 GOSUB 900:K1=D:Y=YY+K1*DX/2:GOSUB 900:K2=D
780 X=XX+DX:Y=YY+K2*DX:GOSUB 900:K3=D
790 DY=DX*(K0+2*K1+2*K2+K3)/6
800 YY=YY+DY:XX=XX+DX:GOSUB 160
810 GOTO 750
820 PRINT:
    PRINT"*** Error! -- You have not defined"
830 PRINT SPC( 11);"the differential equation"
840 PRINT SPC( 11);"in line 900.":BEEP:END
850 REM *********************************************
    ******************
860 REM Define the differential equation
    between lines 900 and 999
870 REM -------------------------------------------
    ------------------
880 REM Line 900 must be made the first line of
    the equation
890 REM *********************************************
    ******************
900 GOTO 820:REM-Redefine this line to be
    D=(Your function of X,Y)
999 RETURN
```

EASY CHANGES

1. If you have already entered the differential equation and wish to skip the introductory output, change line 280 to

    280 GOTO 430

    This will immediately begin the input dialog.

2. If you wish to use negative stepsizes, line 750 must be changed to:

    750 Q = XX + DX:IF Q < XF − 9.999999E − 06 THEN END

MAIN ROUTINES

150	Begins execution.
160-210	Displays output.
220-240	Subroutine to format messages.
250-270	Subroutine to stop and start output.
280-400	Displays initial messages.
410-570	Gets user's inputs.
580-650	Displays additional messages.
660-700	Initializes output display.
710-740	Waits for user to hit a key to start the output.
750-810	Computes each step.
820-840	Error message.
900-999	User supplied subroutine to define D.

MAIN VARIABLES

D	Value of dY/dX.
X,Y	Values of X,Y on current step.
XX,YY	Values of X,Y on last step.
DX	Stepsize in X.
XF	Final value of X.
F$	Output flag string (T = table, G = graph).
YL,YH	Minimum, maximum values of Y plot axis.
F	Fractional distance of graphical point along Y axis.
V	Tab position for graphical output.
C	Used with CHR$; represents an ASCII value of a graphics character.
K0,K1, K2,K3	Runge-Kutta coefficients.
R$	User entered string.
Q	Work variable.

SUGGESTED PROJECTS

1. Modify the program to display the tabular output followed by the graphical output. During the tabular phase, the minimum and maximum values of Y can be saved and automatically used as the plot limits for the graphical output.
2. The value of dY/dX as a function of X is often a useful quantity to know. Modify the program to add it to the columnar display and/or the graphical display.
3. The inherent error in the calculation depends on the stepsize chosen. Most cases should be run with different stepsizes to insure the errors are not large. If the answers do not change much, you can be reasonably certain that your solutions are accurate. Better yet, techniques exist to vary the stepsize during the calculation to insure the error is sufficiently small during each step. Research these methods and incorporate them into the program.
4. The program can be easily broadened to solve a set of coupled, first order, differential equations simultaneously. This would greatly increase the types of problems that could be solved. Research this procedure and expand the program to handle it.

GRAPH

PURPOSE

Is a picture worth a thousand words? In the case of mathematical functions, the answer is often yes. A picture, i.e. a graph, enables you to see the important behavior of a function quickly and accurately. Trends, minima, maxima, etc. become easy and convenient to determine.

GRAPH produces a two-dimensional plot of a function that you supply. The function must be in the form Y = (any function of X). The independent variable X will be plotted along the abscissa (horizontal axis). The dependent variable Y will be plotted along the ordinate (vertical axis). You have complete control over the scaling that is used on the X and Y axes.

HOW TO USE IT

A graphics interface card is required to run this program. You must enter the function to be plotted before this program will run. This is done as a subroutine beginning at line 800. It must define Y as a function of X. The subroutine will be called with X define Y as a function of X. The subroutine will be called with X set to various values. It must then set the variable Y to the correct corresponding value. The subroutine may be as simple or as complex as necessary to define the function. It can take one line or several lines. Line 999 is already set as a RETURN statement, so you need not add another one.

Having entered this subroutine, you are ready to run the program. The program begins by warning you that it assumes the function has already been entered at line 800. It will then ask you for the domain of X, i.e., the lowest and highest values of X that you wish to have plotted. Values can be positive or negative as long as the highest value is actually larger than the lowest one.

Now you must choose the scale for Y. To do this intelligently, you probably need to know the minimum and maximum values of Y over the domain of X selected. The program finds these values and displays them for you. You must then choose the minimum and maximum values you wish to have on the Y scale. Again, any two values are acceptable as long as the maximum scale value of Y is larger than the minimum scale value of Y.

The program will now display the plot of your function. Each axis is twenty tick intervals long, with the origin defined as the minimum scale values of both X and Y. The minimum, middle, and maximum values on each axis are displayed appropriately. (Note: in certain cases, the program will not display the middle scale value on the X-axis.)

The actual plot is drawn with eight times the resolution shown by the tick-marks on the axes. That is, 160 values of X and Y are plotted. Medium resolution graphics are employed.

All axis labelling and "in-bounds" plotting are done in black and white. If a value for Y should be "off-scale" however, a special colored line will be displayed at the appropriate value of X. If the actual value of Y is too large, it will be plotted at the maximum Y value. Similarly, it will be drawn at the minimum Y value if it is too low. (See Easy Change 3.) These colored lines can be detected on a black and white monitor for they have a different texture than the normal white lines. In addition, the speaker is sounded whenever an off-scale point is plotted.

After the plot is drawn, the program will tell you to hit any key to erase the graph and return to text display mode.

Graph   263

SAMPLE RUN

```
Ok
800 Y=SIN(X)
RUN
```

After loading the program, the operator enters line 800 to request the graph Y = SIN(X). RUN is typed to begin the program.

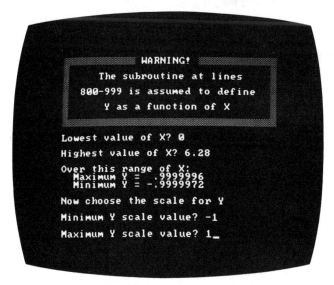

```
                  WARNING!
            The subroutine at lines
        800-999 is assumed to define
             Y as a function of X

Lowest value of X? 0
Highest value of X? 6.28
Over this range of X:
   Maximum Y =  .9999996
   Minimum Y = -.9999972
Now choose the scale for Y
Minimum Y scale value? -1
Maximum Y scale value? 1_
```

The input dialog transpires. The operator asks that the domain of X be 0-6.28. The program responds by showing the maximum and minimum value of Y over this domain. The operator chooses an appropriate scale for the Y axis.

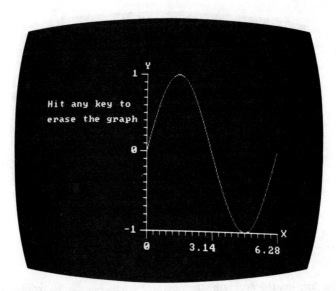

The graph is displayed as requested. The program waits for the operator
to hit any key to end the program.

PROGRAM LISTING

```
100 REM: GRAPH
110 REM: Plot a user supplied function.
120 REM: COPYRIGHT 1982 Phil Feldman and Tom Rugg.
130 REM: Any BASIC, graphics interface card.
140 KEY OFF:SCREEN 0,1,0,0:WIDTH 40:COLOR 7,0,0
150 CLEAR:CLS
160 PRINT TAB(13)"G R A P H":PRINT:D$=CHR$(177)
170 PRINT STRING$(12,177);SPC(1);:COLOR 23
180 PRINT"WARNING!";:COLOR 7:
    PRINT SPC(1);STRING$(12,177)
190 GOSUB 250:PRINT D$;TAB(7);
200 PRINT"The subroutine at lines";TAB(34);D$:
    GOSUB 250
210 PRINT D$;SPC(2);
    "800-999 is assumed to define";
220 PRINT SPC(2);D$:GOSUB 250:PRINT D$;TAB(8);
230 PRINT"Y as a function of X";TAB(34);D$:
    GOSUB 250
240 PRINT STRING$(34,177):GOTO 260
250 PRINT D$;TAB(34);D$:RETURN
260 PRINT:INPUT"Lowest value of X";XL
270 PRINT:INPUT"Highest value of X";XU
```

Graph   265

```
280 IF XU>XL THEN 300
290 PRINT:COLOR 23:BEEP:
    PRINT"** Bad X range **":COLOR 7:GOTO 260
300 XM=(XL+XU)/2
310 DX=(XU-XL)/160:X=XL:GOSUB 800:MN=Y:MX=Y
320 FOR J=1 TO 160:X=XL+J*DX:GOSUB 800:
    IF Y>MX THEN MX=Y
330 IF Y<MN THEN MN=Y
340 NEXT
350 PRINT:PRINT"Over this range of X:"
360 PRINT"  Maximum Y = ";MX
370 PRINT"  Minimum Y = ";MN:PRINT
380 PRINT"Now choose the scale for Y":PRINT
390 INPUT"Minimum Y scale value";YL:PRINT
400 INPUT"Maximum Y scale value";YU
410 IF YU>YL THEN 430
420 PRINT:COLOR 23:BEEP:
    PRINT"** Bad Y range **":COLOR 7:GOTO 350
430 XC=139:YC=172:SCREEN 1:COLOR 0,1:C=1
440 LINE (XC-8,YC)-(XC+160,YC):
    LINE (XC,YC+8)-(XC,YC-160)
450 FOR J=8 TO 160 STEP 8:
    LINE (XC+J,YC)-(XC+J,YC+4)
460 LINE (XC,YC-J)-(XC-4,YC-J):NEXT
470 FOR J=80 TO 160 STEP 80:
    LINE (XC+J,YC)-(XC+J,YC+8)
480 LINE (XC,YC-J)-(XC-8,YC-J):NEXT
490 LOCATE 22,39:PRINT"X":LOCATE 1,18:PRINT"Y"
500 XU$=STR$(XU):XM$=STR$(XM):XL$=STR$(XL)
510 L=LEN(XL$):LOCATE 24,19-L:PRINT XL$;
520 L=LEN(XU$):LOCATE 24,39-L:PRINT XU$;
530 IF L>9 THEN 550
540 L=LEN(XM$):LOCATE 24,29-L:
    IF L<10 THEN PRINT XM$;
550 YM=(YL+YU)/2:YU$=STR$(YU):YM$=STR$(YM):
    YL$=STR$(YL)
560 L=LEN(YU$):LOCATE 2,17-L:PRINT YU$;
570 L=LEN(YM$):LOCATE 12,17-L:PRINT YM$;
580 L=LEN(YL$):LOCATE 22,17-L:PRINT YL$;
590 DY=(YU-YL)/160:F=0:X=XL:GOSUB 800
600 IF Y>YU THEN F=2
610 IF Y<YL THEN F=1
620 V=(Y-YL)/DY:IF F=0 THEN PSET(XC,YC-V):GOTO 650
630 IF F=1 THEN PSET(XC,YC),C:BEEP:GOTO 650
640 PSET(XC,YC-160),C:BEEP
650 FOR J=1 TO 160:X=X+DX:GOSUB 800:F=0
660 IF Y>YU THEN F=2
670 IF Y<YL THEN F=1
680 V=(Y-YL)/DY:IF F=0 THEN LINE -(XC+J,YC-V),3:
    GOTO 710
690 IF F=1 THEN LINE -(XC+J,YC),C:BEEP:GOTO 710
```

```
700 LINE -(XC+J,YC-160),C:BEEP
710 NEXT
720 LOCATE 6,2:PRINT"Hit any key to";
730 LOCATE 8,2:PRINT"erase the graph";
740 DEF SEG:POKE 106,0
750 D$=INKEY$:IF LEN(D$)=0 THEN 750
760 DEF SEG:POKE 106,0
770 SCREEN 0:COLOR 7,0:CLS
780 END
790 REM: ********************************
800 REM: The subroutine to define Y as a
810 REM: function of X begins at line 800
820 REM: ********************************
999 RETURN
```

EASY CHANGES

1. You may want the program to self-scale the Y axis for you.
    That is, you want it to use the minimum and maximum Y
    values that it finds as the limits on the Y axis. This can be ac-
    complished by adding the following lines:

    342 IF MX< =MN THEN 350
    345 YU=MX:YL=MN:GOTO 430

2. Do you sometimes forget to enter the subroutine at line 800
    despite the introductory warning? As is, the program will
    plot the straight line $Y=0$ if you do this. If you want a more
    drastic reaction to prevent this, change line 800 to read

    800 PRINT "FUNCTION NOT DEFINED":END

    Now, if you don't enter the actual subroutine desired, the
    program will stop and print the "function not defined"
    message after you enter the X scaling values.

3. The colors used for the axes function and scale labelling are
    controlled by the COLOR statement in line 430. Currently
    palette 1 is selected with a background color of black. Color
    3 is always selected for the plotting. (This is white with
    palette 1 or brown with palette 0.) You may adjust the
    palette and/or background color by altering the values of
    the parameters used with the COLOR statement. The color
    of off-axis points is set by the variable C in line 430. You
    may change this color by setting $C=2$ and/or changing the
    palette in the COLOR statement. For example, to get brown
    plotting on a cyan background with red off-axis points,
    change line 430 to

Graph   267

430 XC = 139:YC = 172:SCREEN 1:COLOR 3,0:C = 2

4. Currently, legitimate points plotted on the X axis (that is
    with Y equal to exactly Y minimum) are hard to see because
    they lie right on the axis itself. If you wish the speaker to
    sound an alert that this is happening, add the following line

655 IF Y = YL THEN BEEP

MAIN ROUTINES

150-250	Displays introductory warning.
260-290	Gets X scaling from user.
300-420	Determines the minimum, maximum Y values; gets Y scale from user.
430-580	Draws graph axes and scale labeling.
590-730	Plots the function.
740-780	Waits for user to hit a key to return to text display mode.
800-999	User supplied subroutine to evaluate Y as a function of X.

MAIN VARIABLES

XL,XM, XU	Lower, middle, upper scale values of X.
YL,YM, YU	Lower, middle, upper scale values of Y.
DX,DY	Scale increments of X,Y.
X,Y	Current values of X,Y.
F	Plot point status flag (0 = Y in bounds, 1 = Y too low, 2 = Y too high).
V	Offset value of Y in scale units.
MN,MX	Minimum, maximum values of Y.
J	Loop index.
C	Off-axis color code.
L	String length.
XC,YC	X,Y values of graph origin.
D$	Temporary string variable.
XL$,XM$ YU$	String representation of XL, XM, XU.
YL$,YM$ YU$	String representation of YL, YM, YU.

SUGGESTED PROJECTS

1. Determine and display the values of X at which the minimum values of Y occur.
2. After the graph is plotted, allow the user to obtain the exact value of Y for any given X.

INTEGRATE

PURPOSE AND DEFINITION

The need to evaluate integrals occurs frequently in much scientific and mathematical work. This program will numerically integrate a function that you supply using a technique known as Simpson's rule. It will continue to grind out successive approximations of the integral until you are satisfied with the accuracy of the solution.

Mathematical integration will probably be a familiar term to those who have studied some higher mathematics. It is a fundamental subject of second-year calculus. The integral of a function between the limits $x = l$ (lower limit) and $x = u$ (upper limit) represents the area under its curve; i.e., the shaded area in Figure 1.

We may approximate the integral by first dividing up the area into rectangular strips or segments. We can get a good estimate of the total integral by summing the areas of these segments by using a parabolic fit across the top. For those who understand some mathematical theory, Simpson's rule may be expressed as

$$\int_{x=l}^{x=u} f(x)dx \cong \frac{\Delta}{3} \left\{ f(l) + f(u) \right.$$

$$\left. + 4 \sum_{j=1}^{N/2} f[l + \Delta(2j - 1)] + 2 \sum_{j=1}^{(N-2)/2} f[l + 2\Delta j] \right\}$$

Here N is the number of segments into which the total interval is divided. N is 4 in the diagram.

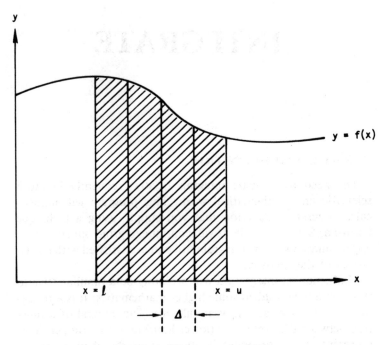

Figure 1. The Integral of f(x)

For a good discussion of the numerical evaluation of integrals see: McCracken, Dorn, *Numerical Methods and Fortran Programming* (New York, Wiley, 1964, pp. 160). Don't let the word "Fortran" scare you away. The discussions in the book are independent of programming language with only some program examples written in Fortran.

HOW TO USE IT

The program begins with a warning! This is to remind you that you should have already entered the subroutine to evaluate Y as a function of X. This subroutine must start at line 2000. More about it shortly.

You will then be asked to provide the lower and upper limits of the integration domain. Any numerical values are acceptable. It is not even necessary that the lower limit of X be smaller than the upper one.

The program will now begin displaying its numerical evaluations of the integral. The number of segments used in the calculation continually doubles. This causes the accuracy of the integral to increase at the expense of additional computation time. For most functions, you should see the value of the integral converging quickly to a constant (or near constant) value. This, of course, will be the best numerical evaluation of the integral at hand.

When you are satisfied with the accuracy of the solution, you must hit the **Ctrl** and **Break** keys to terminate the program. If not, the program will run forever (assuming you can pay the electric bills). The amount of computation is approximately doubled each step. This means it will take the computer about the same amount of time to compute the next step that it took to compute *all* the previous steps. Thus, it will soon be taking the computer hours, days, and weeks to compute steps. Eventually, round-off errors begin degrading the results, causing a nice, constant, converged solution to change. However, the high precision of the computer's floating point arithmetic will postpone this for quite a while. You will probably lose patience before seeing it.

The function to be integrated can be as simple or as complicated as you desire. It may take one line or a few hundred lines of code. In any case, the subroutine to express it must start at line 2000. This subroutine will be continually called with the variable X set. When it returns, it should have set the variable Y to the corresponding value of the function for the given X. The subroutine must be able to evaluate the function at any value of X between the lower and upper bounds of the integration domain.

If your function consists of experimental data at discrete values of X, you must do something to enable the subroutine to evaluate the function at intermediate values of X. We recommend one of two approaches. First, you could write the subroutine to linearly interpolate the value of Y between the appropriate values of X. This will involve searching your data table for the pair of experimental X values that bound the value of X where the function is to be evaluated. Secondly, the program CURVE presented elsewhere in this section can produce an approximate polynomial expression to fit your experimental data. This expression can then be easily entered as the subroutine at line 2000.

By the way, Simpson's rule is *exact* for any polynomial of degree 3 or less. This means that if the function can be written in the form

$$Y = A*X*X*X + B*X*X + C*X + D$$

where A, B, C, D are constants, the program will calculate the integral exactly even with only two segments.

SAMPLE RUN

The sample run illustrates the following integration

$$\int_{x=0}^{x=1} \frac{4}{1+x^2} \, dx$$

This integral has the theoretical value of π (pi) as the correct answer! Pi, as you may know, has the value 3.1415926535.... Before the run is started, the above function is entered at line 2000.

```
Ok
2000 Y=4/(1+X*X)
RUN
```

The integrand function is entered at line 2000 and RUN is typed to start the program.

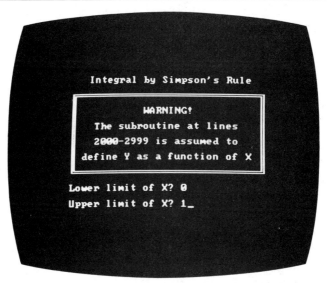

The upper and lower bounds of the integration are input as requested.

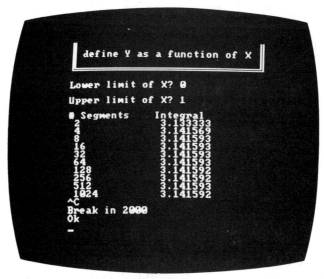

The results are computed up to 1024 segments. Then the **Ctr Break** is pressed to terminate the calculation.

PROGRAM LISTING

```
100 REM: INTEGRATE
110 REM: Compute integrals by Simpson's rule.
120 REM: COPYRIGHT 1982 Phil Feldman and Tom Rugg.
130 REM: Any BASIC, any CRT.
140 KEY OFF:SCREEN 0,0,0,0:WIDTH 40:COLOR 7,0,0
150 CLEAR:CLS
160 N=2
170 PRINT TAB(4)"Integral by Simpson's Rule":B=186
180 PRINT:PRINT CHR$(201)STRING$(29,
    205)CHR$(187):GOSUB 270
190 PRINT CHR$(B)TAB(13)
    "WARNING!"TAB(31)CHR$(B):GOSUB 270
200 PRINT CHR$(B)TAB(5)
    "The subroutine at lines"TAB(31)CHR$(B)
210 GOSUB 270
220 PRINT CHR$(B)TAB(5)
    "2000-2999 is assumed to"TAB(31)CHR$(B)
230 GOSUB 270
240 PRINT CHR$(B)TAB(3)
    "define Y as a function of X"TAB(31)CHR$(B)
250 GOSUB 270:
    PRINT CHR$(200)STRING$(29,205)CHR$(188)
260 GOTO 280
270 PRINT CHR$(B)TAB(31)CHR$(B):RETURN
280 PRINT:INPUT"Lower limit of X";L
290 PRINT:INPUT"Upper limit of X";U
300 PRINT
310 PRINT"# Segments","Integral"
320 DX=(U-L)/N:T=0
330 X=L:GOSUB 2000:T=T+Y
340 X=U:GOSUB 2000:T=T+Y
350 M=N/2:Z=0
360 FOR J=1 TO M
370 X=L+DX*(2*J-1):GOSUB 2000
380 Z=Z+Y:NEXT:T=T+4*Z
390 M=M-1:IF M=0 THEN 430
400 Z=0:FOR J=1 TO M
410 X=L+DX*2*J:GOSUB 2000:Z=Z+Y
420 NEXT:T=T+2*Z
430 A=DX*T/3
440 PRINT N,A
450 N=N*2
460 GOTO 320
1970 REM ****
1980 REM **** Enter Subroutine At Line 2000
1990 REM ****
2000 REM **** Y=F(X) Goes Here ************
2999 RETURN
```

EASY CHANGES

1. You might want the program to stop calculation after the integral has been evaluated for a given number of segments. Adding the following line will cause the program to stop after the integral is evaluated for a number of segments greater than or equal to 100.

    445 IF N> =100 THEN END

    Of course, you may use any value you wish instead of 100.

2. Perhaps you would like to see the number of segments change at a different rate during the course of the calculation. This can be done by modifying line 450. To increase the rate of change, try

    450 N=N*4

    to change it at a constant (and slower) rate, try

    450 N=N+50

    Be sure, however, that the value of N is always even.

3. Take advantage of BASIC's double-precision to compute the results to a high degree of accuracy. Simply add the following line:

    155 DEFDBL A-Z: DEFSNG J,M,N

    How long does it take to compute pi to 15 correct decimal digits?

MAIN ROUTINES

150- 160	Initializes constants.
170- 260	Displays introductory messages and warning.
270	Graphics display subroutine.
280- 290	Gets integration limits from operator.
300- 310	Displays column headings.
320- 340	Computes integral contribution from end points.
350- 380	Adds contribution from one summation.
390- 420	Adds contribution from other summation.
430- 460	Completes integral calculation and displays it. Increases number of segments and restarts calculation.
2000-2999	Operator supplied subroutine to evaluate f(x).

MAIN VARIABLES

N	Number of segments.
J	Loop index.
L,U	Lower, Upper integration limit of x.
DX	Width of one segment.
T	Partial result of integral.
M	Number of summations.
Z	Subtotal of summations.
A	Value of integral.
X	Current value of x.
Y	Current value of the function $y = f(x)$.
B	ASCII value of border character.

SUGGESTED PROJECTS

1. Research other similar techniques for numerical integration such as the simpler trapezoid rule. Then compute the integral with this new method. Compare how the two methods converge toward the (hopefully) correct answer.

SIMEQN

PURPOSE

This program solves a set of simultaneous linear algebraic equations. This type of problem often arises in scientific and numerical work. Algebra students encounter them regularly — many "word" problems can be solved by constructing the proper set of simultaneous equations.

An IBM PC with 5K free bytes of memory can handle up to fifteen unknowns in fifteen equations. This should prove more than sufficient for any practical application.

The equations to be solved can be written mathematically as follows:

$$A_{11}X_1 + A_{12}X_2 + \ldots + A_{1N}X_N = R_1$$
$$A_{21}X_1 + A_{22}X_2 + \ldots + A_{2N}X_N = R_2$$

$$\ldots \qquad \ldots \qquad \ldots \qquad \ldots$$
$$\ldots \qquad \ldots \qquad \ldots \qquad \ldots$$

$$A_{N1}X_1 + A_{N2}X_2 + \ldots + A_{NN}X_N = R_N$$

N is the number of equations and thus the number of unknowns also. The unknowns are denoted X_1 through X_N.

Each equation contains a coefficient multiplier for each unknown and a right-hand-side term. These coefficients (the A matrix) and the right-hand-sides (R_1 through R_N) must be constants — positive, negative, or zero. The A matrix is denoted with doubled subscripts. The first subscript is the equation number and the second one is the unknown that the coefficient multiplies.

HOW TO USE IT

The program will prompt you for all necessary inputs. First, it asks how many equations (and thus how many unknowns) comprise your set. This number must be at least 1. If it is too large, an "Out of memory" or "Subscript out of range" error will immediately result.

Next, you must enter the coefficients and right-hand-sides for each equation. The program will request these one at a time, continually indicating which term it is expecting next.

Once it has all your inputs, the program begins calculating the solution. This may take a little while if the value of N is high. The program ends by displaying the answers. These, of course, are the values of each of the unknowns, X_1 through X_N.

If you are interested, the numerical technique used to solve the equations is known as Gaussian elimination. Row interchange to achieve pivotal condensation is employed. (This keeps maximum significance in the numbers.) Then back substitution is used to arrive at the final results. This technique is much simpler than it sounds and is described well in the numerical analysis books referenced in the bibliography.

SAMPLE PROBLEM AND RUN

Problem: A painter has a large supply of three different colors of paint: dark green, light green, and pure blue. The dark green is 30% blue pigment, 20% yellow pigment, and the rest base. The light green is 10% blue pigment, 35% yellow pigment, and the rest base. The pure blue is 90% blue pigment, no yellow pigment, and the rest base. The painter, however, needs a medium green to be composed of 25% blue pigment, 25% yellow pigment, and the rest base. In what percentages should he mix his three paints to achieve this mixture?

Solution: Let $X_1 =$ percent of dark green to use,
$X_2 =$ percent of light green to use,
$X_3 =$ percent of pure blue to use.

The problem leads to these three simultaneous equations to solve:

$$0.3\,X_1 + 0.1\ \ X_2 + 0.9\,X_3 = 0.25$$
$$0.2\,X_1 + 0.35\,X_2 \qquad\qquad = 0.25$$
$$X_1 + \qquad X_2 + \qquad X_3 = 1.0$$

The first equation expresses the amount of blue pigment in the mixture. The second equation is for the yellow pigment. The third equation states that the mixture is composed entirely of the three given paints. (Note that all percentages are expressed as numbers from 0-1.) The problem leads to the following use of SIMEQN.

SAMPLE RUN

```
        A SIMULTANEOUS LINEAR EQUATION
                    SOLVER
Number of equations? 3

The 3 unknowns will be denoted
X1 through X3
_____


Enter values for equation 1

Coefficient of X1? .3
Coefficient of X2? .1
Coefficient of X3? .9
Right hand side? .25_
```

The operator chooses to solve a set of three simultaneous equations and then enters the coefficients for the first equation.

```
Coefficient of X1? .3
Coefficient of X2? .1
Coefficient of X3? .9
Right hand side? .25


Enter values for equation 2

Coefficient of X1? .2
Coefficient of X2? .35
Coefficient of X3? 0
Right hand side? .25


Enter values for equation 3

Coefficient of X1? 1
Coefficient of X2? 1
Coefficient of X3? 1
Right hand side? 1_
```

The coeffiecients for the remaining two equations are entered.

```
Coefficient of X2? .35
Coefficient of X3? 0
Right hand side? .25


Enter values for equation 3

Coefficient of X1? 1
Coefficient of X2? 1
Coefficient of X3? 1
Right hand side? 1


The solution is

   X1= .55
   X2= .4
   X3= .05
Ok
-
```

The computer provides the solution. The painter should use a mixture
of 55% dark green, 40% light green, and 5% pure blue.

PROGRAM LISTING

```
100 REM: SIMEQN
110 REM: A simultaneous linear equation solver.
120 REM: COPYRIGHT 1982 Phil Feldman and Tom Rugg.
130 REM: Any BASIC, any CRT.
140 KEY OFF:SCREEN 0,0,0,0:WIDTH 40:COLOR 7,0,0
150 CLEAR:CLS:DEFINT J,K,L,M,N
160 PRINT TAB(5) "A SIMULTANEOUS LINEAR EQUATION"
170 PRINT TAB(17) "SOLVER"
180 PRINT
190 INPUT "Number of equations";N
200 IF N>0 THEN 230
210 PRINT:BEEP
220 PRINT "There must be at least 1 !":GOTO 180
230 DIM A(N,N),R(N),V(N)
240 PRINT
250 PRINT"The";N;"unknowns will be denoted"
260 PRINT"X1 through X";MID$(STR$(N),2)
270 GOSUB 380:FOR J=1 TO N
280 PRINT"Enter values for equation";J
290 PRINT:FOR K=1 TO N
300 PRINT"Coefficient of X";MID$(STR$(K),2);
310 INPUT A(J,K):NEXT
320 INPUT"Right hand side";R(J)
330 GOSUB 380:NEXT:GOSUB 390
340 PRINT"The solution is"
350 PRINT:FOR J=1 TO N
360 PRINT"  X";MID$(STR$(J),2);"=";V(J)
370 NEXT:END
380 PRINT:PRINT STRING$(40,205):PRINT:RETURN
390 IF N>1 THEN 410
400 V(1)=R(1)/A(1,1):RETURN
410 FOR K=1 TO N-1:M=K+1
420 L=K
430 Q=ABS(A(M,K))-ABS(A(L,K))
440 IF Q>0 THEN L=M
450 IF M<N THEN M=M+1:GOTO 430
460 IF L=K THEN 490
470 FOR J=K TO N:SWAP A(K,J),A(L,J):NEXT
480 SWAP R(K),R(L)
490 M=K+1
500 Q=A(M,K)/A(K,K):A(M,K)=0
510 FOR J=K+1 TO N
520 A(M,J)=A(M,J)-Q*A(K,J):NEXT
530 R(M)=R(M)-Q*R(K)
540 IF M<N THEN M=M+1:GOTO 500
550 NEXT
560 V(N)=R(N)/A(N,N)
570 FOR M=N-1 TO 1 STEP -1
580 Q=0:FOR J=M+1 TO N:Q=Q+A(M,J)*V(J)
590 V(M)=(R(M)-Q)/A(M,M):NEXT:NEXT:RETURN
```

EASY CHANGES

You may be surprised sometime to see the program end after indicating that division by zero has occured; or display meaningless results after indicating that overflow has occured. This means your input coefficients (the A array) were ill-conditioned and no solution was possible. This can arise from a variety of causes; e.g., if one equation is an exact multiple of another, or if *every* coefficient of one particular unknown is zero. If you would like the program to print a diagnostic message in most of these cases and suppress the answers, add these lines:

```
552 IF A(N,N)< >0 THEN 560
554 PRINT "Bad input—no solution possible"
556 BEEP:END
585 IF A(M,M)=0 THEN 554
```

MAIN ROUTINES

150-180	Clears screen and displays program title.
190-330	Gets input from user and calculates the solution.
340-370	Displays the solution.
380	Subroutine to space and separate the output.
390-590	Subroutine to calculate the solution; consisting of the following parts:
390-400	Forms solution if $N=1$.
410-550	Gaussian elimination.
420-490	Interchanges rows to achieve pivotal condensation.
560-590	Back substitution.

MAIN VARIABLES

J,K,L,M	Loop indices and subscripts.
N	Number of equations (thus number of unknowns also).
A	Doubly dimensioned array of the coefficients.
R	Array of right-hand-sides.
V	Array of the solution.
Q	Work variable.

SUGGESTED PROJECTS

1. The program modifies the A and R arrays while computing the answer. This means the original input cannot be dis-

played after it is input. Modify the program to save the information and enable the user to retrieve it after the solution is given.

2. Currently, a mistake in typing input cannot be corrected once the **ENTER** key is pressed after typing a number. Modify the program to allow correcting previous input.

STATS

PURPOSE

Ever think of yourself as a statistic? Many times we lament at how we have become just numbers in various computer memories, or we simply moan at our insurance premiums. To most people, the word "statistics" carries a negative connotation. To invoke statistics is almost to be deceitful, or at least dehumanizing. But really, we all use statistical ideas regularly. When we speak of things like "she was average height" or the "hottest weather in years," we are making observations in statistical terms. It is difficult not to encounter statistics in our lives, and this book is no exception.

Of course, when used properly, statistics can be a powerful, analytical tool. STATS analyzes a set of numerical data that you provide. It will compile your list, order it sequentially, and/or determine several statistical parameters which describe it.

This should prove useful in a wide variety of applications. Teachers might determine grades by analyzing a set of test scores. A businessman might determine marketing strategy by studying a list of sales to clients. Little leaguers always like to pore over the current batting and pitching averages. You can probably think of many other applications.

HOW TO USE IT

First, press the CAPS LOCK key before beginning data entry. The program starts by asking whether or not you wish to use identifiers with the data values. These identifiers can be anything associated with the data: e.g., names accompanying test scores, cities accompanying population values, corporations accompanying sales figures, etc. Hit the **Y** or **N** key (and **ENTER**) to indicate your choice.

Next, your data list must be entered. The program will prompt you for each value with a question mark. If identifiers are being used, you will be prompted for them before being asked for the associated data value. You may use any length character strings you desire for identifiers. However, if you limit them to a maximum of 18 characters, the formatting of later output will be "cleaner." Two special inputs, *END and *BACK, may be used at any time during this data input phase. They're applicable whether or not identifiers are being used. To signal the end of data, input the four character string, *END, in response to the (last) question mark. You must, of course, enter at least one data value.

If you discover that you have made a mistake, the five character string, *BACK, can be used to back up the input process. This will cause the program to re-prompt you for the previous entry. By successive uses of *BACK you can return to any previous position.

With the input completed, the program enters a command mode. You have four options to continue the run:

       1) List the data in the order input
       2) List the data in ranking order
       3) Display statistical parameters
       4) End the program

Simply input the number **1, 2, 3,** or **4** to indicate your choice. If one of the first three is selected, the program will perform the selected function and return to this command mode to allow another choice. This will continue until you choose **4** to terminate the run. A description of the various options now follows.

Options 1 and 2 provide lists of the data. Option 1 does it in the original input order while Option 2 sorts the data from highest value to lowest. In either case the identifiers, if used, will be shown alongside their associated values.

You start the lists by hitting any key (when told to do so). Either list may be temporarily halted by hitting any key while the list is being displayed. This allows you to leisurely view data that might otherwise start scrolling off the screen. Simply hit any key to resume the display. This starting and stopping can be repeated as often as desired. When the display is completed, you must again hit a key to re-enter the command mode.

Option 3 produces a statistical analysis of your data. Various statistical parameters are calculated and displayed. The following is an explanation of some that may not be familiar to you.

Three measures of location, or central tendency, are provided. These are indicators of an "average" value. The *mean* is the sum of the values divided by the number of values. If the values are arranged in order from highest to lowest, the *median* is the middle value if the number of values is odd. If it is even, the median is the number halfway between the two middle values. The *midrange* is the number halfway between the largest and smallest values.

These measures of location give information about the average value of the data. However, they give no idea of how the data is dispersed or spread out around this "average." For that we need "measures of dispersion" or as they are sometimes called, "measures of variation." The simplest of these is the *range* which is just the difference between the highest and lowest data values. Two other closely related measures of dispersion are given: the *variance* and the *standard deviation*. The variance is defined as:

$$VA = \frac{\sum_{i=1}^{N} (V_i - M)^2}{N - 1}$$

Here N is the number of values, V_i is value i, M is the mean value. The standard deviation is simply the square root of the variance. We do not have space to detail a lengthy discussion of their theoretical use. For this refer to the bibliography. Basically, however, the smaller the standard deviation, the more all the data tends to be clustered close to the mean value.

One word of warning—the first time Option 2 or 3 is selected, the program must take some time to sort the data into numerical order. The time this requires depends upon how many items are on the list and how badly they are out of sequence. Average times are fifteen seconds for twenty-five items, almost one minute for fifty items, about three and one-half minutes for a hundred items. The IBM PC will pause while this is occurring, so don't think it has hung up or fallen asleep! If you have several items on your list, this is the perfect chance to rob your refrigerator, make a quick phone call, or whatever.

SAMPLE RUN

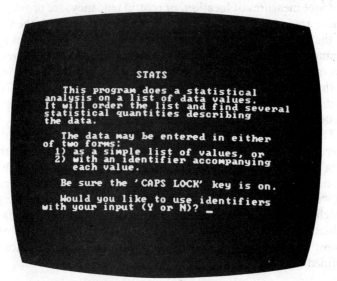

```
                    STATS
         This program does a statistical
    analysis on a list of data values.
    It will order the list and find several
    statistical quantities describing
    the data.

         The data may be entered in either
    of two forms:
       1) as a simple list of values, or
       2) with an identifier accompanying
          each value.

         Be sure the 'CAPS LOCK' key is on.

         Would you like to use identifiers
    with your input (Y or N)? _
```

The program describes its wares. It asks whether or not the operator wishes to use identifiers with the input data.

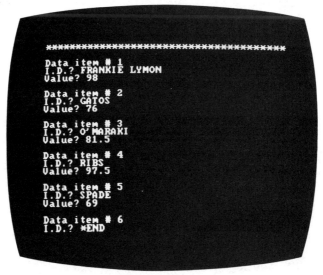

The operator wishes to use identifiers. The program explains how data is to be entered; it is ready to receive the operator's input.

The operator enters the names and scores of those who took a programming aptitude test. The actual test was given to many people, but for demonstration purposes, only five names are used here. The special string, *END, is used to signal the end of data.

```
******************************************
-- CONTINUATION OPTIONS --

  1) List data in original order
  2) List data in ranking order
  3) Display statistics
  4) End program

What next (1, 2, 3, or 4)? 2

******************************************

  The data in ranking order

  5 total entries

      While the list is displaying, you
  can hit any key to cause a temporary
  halt.  The display will resume when you
  hit another key.

      Hit any key to start the display.
```

The operator requests that the list be sorted into numerical order. The
program waits for a key to be pressed to continue the run.

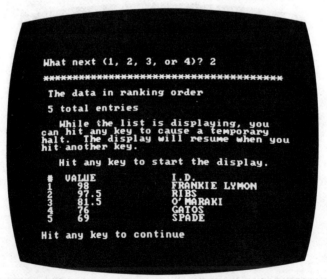

```
What next (1, 2, 3, or 4)? 2

******************************************

  The data in ranking order

  5 total entries

      While the list is displaying, you
  can hit any key to cause a temporary
  halt.  The display will resume when you
  hit another key.

      Hit any key to start the display.
  #   VALUE              I.D.
  1    98               FRANKIE LYMON
  2    97.5             RIBS
  3    81.5             O'MARAKI
  4    76               GATOS
  5    69               SPADE

Hit any key to continue
```

The operator hits a key and is shown the data list in ranking order. The
program waits for a key to be pressed to continue.

```
What next (1, 2, 3, or 4)? 3

******************************************
        STATISTICAL ANALYSIS
Your list has 5 values
   5 Positive; 0 Negative; 0 Zero

Minimum value = 69
Maximum value = 98
Range = 29
Sum of the values = 422

Mean = 84.4
Median = 81.5
Mid-range = 83.5

Std. Deviation = 12.96822
Variance = 168.1748

Hit any key to continue
```

Later in the run, the operator selects continuation Option 3. This calculates and displays the various statistical quantities.

PROGRAM LISTING

```
100 REM: STATS
110 REM: Statistically analyze user's data.
120 REM: COPYRIGHT 1982 Phil Feldman and Tom Rugg.
130 REM: Any BASIC, any CRT.
140 KEY OFF:SCREEN 0,0,0,0:WIDTH 40:COLOR 7,0,0
150 CLEAR:CLS
160 B$="*BACK":E$="*END"
170 MX=100
180 DIM D$(MX),V(MX),Z(MX)
190 Z(0)=0:N$=CHR$(32)
200 PRINT:PRINT
210 PRINT TAB(16);"STATS": PRINT
220 PRINT"   This program does a statistical"
230 PRINT"analysis on a list of data values."
240 PRINT"It will order the list and find several"
250 PRINT"statistical quantities describing"
260 PRINT"the data.": PRINT
270 PRINT"   The data may be entered in either"
280 PRINT"of two forms:"
290 PRINT"  1) as a simple list of values, or"
300 PRINT"  2) with an identifier accompanying"
310 PRINT"     each value.": PRINT
```

```
320 PRINT
    "   Be sure the 'CAPS LOCK' key is on.":PRINT
330 PRINT"   Would you like to use identifiers"
340 INPUT"with your input (Y or N)";R$
350 R$=LEFT$(R$,1)
360 IF R$="Y" OR R$="y" THEN F = 1: GOTO 390
370 IF R$="N" OR R$="n" THEN F = 0: GOTO 390
380 PRINT:GOTO 330
390 GOSUB 1240:PRINT
400 PRINT"   The data must now be entered."
410 PRINT:IF F=1 THEN 450
420 PRINT"   Enter each value separately in"
430 PRINT"response to the question mark."
440 GOSUB 1200:GOTO 490
450 PRINT"   For each data item, enter its"
460 PRINT"identifier (abbreviated I.D.) and its"
470 PRINT"value in response to the separate"
480 PRINT"question marks.": GOSUB 1200
490 GOSUB 1240:DEF SEG:POKE 106,0:N=1
500 IF N<1 THEN N=1
510 PRINT:PRINT"Data item #";N
520 IF F=0 THEN D$(N)=N$:GOTO 560
530 INPUT "I.D.";R$: IF R$ = E$ THEN 620
540 IF R$=B$ THEN N=N-1:GOTO 500
550 D$(N)=R$
560 INPUT "Value";R$: IF R$ = E$ THEN 620
570 IF R$=B$ AND F=1 THEN 510
580 IF R$=B$ THEN N=N-1:GOTO 500
590 V(N)=VAL(R$)
600 IF N=MX THEN PRINT:PRINT"** No more data
    allowed! **":N=N+1:BEEP:GOTO 620
610 N=N+1:GOTO 500
620 N=N-1:IF N=0 THEN PRINT
630 IF N=0 THEN PRINT
    "** No data -- run aborted **":BEEP:END
640 GOSUB 1240
650 PRINT:PRINT"-- CONTINUATION OPTIONS --": PRINT
660 PRINT" 1) List data in original order"
670 PRINT" 2) List data in ranking order"
680 PRINT" 3) Display statistics"
690 PRINT" 4) End program"
700 PRINT:INPUT"What next (1, 2, 3, or 4)";R
710 R=INT(R):IF R<1 OR R>4 THEN 650
720 IF R=4 THEN END
730 ON R GOSUB 750,850,960
740 GOTO 640
750 GOSUB 1240:PRINT
760 PRINT" The original data order": PRINT
770 PRINT N;"total entries": GOSUB 1250
780 PRINT:PRINT TAB(2);"#";TAB(5);"VALUE";
790 IF F=0 THEN PRINT
```

```
 800 IF F=1 THEN PRINT TAB(22);"I.D."
 810 FOR J=1 TO N
 820 PRINT J;TAB(6);V(J);TAB(22);D$(J)
 830 GOSUB 1320
 840 NEXT:GOSUB 1410:RETURN
 850 GOSUB 1240:PRINT
 860 PRINT" The data in ranking order": PRINT
 870 PRINT N;"total entries"
 880 GOSUB 1350
 890 GOSUB 1250:PRINT:
     PRINT TAB(2);"#";TAB(5);"VALUE";
 900 IF F=0 THEN PRINT
 910 IF F=1 THEN PRINT TAB(22);"I.D."
 920 FOR J=1 TO N
 930 PRINT J;TAB(6);V(Z(J));TAB(22);D$(Z(J))
 940 GOSUB 1320
 950 NEXT:GOSUB 1410:RETURN
 960 GOSUB 1240:PRINT
 970 PRINT TAB(6);"STATISTICAL ANALYSIS":PRINT
 980 PRINT"Your list has";N;"values"
 990 NP=0:NN=0:NZ=0:SQ=0:W=0
1000 FOR J=1 TO N:W=W+V(J):SQ=SQ+V(J)*V(J)
1010 IF V(J)>0 THEN NP=NP+1
1020 IF V(J)<0 THEN NN=NN+1
1030 IF V(J)=0 THEN NZ=NZ+1
1040 NEXT:M=W/N:VA=0:IF N=1 THEN 1060
1050 VA=(SQ-N*M*M)/(N-1)
1060 SD=SQR(VA)
1070 PRINT NP;
     "Positive;";NN;"Negative;";NZ;"Zero":PRINT
1080 GOSUB 1350:PRINT"Minimum value =";V(Z(N))
1090 PRINT"Maximum value =";V(Z(1))
1100 PRINT"Range =";V(Z(1))-V(Z(N))
1110 PRINT"Sum of the values =";W: PRINT
1120 PRINT"Mean =";M
1130 Q=INT(N/2)+1:MD=V(Z(Q)):
     IF N/2>INT(N/2) THEN 1150
1140 MD=(V(Z(Q))+V(Z(Q-1)))/2
1150 PRINT"Median =";MD
1160 PRINT"Mid-range =";(V(Z(1))+V(Z(N)))/2
1170 PRINT:PRINT"Std. Deviation =";SD
1180 PRINT"Variance =";VA
1190 GOSUB 1410:RETURN
1200 PRINT:PRINT"   If you make a mistake, type"
1210 PRINT B$;" to re-enter the last datum."
1220 PRINT:
     PRINT"   When the list is completed, type"
1230 PRINT E$;" to terminate the list.": RETURN
1240 PRINT:PRINT STRING$(38,42):RETURN
1250 PRINT:
     PRINT"   While the list is displaying, you"
```

```
1260 PRINT"can hit any key to cause a temporary"
1270 PRINT
     "halt.  The display will resume when you"
1280 PRINT"hit another key."
1290 PRINT:
     PRINT"  Hit any key to start the display."
1300 R$=INKEY$:IF LEN(R$)=0 THEN 1300
1310 RETURN
1320 R$=INKEY$:IF LEN(R$)=0 THEN RETURN
1330 R$=INKEY$:IF LEN(R$)=0 THEN 1330
1340 RETURN
1350 IF Z(0)=1 THEN RETURN
1360 FOR J=1 TO N:Z(J)=J:NEXT:IF N=1 THEN RETURN
1370 NM=N-1:FOR K=1 TO N:FOR J=1 TO NM:N1=Z(J)
1380 N2=Z(J+1):IF V(N1)>V(N2) THEN 1400
1390 Z(J+1)=N1:Z(J)=N2
1400 NEXT:NEXT:Z(0)=1:RETURN
1410 PRINT:PRINT"Hit any key to continue"
1420 R$=INKEY$:IF LEN(R$)=0 THEN 1420
1430 RETURN
```

EASY CHANGES

1. The program arrays are currently dimensioned to allow a maximum of 100 data items. The total storage required for the program depends on the maximum dimension parameter MX, whether or not identifiers are being used, and if so, on the length of a typical identifier. If your system has at least 7K bytes free (see the Appendix), you should be able to use up to 100 data values with identifiers averaging 10 characters each. If no identifiers are used, this dimensioning would require a system with about 5.5 bytes free. Should your application require more than 100 data values, you will have to increase the value of MX in line 170 accordingly. To accommodate up to 300 data items, make this change:

    170 MX = 300

    Of course you will have to have enough RAM available (about 8K bytes free with no identifiers and 10K bytes free with 10 character identifiers).

2. You may wish to change the special strings that signal termination of data input and/or the backing up of data input. These are controlled by the variables E$ and B$, respectively. They are set in line 160. If you wish to terminate the data with /DONE/ and to back up with /LAST/ for example, line 160 should be:

    160 B$ = "/LAST/":E$ = "/DONE/"

3. You may wish to see your lists sorted from smallest value to largest value instead of the other way around, as it's done now. This can be accomplished by changing the "greater than" sign ($>$) in line 1380 to a "less than" sign ($<$). Thus:

1380 N2 = Z(J + 1):IF V(N1) < V(N2) THEN 1400

This will, however, cause a few funny things to happen to the statistics. The real minimum value will be displayed under the heading "maximum" and vice-versa. Also, the range will have its correct magnitude but with an erroneous minus sign in front. To cure these afflictions, make these changes also:

1080 GOSUB 1350:PRINT "Minimum value = ";V(Z(1))
1090 PRINT "Maximum value = ";V(Z(N))
1100 PRINT "Range = ";V(Z(N)) − V(Z(1))

MAIN ROUTINES

150- 190	Initializes constants and dimensioning.
200- 380	Displays messages, determines if identifiers will be used.
390- 610	Gets data from the user.
620- 630	Checks that input contains at least one value.
640- 740	Command mode—gets user's next option and does a GOSUB to it.
750- 840	Subroutine to list data in the original order.
850- 950	Subroutine to list data in ranking order.
960-1190	Subroutine to calculate and display statistics.
1200-1310	Subroutine to display various messages.
1320-1340	Subroutine to allow user to temporarily start and stop display listing.
1350-1400	Subroutine to sort the list in ranking order.
1410-1430	Subroutine to detect if user has hit a key to continue.

MAIN VARIABLES

MX	Maximum number of data values allowed.
D$(MX)	String array of identifiers.
V(MX)	Array of the data values.
Z(MX)	Array of the sorting order.
N	Number of data values in current application.
B$	Flag string to back up the input.

E$	Flag string to signal end of the input.
R$	User input string.
NM	N − 1.
R	Continuation option.
NP	Number of positive values.
NN	Number of negative values.
NZ	Number of zero values.
W	Sum of the values.
SQ	Sum of the squares of the values.
M	Mean value.
MD	Median of the values.
VA	Variance.
SD	Standard deviation.
J,K	Loop indices.
N1,N2	Possible data locations to interchange during sorting.
Q	Work variable.
N$	String for a null identifier.
F	Flag on identifier usage (1 = yes, 0 = no).

SUGGESTED PROJECTS

1. The sorting algorithm used in the program is efficient only when the number of list items is fairly small — less than twenty-five or so. This is because it does not do checking along the way to see when the list becomes fully sorted. If your lists tend to be longer than twenty-five items, you might wish to use another sorting algorithm more ap-propriate for longer lists. Try researching other sorts and in-corporating them into the program. To get you started, try these changes:

```
1370 Q = 0: FOR J = 1 TO N − 1:N1 = Z(J):N2 = Z(J + 1)
1380 IF V(N1) > = V(N2) THEN 1400
1390 Z(J + 1) = N1:Z(J) = N2:Q = 1
1400 NEXT:IF Q = 1 THEN 1370
1405 Z(0) = 1:RETURN
```

    If your lists are short, this routine will probably be a little slower than the current one. However, for longer lists it will save proportionately more and more time.

2. Many other statistical parameters exist to describe this kind of data. Research them and add some that might be useful to you. One such idea is classifying the data. This consists of dividing the range into a number of equal classes and then counting how many values fall into each class.

Section 6

Miscellaneous Programs

These programs show how simple programs can do interesting things. Most of them have a mathematical flavor. They are short and, as such, would be useful for study for those just learning BASIC in particular or programming in general.

Monte Carlo simulation involves programming the computer to conduct an experiment. (It doesn't involve high-stakes gambling!) PI shows how this technique can be used to calculate an approximation to the famous mathematical constant pi.

PYTHAG will find all right triangles with integral side lengths. A clever algorithm is utilized to do this.

Have you ever looked around your classroom or club meeting and wondered if any two people had the same birthdate? BIRTHDAY will show you what the surprising odds are.

Very high precision arithmetic can be done using BASIC with the proper "know-how." POWERS will calculate the values of integers raised to various powers; not to the computer's standard six or sixteen digit precision, but up to 250 full digits of precision.

Your computer can play music! TUNE allows you to enter tunes into your computer in a simple, convenient manner. Then your computer will play them for you.

BIRTHDAY

PURPOSE

Suppose you are in a room full of people. What is the probability that two or more of these people have the same birthday? How many people have to be in the room before the probability becomes greater than 50 percent? We are talking only about the month and day of birth, not the year.

This is a fairly simple problem to solve, even without a computer. With a computer to help with the calculations, it becomes very easy. What makes the problem interesting is that the correct answer is nowhere near what most people immediately guess. Before reading further, what do you think? How many people have to be in the room before there is better than a 50-50 chance of birthday duplication? 50? 100? 200?

HOW TO USE IT

When you run the program, it starts by displaying headings over two columns of numbers that will be shown. The left column is the number of people in the room, starting with one. The right column is the probability of birthday duplication.

For one person, of course, the probability is zero, since there is no one else with a possible duplicate birthday. For two people, the probability is simply the decimal equivalent of $1/365$ (note that we assume a 365 day year, and an equal likelihood that each person could have been born on any day of the year).

What is the probability of duplication when there are three people in the room? No, not just $2/365$. It's actually

$$1 - (^{364}\!/_{365} \text{ times } ^{363}\!/_{365})$$

This is simply one minus the probability of *no* duplicate birthdays.

The probability for four people is

$$1 - (\tfrac{364}{365} \text{ times } \tfrac{363}{365} \text{ times } \tfrac{362}{365})$$

The calculation continues like this, adding a new term for each additional person in the room. You will find that the result (probability of duplication) exceeds .50 surprisingly fast.

The program continues with the calculation until there are 60 people in the room. You will have to press **Ctrl Break** to stop the program long before that to see the point where the probability first exceeds 50 percent. You can also press the **NumLock** key while holding **CTRL** down to make the computer pause.

SAMPLE RUN

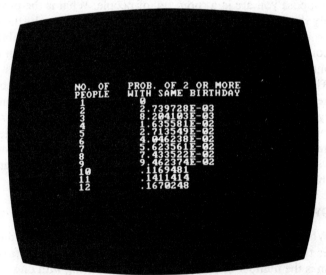

```
NO. OF      PROB. OF 2 OR MORE
PEOPLE      WITH SAME BIRTHDAY
1           0
2           2.739728E-03
3           8.204103E-03
4           1.635581E-02
5           2.713549E-02
6           4.046238E-02
7           5.623561E-02
8           7.433522E-02
9           9.462374E-02
10          .1169481
11          .1411414
12          .1670248
```

The program shows the probabilities for up to 12 people in the room before the operator presses the "Ctrl" and "Num Lock" keys to freeze the display.

PROGRAM LISTING

```
100 REM: BIRTHDAY
110 REM: Probability of birthday coincidence.
120 REM: COPYRIGHT 1982 Tom Rugg and Phil Feldman.
130 REM: Any BASIC, any CRT.
```

```
140 KEY OFF:SCREEN 0,0:COLOR 7,0:CLS
150 PRINT"NO. OF    PROB. OF 2 OR MORE"
160 PRINT"PEOPLE    WITH SAME BIRTHDAY"
170 Q=1
180 FOR N=1 TO 60
190 PRINT N;TAB(11);1-Q
200 Q=Q*(365-N)/365
210 NEXT N
220 END
```

EASY CHANGES

1. Change the constant value of 60 at the end of line 180 to alter the range of the number of people in the calculation. For example, change it to 100 and watch how fast the probability approaches 1.
2. To avoid displaying the first probabilities in scientific notation format, make these changes:

   190 PRINT N; TAB(11);
   195 PRINT USING "#.#######"; 1-Q

3. To make more precise calculations, make this change to use double precision arithmetic:

   145 DEFDBL Q

MAIN ROUTINES

140-160   Displays headings.
170   Initializes Q to 1.
180-210   Calculates probability of no duplication, then displays probability of duplication.

MAIN VARIABLES

N   Number of people in the room.
Q   Probability of no duplication of birthdays.

SUGGESTED PROJECTS

Modify the program to allow for leap years in the calculation, instead of assuming 365 days per year.

PI

PURPOSE AND DISCUSSION

The Greek letter pi, π, represents probably the most famous constant in mathematical history. It occurs regularly in many different areas of mathematics. It is best known as the constant appearing in several geometric relationships involving the circle. The circumference of a circle of radius r is $2\pi r$, while the area enclosed by the circle is πr^2.

Being a transcendental number, pi cannot be expressed exactly by any number of decimal digits. To nine significant digits, its value is 3.14159265. Over many centuries, man has devised many different methods to calculate pi.

This program uses a valuable, modern technique known as computer simulation. The name "simulation" is rather self-explanatory; the computer performs an experiment for us. This is often desirable for many different reasons. The experiment may be cheaper, less dangerous, or more accurate to run on a computer. It may even be impossible to do in "real life." Usually, however, the reason is that the speed of the computer allows the simulation to be performed many times faster than actually conducting the real experiment.

This program simulates the results of throwing darts at a specially constructed dartboard. Consider Figure 1 which shows the peculiar square dartboard involved. The curved arc, outlining the shaded area, is that of a circle with the center in the lower left hand corner. The sides of the square, and thus the radius of the circle, are considered to have a length of 1.

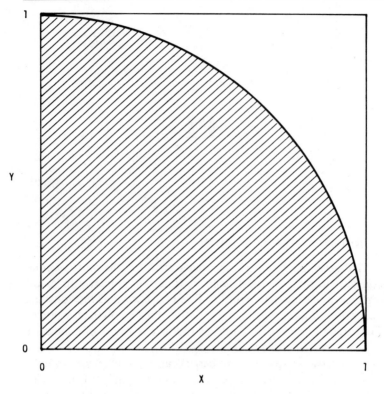

Figure 1. The PI Dartboard

Suppose we were able to throw darts at this square target in such a way that each dart had an equal chance of landing anywhere within the square. A certain percentage of darts would result in "hits," i.e., land in the shaded area. The expected value of this percentage is simply the area of the shaded part divided by the area of the entire square.

The area of the shaded part is one fourth of the area the entire circle would enclose if the arc were continued to completely form the circle. Recall the area of a circle is πr^2 where r is the radius. In our case, $r = 1$, and the area of the entire circle would simply be π. The shaded area of the dartboard is one fourth of this entire circle and thus has an area of $\pi/4$. The area of the square is s^2, where s is the length of a side. On our dartboard, $s = 1$, and the area of the whole dartboard is 1.

Now the expected ratio of "hits" to darts thrown can be expressed

$$\text{RATIO} = \frac{\# \text{ hits}}{\# \text{ thrown}} = \frac{\text{shaded area}}{\text{entire area}} = \frac{\pi/4}{1} = \frac{\pi}{4}$$

So we now have an experimental way to approximate the value of π. We perform the experiment and compute the ratio of "hits" observed. We then multiply this number by 4 and we have calculated π experimentally.

But instead of actually constructing the required dartboard and throwing real darts, we will let the computer do the job. The program "throws" each dart by selecting a separate random number between 0 and 1 for the X and Y coordinates of each dart. This is accomplished by using the built-in RND function of BASIC. A "dart" is in the shaded area if $X^2 + Y^2 < 1$ for it.

So the program grinds away, continually throwing darts and determining the ratio of "hits." This ratio is multiplied by 4 to arrive at an empirical approximation to π.

HOW TO USE IT

After you type **RUN**, the program will request that you hit a key to begin. This allows the random number generator to be seeded. After this is done, the program requests one input from you. This is the "sample size for printing," i.e., how many darts it should throw before printing its current results. Any value of one or higher is acceptable.

After you input this number, the program will commence the simulation and display its results. A cumulative total of "hits," darts thrown, and the current approximation to π will be displayed for each multiple of the sample size.

This will continue until you stop the program. When you are satisfied with the total number of darts thrown, press the **Ctrl** and **Break** keys simultaneously to terminate the program execution.

SAMPLE RUN

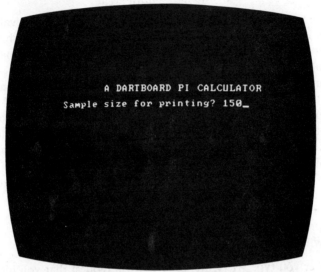

After hitting a key to begin, the operator selects 150 for the printing sample size.

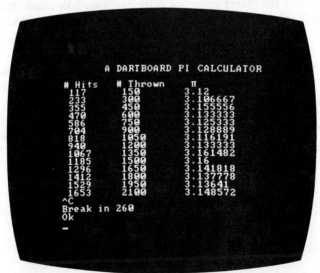

After 2100 darts are "thrown," the BREAK key is pressed to terminate the run.

PROGRAM LISTING

```
100 REM: PI
110 REM: A dartboard pi calculator.
120 REM: COPYRIGHT 1982 Phil Feldman and Tom Rugg.
130 REM: Any BASIC, any CRT.
140 CLEAR:DEF SEG:POKE 106,0:T=0:TH=0
150 KEY OFF:SCREEN 0,1,0,0:COLOR 7,0,0:WIDTH 40
160 GOSUB 290:PRINT"Hit any key to begin."
170 Q$=INKEY$:Q=Q+1:IF LEN(Q$)=0 THEN 170
180 Q=RND(-Q):GOSUB 290
190 INPUT"Sample size for printing";NP
200 NP=INT(NP):IF NP<1 THEN 180
210 GOSUB 290:PRINT"# Hits";TAB(10);
220 PRINT"# Thrown";TAB(22);CHR$(227)
230 GOSUB 260:TH=TH+NH:T=T+NP:P=4*TH/T
240 PRINT TH;TAB(10);T;TAB(20);P
250 GOTO 230
260 NH=0:FOR J=1 TO NP:X=RND:Y=RND
270 IF (X*X+Y*Y)<1 THEN NH=NH+1
280 NEXT:RETURN
290 CLS:PRINT TAB(8);
300 PRINT"A DARTBOARD PI CALCULATOR"
310 PRINT:RETURN
```

EASY CHANGES

1. If you want the program to always use a fixed sample size, change line 190 to read

   190 NP = 150

   Of course, the value of 150 given here may be changed to whatever you wish.

2. If you want the program to stop by itself after a certain number of darts have been thrown, add the following two lines:

   205 INPUT"TOTAL # DARTS TO THROW";ND
   245 IF T> = ND THEN END

   This will ask the operator how many total darts should be thrown, and then terminate the program when they have been thrown.

3. The calculated values of pi will be shown with seven digits of precision as is standard for single precision variables in BASIC. This is sufficient for the degree of accuracy possible in this simulation. However, you might want to try the following change to see the effects of computing pi to double precision:

   145 DEFDBL P – Z

MAIN ROUTINES

140-150	Initializes constants.
160-220	Gets operator input, displays column headings.
230-250	Calculates and displays results.
260-280	Throws NP darts and records number of "hits."
290-310	Clears screen and displays program title.

MAIN VARIABLES

T	Total darts thrown.
TH	Total "hits."
NP	Sample size for printing.
NH	Number of hits in one group of NP darts.
P	Calculated value of pi.
Q$	Temporary string variable.
Q	Work variable.
X,Y	Random-valued coordinates of a dart.
J	Loop index.

SUGGESTED PROJECTS

1. Calculate the percentage error in the program's calculation of pi and display it with the other results. You will need to define a variable, say PI, which is set to the value of pi. Then the percentage error, PE, can be calculated as:

$$PE = 100*ABS(P - PI)/PI$$

2. The accuracy of this simulation is highly dependent on the quality of the computer's random number generator. Try researching different algorithms for pseudo random number generation. Then try incorporating them into the program. Change line 260 to use the new algorithm(s). This can actually be used as a test of the various random number generators. Gruenberger's book, referenced in the bibliography, contains good material on various pseudo random number generators.

POWERS

PURPOSE

By now you have probably learned that your computer keeps track of six significant digits when dealing with numbers. For integers less than one million (1,000,000), the computer can retain the precise value of the number. But for larger integers the computer only keeps track of the most significant (leftmost) six digits, plus the exponent. This means, of course, that there is no way you can use the computer to deal with precise integers greater than one million, right?

Wrong.

Of course, you say. You can use double precision variables to get precise results up to 16 digits. So, undoubtedly, the computer's limit in BASIC is 16 digit integers, right?

Wrong again.

This program calculates either factorials or successive powers of an integer, and can display precise results that are up to 250 digits long. By using a "multiple-precision arithmetic" technique, this program can tell you *exactly* what 973 to the 47th power is, for example.

HOW TO USE IT

The program first asks you how many digits long you want the largest number to be. This can be any integer from 1 to 250. So, for example, if you enter 40, you will get answers up to forty digits long.

Next you are asked for the value of N. If you respond with a value of 1, you are requesting to be shown all the factorials that

will fit in the number of digits you specified. First you will get
one factorial, then two factorial, and so on. In case you have
forgotten, three factorial is 3 times 2 times 1, or 6. Four factorial
is 4 times 3 times 2 times 1, or 24.

If you enter an N in the range from 2 through 100,000, you are
requesting the successive powers of that number up to the limit
of digits you specified. So, if you provide an N of 23, you will
get 23 to the first power, then 23 squared, then 23 cubed, and so
on.

Finally, after it has displayed the largest number that will fit
within the number of digits you entered, the program starts
over. The larger the number of digits you ask for, the longer it
will take the program to calculate each number. If you enter
zero, the program ends.

SAMPLE RUN

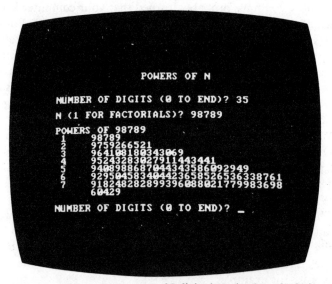

The operator wants answers up to 35 digits long in the calculations of
the powers of 98789. The program calculates numbers up to 98789[7] and
then asks for the number of digits again (in preparation for the next
calculation the operator requests).

PROGRAM LISTING

```
100 REM: POWERS
110 REM:
      Compute high precision powers and factorials.
120 REM: COPYRIGHT 1982 Tom Rugg and Phil Feldman.
130 REM: Any BASIC, any CRT.
140 KEY OFF:SCREEN 0,0:WIDTH 40:COLOR 7,0:CLS
150 PRINT TAB(15);"POWERS OF N"
160 DEFINT D,J,L:PRINT:PRINT
170 L=250
180 DIM N(L+5):I=1
190 INPUT "NUMBER OF DIGITS (0 TO END)";M
200 IF M=0 THEN END
210 M=INT(M):IF M>L OR M<1 THEN 190
220 PRINT:INPUT "N (1 FOR FACTORIALS)";N
230 N=INT(N)
240 IF N<1 OR N>100000! THEN 220
250 PRINT
260 F=0:IF N=1 THEN F=1:PRINT"FACTORIALS"
270 IF F=0 THEN PRINT"POWERS OF";N
280 T=10:K=1:N(0)=N
290 FOR J=0 TO M
300 IF N(J)<T THEN 330
310 Q=INT(N(J)/T):W=N(J)-Q*T
320 N(J)=W:N(J+1)=N(J+1)+Q
330 NEXT
340 J=M+1
350 IF N(J)=0 THEN J=J-1:GOTO 350
360 IF J>=M THEN 450
370 D=0:PRINT K;TAB(7);
380 N$=RIGHT$(STR$(N(J)),1)
390 D=D+1:IF D>30 THEN D=1:PRINT:PRINT TAB(7);
400 PRINT N$;:J=J-1:IF J>=0 THEN 380
410 N=N+F
420 K=K+1:PRINT
430 FOR J=0 TO M:N(J)=N(J)*N:NEXT
440 GOTO 290
450 FOR J=1 TO L+5:N(J)=0:NEXT
460 M=0:N=0:PRINT:GOTO 190
```

EASY CHANGES

1. To change the program so that it always uses, say, fifty digit
   numbers, remove lines 190 and 200, and insert this line:

   190 M = 50

2. To clear the screen before the output begins being displayed,
   insert this line:

   255 CLS

3. If 250 digits isn't enough for you, you can go higher. For 500 digits, make this change:

    $$170 \ L = 500$$

4. To use the full width of an 80 column display screen, change WIDTH 40 to WIDTH 80 in line 140, and change the 30 in line 390 to 70. This will cause the program to display 70 digits per line.

MAIN ROUTINES

140-180	Displays title. Sets up array for calculations.
190-270	Asks for number of digits and N. Checks validity of responses. Displays heading.
280	Initializes variables for calculations.
290-330	Performs "carrying" in N array so each element has a value no larger than 9.
340-350	Scans backwards through N array for first non-zero element.
360	Checks to see if this value would be larger than the number of digits requested.
370-400	Displays counter and number. Goes to second line if necessary.
410-420	Prepares to multiply by N to get next number.
430-440	Multiplies each digit in N array by N. Goes back to line 290.
450-460	Zeroes out N array in preparation for next request. Goes back to 190.

MAIN VARIABLES

L	Maximum length allowed for numbers.
N	Array in which calculations are made.
M	Number of digits of precision requested by operator.
N	Starting value. If 1, factorials. If greater than 1, powers of N.
F	Set to zero if powers, 1 if factorials.
T	Constant value of 10.
K	Counter of current power or factorial.
J	Subscript variable.
Q,W	Temporary variables used in reducing each integer position in the N array to a value from 0 to 9.

D   Number of digits displayed so far on the current
             line (maximum is 30).

N$ String variable used to convert each digit into dis-
             playable format.

SUGGESTED PROJECTS

1. Determine the largest N that could be used without errors
    entering into the calculation (because of intermediate results
    exceeding one million), then modify line 240 to permit
    values that large to be entered.

2. Create a series of subroutines that can add, subtract, multi-
    ply, divide, and exchange numbers in two arrays, using a
    technique like the one used here. Then you can perform high
    precision calculations by means of a series of GOSUB
    statements.

PYTHAG

PURPOSE

Remember the Pythagorean Theorem? It says that the sum of the squares of the two legs of a right triangle is equal to the square of the hypotenuse. Expressed as a formula, it is $a^2 + b^2 = c^2$. The most commonly remembered example of this is the 3-4-5 right triangle ($3^2 + 4^2 = 5^2$). Of course, there are an infinite number of other right triangles.

This program displays integer values of a, b, and c that result in right triangles.

HOW TO USE IT

To use this program, all you need to do is RUN it and watch the "Pythagorean triplets" (sets of values for a, b, and c) come out. The program displays twenty sets of values on each screen, and then waits for you to press the space bar before it continues with the next twenty. It will go on indefinitely until you press the **Esc** key.

The left-hand column shows the count of the number of sets of triplets produced, and the other three columns are the values of a, b, and c.

The sequence in which the triplets are produced is not too obvious, so we will explain how the numbers are generated.

It has been proved that the following technique will generate all *primitive* Pythagorean triplets. ("Primitive" means that no set is an exact multiple of another.) If you have two positive integers called R and S such that:

1. R is greater than S,

2. R and S are of opposite parity (one is odd and the other is even), and
3. R and S are relatively prime (they have no common integer divisors except 1),

then a, b, and c can be found as follows:

$$a = R^2 - S^2$$
$$b = 2RS$$
$$c = R^2 + S^2$$

The program starts with a value of 2 for R. It generates all possible S values for that R (starting at R − 1 and then decreasing) and then adds one to R and continues. So, the first set of triplets is created when R is 2 and S is 1, the second set when R is 3 and S is 2, and so on.

SAMPLE RUN

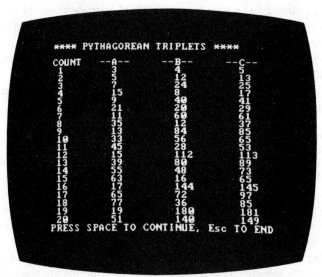

The program shows the first screen of Pythagorean triplets.

PROGRAM LISTING

```
100 REM: PYTHAG
110 REM: Calculate Pythagorean triplets.
120 REM: COPYRIGHT 1982 Tom Rugg and Phil Feldman.
130 REM: Any BASIC, any CRT.
140 KEY OFF:SCREEN 0,0:WIDTH 40:COLOR 7,0:CLS
```

```
150 DEFDBL A-Z
160 R=2:K=1:D=0
170 GOSUB 310
180 S=R-1
190 A=R*R-S*S
200 B=2*R*S
210 C=R*R+S*S
220 PRINT K;TAB(10);A;TAB(20);B;TAB(30);C
230 K=K+1:D=D+1:GOTO 360
240 S=S-2:IF S<=0 THEN R=R+1:GOTO 180
250 S1=S:B1=R
260 N=INT(B1/S1)
270 R1=B1-(S1*N)
280 IF R1<>0 THEN B1=S1:S1=R1:GOTO 260
290 IF S1<>1 THEN 240
300 GOTO 190
310 CLS
320 PRINT"**** PYTHAGOREAN TRIPLETS ****"
330 PRINT
340 PRINT"COUNT";TAB(9);"--A--";TAB(19);"--B--";
    TAB(29);"--C--"
350 RETURN
360 IF D<20 THEN 240
370 DEF SEG:POKE 106,0
380 PRINT"PRESS SPACE TO CONTINUE, Esc TO END ";
390 R$=INKEY$:IF LEN(R$)=0 THEN 390
400 IF ASC(R$)=27 THEN END
410 POKE 106,0
420 GOSUB 310:D=0
430 GOTO 240
```

EASY CHANGES

1. Alter the starting value of R in line 160. Instead of 2, try 50 or 100.

2. If you want, you can change the number of sets of triplets displayed on each screen. Change the 20 in line 360 to a 10, for example. You probably won't want to try a value greater than 20, since that would cause the column headings to roll off the screen.

3. To make the program continue without requiring you to press a key for the next screen of values, insert either of these lines:

    365 GOTO 420

    or

    365 GOTO 430

The first will display headings for each screen. The second
will only display the headings at the beginning of the run. In
either case you will have to press **Ctrl Break** to stop the
program.

MAIN ROUTINES

140-160	Initializes variables and sets up screen.
170	Displays the title and column headings.
180	Calculates first value of S for current R value.
190-210	Calculates A, B, and C.
220-230	Displays one line of values. Adds to counters.
240	Calculates next S value. If no more, calculates next R value.
250-300	Determines if R and S are relatively prime.
310-350	Subroutine to display title and column headings.
360-430	Checks if screen is full yet. If so, waits for key to be pressed.

MAIN VARIABLES

R,S	See explanation in "How To Use It."
K	Count of total number of sets displayed.
D	Count of number of sets displayed on one screen.
A,B,C	Lengths of the three sides of the triangle.
S1,B1, R1,N	Used in determining if R and S are relatively prime.
R$	Key pressed by operator.

SUGGESTED PROJECTS

1. In addition to displaying K, A, B, and C on each line, dis-
    play R and S. You will have to change the WIDTH to 80 to
    have room on each line of the screen.
2. Because this program uses integer values that get increas-
    ingly large, eventually some will exceed BASIC's double
    precision integer capacity and produce incorrect results. Can
    you determine when this will be? Modify the program to
    stop when this occurs.

TUNE

PURPOSE

The BASIC manual that came with your computer explains in detail how the PLAY statement of Advanced BASIC can be used to play music. However, the manual provides no programs or detailed examples to make it easy to play tunes. This simple program lets you experiment with simple computer tune-playing if you have Advanced BASIC (BASICA).

HOW TO USE IT

As shown in the program listing, TUNE currently plays a familiar portion of the "Blue Danube" waltz. We'll explain how to enter other tunes in a moment.

When you run the program, it displays its title at the top of the screen, and shows you three options you have to choose from. Option 1 plays the tune once, and then returns to the menu of options. Option 2 plays the tune continuously. Pressing the **ESC** (escape) key will end the tune after the next complete playing, and return to the menu. Option 3 ends the program.

After you get tired of hearing the "Blue Danube", you will probably want to enter some tunes of your own choosing. By reading the PLAY explanation in the BASIC manual, and having a little musical knowledge, you can easily play other tunes. All you need to do is delete lines 460 through 540, and insert your own PLAY data. You may also want to change line 440, which sets the tempo (speed) of the tune. Leave line 550 as it is—it indicates the end of the tune. If you need more line

numbering space (because you are entering a longer tune), you
can delete line 550 and insert a higher numbered line, such as

990 DATA XXX

Here's an example of how you would enter the always-exciting
tune, "Mary Had a Little Lamb":

1. Delete lines 460 through 540.
2. Insert these lines:

> 460 DATA L4EDCDEEL2EL4DDL2DL4EGL2G
> 470 DATA L4EDCDEEEEDDEDL2C

It isn't necessary to use multiples of ten for the line numbers,
but it's common to do it that way to simplify entering more lines
later if needed.

To learn the fundamentals of reading sheet music, refer to an
introductory music text, or possibly a beginning piano or guitar
instruction book.

SAMPLE RUN

The operator selects option 1, and the data for the tune is displayed as
the tune plays.

PROGRAM LISTING

```
100 REM: TUNE
110 REM: Play a tune using DATA statements.
120 REM: COPYRIGHT 1982 Tom Rugg and Phil Feldman.
130 REM: Advanced BASIC, any CRT.
140 KEY OFF:SCREEN 0,0:COLOR 7,0:CLS
150 PRINT"**** TUNE ****":I=1
160 PRINT:PRINT
170 PRINT"--OPTIONS--"
180 PRINT
190 PRINT"1 - PLAY TUNE ONCE"
200 PRINT"2 - PLAY TUNE CONTINUOUSLY"
210 PRINT"3 - END PROGRAM"
220 PRINT
230 DEF SEG:POKE 106,0
240 R$=INKEY$:IF LEN(R$)=0 THEN 240
250 IF R$<"1" OR R$>"3" THEN 240
260 PRINT R$
270 R=VAL(R$)
280 ON R GOTO 300,300,400
290 PRINT"**ERROR**":BEEP:STOP
300 FOR J=1 TO 2000:NEXT
310 RESTORE
320 READ T$
330 PRINT T$
340 IF T$="XXX" OR T$="xxx" THEN 370
350 PLAY T$
360 GOTO 320
370 A$=INKEY$:IF LEN(A$)=0 THEN 390
380 IF ASC(A$)=27 THEN 160
390 IF R$="1" THEN 160 ELSE GOTO 300
400 PRINT
410 END
420 REM - DATA statements follow this
430 REM - Don't mix up letter "O" with number "0"
440 DATA T180
450 DATA MF
460 DATA MNL4O3DF#AL2AL4O4AAP4F#F#P4O3D
470 DATA DF#AL2AL4O4AAP4GGP4O3C#
480 DATA C#EBL2BL4O4BBP4GGP4O3C#
490 DATA C#EBL2BL4O4BBP4F#F#P4O3D
500 DATA DF#AL2O4DL4O5DDP4O4AAP4O3D
510 DATA DF#AL2O4DL4O5DDP4O4BBP4E
520 DATA EGL8BP8MLL2B.L4BMNG#AMLL2O5F#.
530 DATA L4F#MNDO4F#MLL2F#MNL4EMLL2BMNL4A
540 DATA DP8L8DL4D
550 DATA XXX
560 REM: BLUE DANUBE
```

EASY CHANGES

1. Eliminate the display of each string of data that is played by deleting line 330.
2. Lengthen the delay after each time the tune is played in the continuous mode by changing the 2000 in line 300 to, say, 5000. Eliminate the delay by changing it to 1.
3. To display the title of the tune to be played, insert this line:

       165 PRINT"BLUE DANUBE":PRINT

MAIN ROUTINES

140-150	Initializes screen and displays title.
160-220	Displays menu of options.
230-290	Gets reply from operator and goes to corresponding routine.
300	Delays briefly before starting to play tune.
310-360	Reads DATA statements, displays and plays data until XXX is encountered.
370-390	Checks if escape key was pressed. If not and if Option 2 is in effect, goes back to play again.
400-410	Ends program.
440-450	Sets tempo and music foreground.
460-540	DATA statements with tune data.
550	DATA statement indicating end of tune.

MAIN VARIABLES

R$	Reply from operator saying which option selected.
R	Numeric value of R$.
J	Loop variable.
T$	Tune data read from DATA statement.
A$	Key pressed by operator during playing of tune.

SUGGESTED PROJECTS

1. If you have a graphics interface, display something corresponding with each note as it is played. For example, display a piano keyboard and indicate each note as it is played. Or, display a musical score and graphically draw each note.
2. Revise the program to *compose* melodies, rather than simply play tunes that you enter. Use the RND function to randomly select possible notes and lengths, and use only those that will rhythmically and harmoniously produce pleasing music.

Appendix

Memory and Configuration Requirements

All of the programs in this book will run on an IBM Personal Computer with 64K of user memory (RAM), one disk drive (or two), and the color/graphics display interface with an 80 column video monitor (either black and white or color). However, nearly all the programs will also work with other hardware configurations, such as the monochrome display, or without any disk drives. In addition, some of the programs will work in a limited way without certain hardware. For example, MILEAGE and SORTLIST work fine without having a disk drive as long as you don't try to use the options that read or write disk files.

Here is a summary of the programs that require certain hardware or memory configurations. All other programs will work on even the minimum configuration (a 16K cassette system with either video display interface). Some of the programs require easy changes (detailed in the chapters) to run on certain configurations.

Programs requiring the color/graphics display interface
NUMBERS, SPIRALS, WALLOONS, GRAPH

Programs requiring an 80 column video display
LOAN, ARGO

Programs requiring a disk drive to use all options
MILEAGE, SORTLIST

Programs requiring advanced disk basic (BASICA)
WALLOONS, TUNE

Programs requiring extra memory (over 16K for a cassette system, or over 48K for a disk system with PC-DOS 1.0 or 1.1, or over 64K for a disk system with PC-DOS 2.0)
none

Line 130 of each program listing indicates which version of BASIC is required for the program. Most programs say "Any BASIC", which means Cassette BASIC, Disk BASIC, or Advanced BASIC. It does *not* necessarily mean the program will work with the BASIC Compiler, which has many differences from the other versions of BASIC.

Some of the chapters mention limitations of the programs based on the number of "bytes free" in your system. This refers to the amount of memory available when BASIC is started on your system, before a BASIC program has been entered or loaded. This number is displayed on the screen when BASIC is initialized. If you have 11000 bytes free (or more), you should have enough memory to run any of these programs. For most of the programs, 6000 is plenty.

Bibliography

BOOKS

Bell, R. C., *Board and Table Games From Many Civilizations*, Oxford University Press, London, 1969. (WARI)

Cohen, Daniel, *Biorhythms in Your Life*, Fawcett Publications, Greenwich, Connecticut, 1976. (BIORHYTHM)

Crow, E. L., David, F. A., and Maxfield, M. W., *Statistics Manual*, Dover Publications, New York, 1960. (STATS)

Croxton, F. E., Crowden, D. J., and Klein, S., *Applied General Statistics* (Third Edition), Prentice-Hall, Englewood Cliffs, N. J., 1967. (STATS)

Elson, Louis C., *Elson's Pocket Music Dictionary*, Oliver Ditson Company, Bryn Mawr, Pennsylvania, 1909. (TUNE)

Gruenberger, Fred J., and Jaffray, George, *Problems for Computer Solution*, John Wiley and Sons, New York, 1965. (BIRTHDAY, PI, SORTLIST)

Gruenberger, Fred J., and McCracken, Daniel D., *Introduction to Electronic Computers*, John Wiley and Sons, New York, 1961. (MILEAGE, PI, PYTHAG, WARI as Oware)

Hildebrand, F. B., *Introduction to Numerical Analysis*, McGraw-Hill, New York, 1956. (CURVE, DIFFEQN, INTEGRATE, SIMEQN)

Knuth, Donald E., *The Art of Computer Programming (Volume 3)*, Addison-Wesley, Reading, Massachusetts, 1973. (SORTLIST)

Kuo, S. S., *Computer Applications of Numerical Methods*, Addison-Wesley, Reading, Massachusetts, 1972. (CURVE, DIFFEQN, INTEGRATE, SIMEQN)

McCracken, Daniel D., and Dorn, W. S., *Numerical Methods And FORTRAN Programming*, John Wiley and Sons, New York, 1964. (CURVE, DIFFEQN, INTEGRATE, SIMEQN)

Orr, William I., *Radio Handbook* (19th Edition), Howard W. Sams & Co., Inc., Indianapolis, Indiana, 1972. (HAMCODE)

Shefter, Harry, *Faster Reading Self-Taught*, Washington Square Press, New York, 1960. (TACHIST)

PERIODICALS

Feldman, Phil, and Rugg, Tom, "Pass the Buck," *Kilobaud*, July 1977, pp. 90-96. (DECIDE)

Fliegel, H. F., and Van Flandern, T. C., "A Machine Algorithm for Processing Calendar Dates," *Communications of the ACM*, October, 1968, P. 657. (BIORHYTHM)

Errata Offer

All of the programs in this book have been tested carefully and are working correctly to the best of our knowledge. However, we take no responsibility for any losses which may be suffered as a result of errors or misuse. You must bear the responsibility of verifying each program's accuracy and applicability for your purposes.

If you want to get a copy of an errata sheet that lists corrections for any errors or ambiguities we have found to date, send one dollar ($1.00) and a self addressed stamped envelope (SASE) to the address below. Ask for errata for this book (by name). We hope we won't have any errors to tell you about, in which case we'll try to send you some other worthwhile information about the IBM PC.

If you think you've found an error, please let us know. If you want an answer, include a SASE.

Please keep in mind that the most likely cause of a program working incorrectly is a typing error. Please check your typing *very* carefully before you send us an irate note about an error in one of the programs. Reread the "How To Use This Book" section, too.

Tom Rugg or Phil Feldman
Errata—More Than 32 Pgms for the IBM PC
P.O. Box 24815
Los Angeles, CA 90024

ABOUT THE AUTHORS:

Tom Rugg and Phil Feldman have a long-standing association with the microcomputer industry. Together they wrote the popular column "Games and Things" in Southern California Computer Society Interface, and have written numerous articles for other publications. They are authors of several other books in the '32 BASIC' series published by dilithium Press.

☐ **Yes,** send me your free catalog,
BRAINFOOD, which lists over 90
microcomputer books covering
software, hardware, business
applications, general computer literacy
and programming languages.

NAME _____

ADDRESS _____

CITY, STATE, ZIP _____

- -

☐ **Yes,** send me your free catalog,
BRAINFOOD, which lists over 90
microcomputer books covering
software, hardware, business
applications, general computer literacy
and programming languages.

NAME _____

ADDRESS _____

CITY, STATE, ZIP _____

- -

☐ **Yes,** send me your free catalog,
BRAINFOOD, which lists over 90
microcomputer books covering
software, hardware, business
applications, general computer literacy
and programming languages.

NAME _____

ADDRESS _____

CITY, STATE, ZIP _____

FREE CATALOG FREE
CATALOG FREE CATA
LOG FREE CATALOG
FREE CATALOG FREE
CATALOG FREE CATA
LOG FREE CATALOG
FREE CATALOG FREE
CATALOG FREE CATA
LOG FREE CATALOG
FREE CATALOG FREE
CATALOG FREE CATA
LOG FREE CATALOG
FREE CATALOG FREE
CATALOG FREE CATA
LOG FREE CATALOG
FREE CATALOG FREE
CATALOG FREE CATA
LOG FREE CATALOG
FREE CATALOG FREE
CATALOG FREE CATA
LOG FREE CATALOG
FREE CATALOG FREE
CATALOG FREE CATA
LOG FREE CATALOG

Mail To:

dilithium Press
P.O. Box E
Beaverton, OR 97075

Or Call:

800-547-1842

FREE CATALOG FREE
CATALOG FREE CATA
LOG FREE CATALOG
FREE CATALOG FREE
CATALOG FREE CATA
LOG FREE CATALOG
FREE CATALOG FREE
CATALOG FREE CATA
LOG FREE CATALOG
FREE CATALOG FREE
CATALOG FREE CATA
LOG FREE CATALOG
FREE CATALOG FREE
CATALOG FREE CATA
LOG FREE CATALOG
FREE CATALOG FREE
CATALOG FREE CATA
LOG FREE CATALOG
FREE CATALOG FREE
CATALOG FREE CATA
LOG FREE CATALOG
FREE CATALOG FREE
CATALOG FREE CATA
LOG FREE CATALOG
FREE CATALOG FREE